KING
ME

Other books and resources by Michael Thompson

Search and Rescue: The Life and Love That is Looking for You

Search and Rescue Journal Workbook: A Guide for Your Journey through the Larger Story

The Heart of a Warrior: Before You Can Become the Warrior, You Must Become the Beloved Son

The Heart of a Warrior Journal Workbook: A Guide for Your Journey of the Heart

The Heart of a Warrior Expedition Small Group Video Series

The Rendezvous Project 12-Session Video Series

KING
ME

Loving and Leading
in a Wounding World

MICHAEL THOMPSON

Editor: Bob Hartig
Cover Photography: Patrick Dunnagan
Cover & Interior design: Cole Phillips
Author photograph: Oksana Dunnagan

This book is dedicated to all those men to whom God wants to entrust his Kingdom. On you few, you narrow-road travelers, you good and faithful, I pray blessing as you overcome and become, taking your places as small-*k* kings in the Kingdom of God.

Table of Contents

INTRODUCTION

The rain is coming down and I'm inside, poised to go against my younger brother once again in a familiar duel we played for hours as boys. It's an ancient conflict of strategic offense, blocking defense, sacrifice for the good, unfortunate losses—and moves that promise the hope of becoming *more*.

As in any battle, this conflict comes with an adversary across the board who wants to stop you, block you, thwart you, capture your pieces, and eventually take you out.

Checkers may be the oldest game in the world. Original versions date back over three thousand years, with earliest evidence coming from an archeological dig in the ancient city of Ur. The game surfaces in the culture of the Roman Empire; fourth-century Greek philosopher Heraclitus said, "Eternity is a child playing, playing checkers; the kingdom belongs to a child." The game evolved, as you'd expect, with books on its rules and strategy written in Europe in the mid-1500s.

It's a simple game, straightforward: move, survive, move again. Most of us were introduced to checkers when we were young and knew little of strategy or rules. We just understood one thing: If we could get safely to the other side, we would become something else—something new.

It's a weighty moment when you navigate safely across the board and utter the words "King me." In that short but glorious moment, you are transformed. You become *more*. And then . . . you are turned loose.

As a king.

Now you can range the board freely, ruling over it, and the prey becomes the predator, with two important results. You can see what your enemy is trying to do and take him out before he attacks your other pieces. And you can help those pieces become kings in their own right.

Introduction

The request "King me" lives deep in every man. It is a hope that endures, as we navigate the obstacles of life, that one day we will be initiated into a life of more, validated as men. But even when a man becomes a king—when he has arrived at the zenith of his influence, understanding, and authority—he is still hunted. His adversaries know that if they can take out a king, they can make his whole kingdom pay.

What a man offers those he loves and the world around him in his forties, fifties, and sixties is largely shaped by all that has happened to him during the first two decades of his life, the years when a young heart is subject to another kingdom whose evil ruler is pitted against him and who works through others to compromise parts of his heart. The chance that we were captured in our youth and held captive on the enemy's side of the board is 100 percent. That's how our adversary gets a head start: by using other kings to usher guilt, shame, and fear into a boy's story, take hold of his heart, and compromise his ability to reign in his own sphere of influence when his turn comes as a man.

These are difficult times to be a man. But it has been difficult since the garden, mostly because men as a whole haven't played their part well. We have not learned how to provide for and protect others, because to some degree, we were not protected or provided for. And so, we have unfortunately continued and confirmed our reputation that men aren't safe, cannot be trusted, and therefore are a large part of the problem with the world.

Because most men have not been loved well—have not been healed, trained, validated, and initiated by the kings who came before them—there are very few good kings in the game today.

But if men are largely the problem, then maybe, just maybe, men are also a key part of the solution. I believe this is what God is wanting and calling this generation of men to be: men loved by God so they can be entrusted to love the hearts of others. With God's help, good kings recover their lost and assaulted hearts and trust God to restore what was stolen on their masculine journey.

This is the calling of godly kings, of the sons of God written into a larger story. No one king can fulfill that calling by himself; it will take kings of all races and kinds allying with one another. But this is nothing new. It is a wildly ancient way that must be recovered. And you are (or soon enough will be) of that age, the age when a warrior attains the influence and understanding of a king. Time now to cross the board and claim your crown.

Book Overview

Let's start with a broad glimpse of the whole checkerboard. If you've read my previous book, *The Heart of a Warrior*, concepts such as *oriented, Larger Story, false self, initiation, validation, agreements,* and others will be familiar to you. If not, don't worry—they'll be explained as we move along. Using the same language, *King Me* takes up where the earlier book left off to give all men, particularly those in their forties and beyond, an in-depth, life-changing view of the masculine journey: its stages, its dangers, its training, and its kingdom impact.

This book is divided into four parts. The first two are conceptual, unpacking biblical, developmental, and personal insights that will form the basis for parts 3 and 4, which help you put your boots on and walk it out.

Part 1, *The Heart of a King*, looks at how the hope of becoming a king dwells in us from boyhood; at what makes a good king and how Jesus, the King of kings, embodies those qualities as our model and our very life; and at how the story of a man's journey fits into the Larger Story of what God has done, is doing, and is going to do in establishing his kingdom on earth as it is in heaven.

Part 2, *The Journey of a King*, takes you through the six stages of the masculine journey. The characteristics of every stage, the questions that define it, the strengths it offers, the wounds a man experiences in it, and how the stages build on and interact with each other . . . these lay the foundation for redemption and restoration and for the practical steps of healing and training that follow.

Part 3, *The Glory of a King*, takes what you've read in parts 1 and 2 and shows you how to actually apply it to getting your heart back and walking in your glory as an image bearer, as a king entrusted with the hearts of others. With real-life examples of men's restorative experiences with God, this section helps you turn in wounding and losses for healing through validation and initiation. That is how the battle for the heart is won and how the Father works all things for good in the life of a man whose heart belongs to God.

Part 4, *The Reign of a King*, pays special attention to understanding, fighting for, and cultivating the two most important relationships in the life of most good kings: their queen and the heirs to their throne—a man's wife and kids. This section packs tremendous value for unmarried men as well. So if you are single, *please* do not overlook it. Part 4 is about turning a man loose to see others become who they are in the kingdom.

Throughout the book, you'll read the stories of men like yourself—men from all walks of life who know firsthand what it means to struggle with wounds, fight to get their hearts back, and, as good kings, love, provide for, initiate, and fight for the hearts of others in their kingdom. Chances are good you'll see yourself in some of their stories. Chances are equally good that other men will see themselves in yours. That's how God intends it.

Life is much more than a game. It is a battle between good and evil. It's time for good men to engage with God, getting free from anything and everything that encumbers them so they can align with one another and advance God's kingdom together. That's God's plan: a shared enterprise entrusting men with more. More of the Life and Love of God—the very thing we were promised. The thing that is ours . . . if we will fight for it.

PART ONE
The Heart of a King

You can tell a lot about something when you know what it was made for. I've tried to use a lot of different things to put a nail in a wall: a rock, a shoe, the back of a screwdriver. But there's nothing like a hammer for driving in a nail. What something is made for gives it function, meaning—purpose. And purpose is a good thing.

The purpose for which God made man will probably always remain a bit of a mystery. But things get created either to fulfill a desire or to fix a problem. I believe God created us for both. For the triune God, desire was expressed in the question "Whom can we love?" And the problem (if God can have a problem) was "With whom can we share, entrust, the running of creation?" To both of those questions, we were created to be the answer.

And therein lies your purpose and your worth.

As one of God's image bearers (Genesis 1:26), you were made to love and be loved by God and given dominion over the earth. In the intimacy of that relationship, you are created to reign and rule over many of the works of the Creator's hands.

Jesus reigns over it all—all creation, including us. In the book of Revelation, he is called the King of kings: capital-*K* King over small-*k* kings. And yet, remarkably, Jesus shares his authority with his friends. That's what the scrimmage in Luke 10 is all about. You know the story: Jesus sends seventy-two of his friends out in pairs to do what he does. They go, and they do, and they come back so excited. Jesus then basically says, "Yep, it's going to work. I'm going to share with you my power and authority, and the enemy won't stand a chance."

That's what the Great Commission is really about. It goes far beyond saving people from eternal judgment (though that in itself is wonderful); the Great Commission is about empowering friends of Christ to reign and rule in love, the kind of love that transforms people and circumstances. And it's about wielding power and authority against evil to advance God's kingdom for good. It's about living a certain way, the powerful, loving way of Jesus. In sharing his authority with us, his intention isn't merely to honor us; it's to equip us to live as he lived (1 John 2:6). He arms us as if we'll need it—because the truth is, we do.

So, the million-dollar question is, If we were created for intimacy with Christ and to reign and rule with him here, now, and forever as his coheirs, then why aren't we doing what we were made for?

For two reasons: We don't know who we are, and we don't know why we're here.

It's time we found out—starting with Jesus himself: seeing and experiencing him for who he really is, then exploring what being like him, a good king, is all about. What is the King of kings really like? What does it mean to be an image bearer intimately connected to him? And how does our story fit into a much larger story—*the* Larger Story of what God has done, is doing, and will do? This first part of *King Me* is where good steps and important direction begin.

CHAPTER 1
The Hope of Every Boy's Heart

You have made them a little lower than the angels
and crowned them with glory and honor.
—Psalm 8:5

How strange it is that when I was a child I tried to be like a grownup, yet as soon as I
ceased to be a child I often longed to be like one.
—Leo Tolstoy

I met Rob in early 2016 on a retreat in the mountains of Colorado. I was one of several guides, and he was one of many younger men hungry to experience his true self. It's an all-too-common quest: men looking for who they are and why they are.

When Rob was young, his mother and father divorced, and the drift between father and son began. A young masculine heart seeking identity faces challenges enough when parents stay together; the distance and the incline increase dramatically, and the path becomes all the more elusive, when a dad leaves home and a son is left behind. Masculinity is primarily bestowed by masculinity. Take out the fathers and you get the sons as well.

The result of that father wound in Rob's life later on was a young man who didn't know exactly how to be a dad to his own kids or a husband to his wife. Not that he didn't love them—he did, very much. But his dad's abandonment of him as a boy had left parts of his heart untouched and unwatered at a time when he most needed what only a father can give. Like a knife, that lack had carved a message in his heart: *You're not worth my time or attention.*

Rob carried that message with him as he grew from boyhood into manhood and career and marriage. It left him insecure. Diminished. Uncertain, quiet, hiding. Not qualities that enhance a man's ability to show up effectively for those he loves— because showing up involves the heart, and Rob's heart was blocked. It wasn't that the stuff his wife and kids needed from him wasn't there; he just didn't know what it looked like, or how to release it, or that it was OK and, indeed, vital for him to do so.

But that weekend in 2016 was a turning point for Rob as he revisited his personal story and its impact on him, bringing them along with his heart to God. Most men won't go there; they have written off the significance of their heart and the importance of their story. Rob chose otherwise. He committed himself to discovering and recovering something precious that belonged to him alone: his masculine heart.

Over the next few days, Rob entered with the Father into a great excavation. The things that had happened to Rob when he was young that shouldn't have happened . . . the things that didn't happen that should have . . . the bad words spoken and the good words left unspoken . . . the shovels went deep into the ground of Rob's heart, and a holy work of reconstruction commenced. It was a restorative, life-giving time with something monumental afoot. A man was getting his heart back and hearing who he was in the kingdom from God and trusted friends.

* * *

There is the call of the sea, the call of the mountains, the call of the great ice barriers; but these calls are only heard by the few. . . . The majority of us have no ear for anything but ourselves, we cannot hear a thing God says. To be brought into the zone of the call of God is to be profoundly altered.
—*Oswald Chambers*[1]

Three years later, in mid-2019, I was invited to be part of a ceremony to recognize all the treasures Rob had recovered and the new paths he and the Father had explored. For one night, eight men assembled—experienced, wise men who knew Rob well and were walking alongside him in the same direction.

The hard work had paid off. The excavating had unearthed the long-buried treasure of a good man's heart, unlocked at last and open now to live and love and spend itself freely on others. The books *The Heart of a Warrior* and *Wild at Heart* had introduced Rob to being loved by God and affirmed for who he was.[2] The boy's heart that was unsure if he'd ever known his earthly father's love had experienced as a man what it means to be fathered by God. The wounds had been healed through powerful times of validation of his worth and belovedness as a son and his capability as a man. Now, to his wife and children Rob was offering with growing confidence the things of his heart that they needed, drawing from inner resources that were good and true and wanted and that he had claimed as his own. His marriage was coming alive and his children were thriving—because Rob himself was alive and thriving.

That night was a coronation, a night for us, his friends and brothers, to share how we experienced Rob—who he was to each of us and how we saw the Father shaping him as a beloved son and a warrior man. He was ready to step into the next season of his life as a man, as both a husband and a father. Rob was no longer unfinished or unfathered. He had crossed the game board of fighting for his own heart and the hearts of others. Now it was time for him to be crowned a good king.

It's Not an *S*

In this modern world, it's possible that COVID-19 has changed the lives of more professing Christians than Jesus has. Believers could learn something from the pandemic's effect on our lives. I'm not indicting us; I'm inviting us to allow Jesus to affect us so radically that we would change the world. The great challenge is, Jesus wants to be chosen, not forced. He wants to be more than a vaccination against sin—he wants to bring life and hope.

In the 2013 film *Man of Steel*, Superman is being questioned about who he is and why he is here by a smug, snooty Lois Lane. With observers looking on behind the interrogation glass, she gazes across the table at the symbol on his chest.

> Lois. What's the *S* stand for?
> Superman. It's not an *S*. . . . On my world it means hope.
> Lois, *smirking and raising an eyebrow*. Well, here it's an *S*.

She doesn't get it.

The vast majority of men and women don't get it. There is something more going on, a covert and seductive and beguiling evil, something very large that celebrates appearances, success, bank accounts, and everything tied to this fallen world, which judges and evaluates a man based on his performance.

Nothing wrong with achieving and working hard—except when it defines us or when we allow others' opinions of our attainments to assign our value or lack thereof. Neither is good for a man's heart. A man needs more, and therefore a man can hope for more. But in order to walk in that more, we need training, because we don't know how.

And we need healing, because every masculine heart has taken hits along its journey from boyhood to manhood. Wounded hearts makes healing essential for recovery and eventual reentry into the battle to move forward with what God has for us. We aren't meant to live wounded. And we can't ignore the reality of the battle or remain naïve to the enemy's devices to take us out.

* * *

Hope is a favorable and confident expectation, the pleasurable anticipation of good. In order to hope, we must see that there is something that exists and is meant for us. Something worth pursuing, worth fighting for.

A few years ago I was in a difficult relationship. I prayed and prayed God would change that person, change me, work it out. I hoped God would make it better, easier, more enjoyable. He didn't. The Father seemed to *hope* for something other than a simple fix, and he made it clear to me:

"I want to show you something, Michael. Show you how to forgive, invite you to compassion, and remind you that not everyone sees the world like you do, and that doesn't mean they are wrong. You're going to have to let go of something."

"Wow, can't you just change them? It would be simpler and much more convenient."

"No, that person is in your life to teach you how to love, and right now you're not doing it very well."

"What about *them*? What are you going to do about them?"

"That's my concern, not yours. Now let's go to work."

"OK. What are you going to do?"

"Not me. You."

"OK. What am I going to do?"

"Learn to walk with me and I'll show you."

Walk with God: that's the solution. Maybe not the immediate answer to our specific circumstances, but the path to every answer that matters.

My formula for hope will deeply affect whether I am disappointed or frustrated, glad or excited, with God's invitation to walk with him. I've found that God is more committed to rearranging my hope than my circumstances, and other people's behavior is less important to him than the work he is determined to do in my heart.

It's human nature to wonder, Why am I going through this experience? What are you up to, God? Questions are good if you know whom to ask *and* are ready for the answer—because what that answer is, and how you expect it to come, will influence whether you even recognize it when it arrives. What if the answer is an ongoing invitation to come and see, experience for yourself, taste, feel, and hear, the presence and goodness of God in any and every situation?

With God, there is always going to be some mystery. But mystery isn't a bad thing. It is an invitation to intimacy. That is his ongoing offer. So . . . you can seek answers to a problem, and you may never get them. Or you can seek intimacy with God, which he is delighted to give you, and in time you'll get something better than answers. You'll gain wisdom and understanding.

The fundamental answer to all life's questions, all the time, is God. Walk with God.

It's a Hard Time to Be a Man

I was standing in front of seventy pastors and church leaders. The event was one in a series of five around the state of North Carolina in partnership with a particular church association, and I was there to share about men's ministry and the condition of men today. It was an honor to have been invited. After sharing the disheartening news—the rising statistics regarding men and anxiety, depression, suicide, pornography, adultery, and the insurmountable losses of both marriage and family— I continued:

"Men, it isn't a question of *if* the church is losing the battle for men's hearts. We've lost. Now the question is, Are there enough rebels?—a remnant of oriented*

---

* In my book *The Heart of a Warrior*, I discussed the importance of being *oriented*. In brief, an oriented man knows three things: who he is, where he is, and the good God is up to in his life. *Who*: He knows he is a beloved son of the Father, and his heart is settled in that love. *Where*: He knows he is in a conflict zone between kingdoms, and he walks alert with that in mind. *The Good*: He views his circumstances and relationships with an eye on how he can participate in God's redemptive purpose. Taking a Larger Story mindset (see p. 62–76 of this book), an oriented man seeks to make wise, kingdom-conscious choices in the things he invests himself in.

men who will reassemble, begin reforming the lines of masculinity through redemptive friendships, and rally as brothers on a mission. That mission is to see other men's hearts healed and settled, equipped and trained to fight once again so more and more of us can take back from our enemy what has been lost."

I had never said it like that before, and it wasn't my opinion. A few hours earlier, when I was asking Jesus, *Anything else you want me to share tonight?* he responded, "Tell them they've lost, but it isn't over."

Looking out at the men's faces, I heard in response . . . silence. The long pause that is both sobering and uncomfortable. Half the eyes in the room were glued on me, the rest looked at the floor, and everyone waited for an answer. For some, the question was "What are we going to do now?" For the rest, it was "When does he finish?"

It's always that way. Some are ready, and some are not—not yet. As the Germans taught Europe, when the battle finally comes to your door—when it begins to affect you and those you love—that's when you're ready to fight.

You're Invited

Long before COVID-19, every man was dealing with a crisis, a pandemic that infected or touched us all. Maybe it started with our fathers or our grandfathers before us, but the character of the masculine image bearer has been fading for centuries. Each generation has a chance to reclaim it, though, in a battle that, aided by the Trinity and other oriented men, starts with a man's own heart and extends beyond to the hearts of others—those God has placed in that man's life to share with, encourage, protect, and love.

There is a country for you, and a King who is inviting you to a role only you can play. It's one you both find and that is brought to you. You will know it when you have it. Jesus called it *being fully alive* (John 10:10). And it isn't waiting for you at some future finish line. It is actually the beginning—the trailhead of the path to true masculinity. But like Narnia, Middle-earth, and the Matrix, it must be discovered. How? Through a holy discontent for what is, and in hope of uncovering kingdom treasures by exploring with God the things that could be; by searching out the questions that drive a man's heart—*Who am I?* and *Why am I here?*—and discovering, in the answer, your deepest identity as a beloved son and your part, your mission, in the kingdom.

Sometimes the mission comes after the man; other times, the man must go after the mission. Throughout his journey, missions become rites of passage in which the man is *initiated* by the Father into greater influence and responsibility and *validated* in his belovedness as a son, in his growing capabilities, and in his expanding authority. Missions are, in a sense, ceremonies of initiation and validation. Our masculine hearts need them, and they need us. But because they often are not marked with outward fanfare, the trick is to recognize them.

The Trinity knows how much is riding on our showing up and taking the invitation to *more*. Father, Son, and Spirit are ever calling us to the next trusting step of further up and further in, in a very large story with a very large role for each and every man to play. We long for more because we were made for more. And our longing corresponds with God's longing for us. Remember the invitation of Jesus to ask, seek, and knock? (Matthew 7:7–11) That's not a passage about "salvation"—it is an invitation to *life*, true life. An invitation to come to the Father, engage with Jesus, and be shown by the Spirit how to become more.

Dreams

What did you want to be when you grew up?

We have all been asked that question. Maybe not for a few decades, but think about it, and jot down a few things in this book's margin. Go back to when you were six, seven, or eight. Some clues are available in the toys you played with, the games you enjoyed, the lunch box you took to school, the costumes you wore. What did you pretend to be? A galaxy explorer? A lawman of the Old West? A sports all-star, perhaps, or a world-renowned performing artist? Or maybe an animal doctor, an adventure guide, a builder, or an author. Ask boys what they want to be and it will be daring, adventurous, heroic, and important. It will require strength and courage, and it will come with a uniform and the tools of their calling. "Boys aren't pretending," I once heard John Eldredge say. "They are rehearsing."[3]

In mock contrast, remember the Monster.com commercial? The one with fifth-grade kids saying things like,

> When I grow up, I want to . . .
> file *allll* day.
> climb my way up to middle management.

be replaced on a whim.

have a brown nose.

be a yes-man.

That commercial made Monster.com a household name overnight and launched it into the largest job-posting and career website in the world. I wonder why. Settling for less was never an option when you were eight. That's the age when commencement speeches should be made, because it is the time in a boy's life when he really believes, "I can do anything."

Add ten more years, though, and his young masculine heart isn't so sure anymore. He's not certain who he is, and he is definitely concerned whether he has what it takes.

One Day

Several years ago I was doing a team-building and profile exploration for a pharmaceutical sales team—high-earning executives, top achievers on the corporate ladders, men in their forties and fifties who had second homes, enjoyed family vacations that involved air travel, and drove new vehicles for work and play. I asked the participants, "If you could do anything for a job—*anything*, with no financial responsibility to sway your decision—what would you do?"

Football coach, pilot, forest ranger, science teacher, fishing guide . . . back came the answers, and it didn't take long. And men who over the years had logged hours and hours together in meetings and destination conferences responded to each other, "I had no idea you wanted to be ——."

As amazing as what the men shared was the transparency with which they shared it. Because we had already spent several hours together exploring life and leadership, they felt safe even with their bosses in the room. One man spoke of his regrets; another, the hope of "one day."

Sadly, none of these men were stepping into their dreams, not even as a hobbyist or volunteer or by taking classes or seeking certification. None were actively exploring what their hearts longed for.

Why not?

Time. Family and work responsibilities. When pressed a little harder, money. They couldn't afford to pursue their hearts' desires—it would be "irresponsible."

So back we went to quarterly goals and sales quotas while the dreams that had surfaced shuffled silently back to the dark corners of their hearts. Perhaps in time another opportunity would invite them to come out and play again.

Perhaps. One day.

* * *

The boredom and unhappiness that come from unmet dreams and incarcerated hearts can lead men to do awful things. Alcoholism, pornography, simmering anger—no one wants to live that way. But many men do, and worse. They raid each other's castles, steal one another's wives, divide marriages and families, all by looking beyond their own borders for greener grass. But the grass isn't the problem; broken-heartedness is. The choice of one man to invade another man's kingdom and take his queen—that's not what we dreamed of doing to each other as boys.

What *did* we dream of? What do we dream of still?

To matter. To be seen and wanted, to contribute and make a difference. That's the deep longing of every masculine heart. The hope and desire of every one of us, young and old alike, is to hear validating words:

I see you. I love you. And I love what I see.

I'm proud of you!

What you did and who you are . . . amazing, simply amazing!

Powerful words, those. Life-giving words.

Every man is on a recon mission to receive them, feel them, experience them.

Where we go and to whom we go for validation, for *love*, will shape our lives, determine our direction, and create the destiny of how we reign and rule in our "one day" kingdoms.

Reclaiming Desire

When did desire become synonymous with sin? As image bearers, we were made to desire. That "God-shaped vacuum" described by Blaise Pascal was put there by God to point us to God.

Deep within us, the holy longing resides. Both a rudder and a sail, it can dash us on the rocks when we navigate amiss. Yet navigate we must. As Saint Augustine famously wrote, "God, you have made us for yourself, and our hearts are restless till we find our rest in you." And centuries later, C. S. Lewis observed, "One of the things that distinguish man from the other animals is that he wants to know things, wants to find out what reality is like, simply for the sake of knowing. When that desire is completely quenched in anyone, I think he has become something less than human."[4]

So, what is it we all desire?

What does every human being want, hope for, long to experience in his or her life from the time we arrive till the day we depart?

In a word, *love*. Love is the greatest thing in the world. It is our greatest need and, therefore, our greatest desire. We were made for love, and we are only happy when we are in love.

But among love's different varieties, *unconditional love* is the only love that, when we experience it, transforms us, removes our ache and longing. Settled by that kind of love, we move beyond striving, arranging, and manipulating; grounded in that kind of love, we set aside fear, protection, and isolation. Like water to dryness and warmth to cold, so is unconditional love to the longing heart. Until the heart finds it—a love that never leaves, never forsakes—the heart will continue its restless search. The desire to be seen, invited, wanted, will, like the wind, blow and fill our sails. The problem isn't what we desire, or that we desire, but where we allow our desire to take us.

All our longings are holy at their core. The enemy knows this. He also knows that their most convincing and potent substitute, and our worst downfall, is another image bearer—because image bearers were never meant to be the primary source of love for one another. To fulfill our desire for love—for acceptance, worth, and belonging, to mention a few of love's ingredients—we must go to an unlimited and unconditional source.

Lewis again:

The place for which He designs them [human beings] in His scheme of things is the place they were made for. When they reach it their nature is fulfilled and their happiness attained: a broken bone in the universe has been set, the anguish is over. When we want to be something other than the thing God wants us to be, we must be wanting what in fact, will not make us happy. Those Divine demands which sound to our natural ears most like those of a deposit and least like those of a lover, in fact marshal us where we should want to go if we knew what we wanted.[5]

It is the counterfeits that compromise, and in compromise we are wounded. Minimized. Disappointed. In response, we inevitably develop a self-sufficient, self-protecting, self-promoting system—a system rooted in inner vows to either *never* or *always*.

> *I will never trust again.*
> *I will always know the answer.*
> *I will always win, no matter the cost.*
> *I will never admit I'm wrong.*

And on and on—internal policies we make and whose consequences we live with and impose on others. This is the essence of the *false self*, the *imposter*: the persona that arises as our means of coping with the harsh experiences of life. It's the front we present to others, to ourselves, even to God. We come to believe it's who we really are. But it's a far cry from who God created us to be, and it's a rival to a life of freedom with God—to true life, capital-*L* Life. The life we most deeply desire.

* * *

God wants to redeem desire. He wants back what he created in us for himself.

> It is God Who is all the while effectually at work in you [energizing and creating in you the power and desire], both to will and to work for His good pleasure *and* satisfaction *and* delight. (Philippians 2:13 AMPC)

Good pleasure? Satisfaction? Delight? That is all I ever wanted—to be in a relationship where I am *seen*, *wanted*, and *loved*. Those are powerful, powerful influences. When experienced, they allow an image bearer to eventually partner with God in wielding them. But we must ask the Father to help us first experience them for ourselves before we can offer them with great freedom and transforming impact to others. He is the only One who sees us clearly, wants us more than we can imagine, and loves us for both who we are and who we have it in us to become.

This is what every boy hopes for, what every heart longs for: to be loved. Love is the foundation, the bedrock every man needs in order to become a good king.

Validation

Sadie Sorge, my fifth-grade English teacher, was a cross between Mrs. Doubtfire and Ron's mom, Molly Weasley, in the Harry Potter series. She always wore flowery dresses with a solid-color sweater or jacket over them. The different combinations looked like dress suits. Mrs. Sorge had black, frizzy hair that she teased, which made it look a bit more wild. She had horn-rimmed glasses that, when she wasn't wearing them, hung by a silver chain around her neck.

Mrs. Sorge was a true teacher. She loved teaching, loved cheering students on. She was like a surrogate mother to hundreds of boys and girls, but she always made you feel like *you* were her favorite.

In the 1970s, elementary school teachers often taught several subjects. Sadie Sorge taught reading and English grammar. She made me love diagramming sentences. Can you believe it? Diagramming sentences! I can still do it today.

How'd she do it? Validation.

One by one, Mrs. Sorge would call us to the chalkboard to diagram the short sentence at the top. From the moment we picked up the chalk, she would stand in the wings and—with her shoulders shrugged, and peering over her cat-eye bifocals that rested halfway down her nose—say, "Ohhh, heeere we *goood!*" She more sang her encouragement than said it, and even as you started chalking out the lines of the diagram, you could feel her pleasure.

I would tag the subject, draw the half-line for the verb, and she would comment, "Mr. Thompson, how *clever* of you! My goodness, how impressive." And if I had an adjective or an adverb—or better, a prepositional phrase—watch out! She was going to make sure I hit the jackpot. It was like the hotter/colder game, only with grammar.

Small wonder I still remember those lessons so vividly and even today could be called at any moment to chalk up a simple sentence structure. Because—*validation*. Mrs. Sorge used those blackboard exercises to affirm that I knew what I was doing, that Yes I Could, and that I had what it took.

Moments when we are

> seen
>
> invited
>
> recognized

affirmed

and encouraged

leave a lasting mark. So do scenes when the opposite happens. It's a risky thing being called to the chalkboard—but not if you were in Mrs. Sorge's class. It might not begin well, but with Mrs. Sorge, it always ended well. Even if you didn't know the answer on the long walk *to* the board, she made sure you knew it on the return trip *from* the board.

Teachers like her make you *want* to learn, want to do well, want to rise to the level of their validation. That is teaching at its best, showing love and kindness in helping the student attain an objective. A good teacher reads the situation and treats both the learner's mind and his heart appropriately.

Unfortunately, not all teachers are this way. For years I thought I didn't like playing the piano. Then when I was forty, Jesus showed me, "No, it wasn't the piano you hated. It was being scolded by the teacher you had when you were ten. It was being impatiently corrected and made to feel that what you did was never good enough. You hated the way the teacher handled your heart."

Who knows what many of us might have become, been able to learn or accomplish, with the validation of a good teacher?

* * *

Every masculine heart needs loving and kind validation in order to become *more* and, eventually, a good king for the hearts of others. It is not a need we grow out of, either. Still today, in my late fifties, there is a part of my heart that can only be touched with an encouraging and sincere validating word from God through another image bearer. Receiving love through the compliments and recognition of others never gets old.

I've also seen that principle at work on the giving end when I've recognized and honored men in their seventies and eighties—not just for what they've done, for their contributions and accomplishments, but also for *who they are*. Validate an older man and you will not only access his deep heart, but you may very well water the dry places of his being with tears he himself supplies.

The Father did this for the Son. The Son did this for his friends. And his friends were then commissioned to do it for others. This way has mostly been lost in the church today. Our doctrine and theology may be buttoned up tight, but the way we share it often leaves young hearts feeling like they're taking lessons from my old piano teacher rather than diagramming sentences for Mrs. Sorge.

God's way, validation, is a central theme throughout these pages. We'll look at the importance of validation: its effect on a heart when it is done well, and what happens when validation is missing or done poorly. As we explore those areas in our lives, we will want to remember the good and bring it forward; and we will need healing from the bad and bring that forward as well so we can extend healing to others. We need to harness both the good and the bad in order to recover and move forward in our initiation as sons of God.

That is the other major theme required to make a good king: *initiation*. It is the hope of every boy's heart along his masculine journey.

Initiation

In 2004, at age forty, I was called into a role that made my heart come alive. The setting was a long weekend retreat in the Rocky Mountains with more than three hundred men. I was one of the eight-man conference team.

Every man attending was on a mission to explore the masculine heart with God—scores and scores of missions in process all at once, each one distinct because every man is different. But at the core, we all needed the same thing. We needed God to show up.

I knew the potential that this time of seeking and discovering held for those men. My own life had been deeply impacted by previous such weekends. Now I was back again for more, but this time also to help others on their journey of learning to walk intimately with God.

With our team circled up, the leader proceeded to pray over each man, speaking affirming words about *who* we were, *how* we were seen in the spiritual realm, and *why* we had been chosen for such a time as this. My heart drank in the moment, every word. At the amen, we were invited to take a walk by ourselves, listen to God, and ask him for a gift—for some expression of the Trinity's love and a token commemorating the mission ahead.

I walked down a mountain path for a few minutes, then veered off it into the hillside. Shortly, I came upon a huge, long, flat rock, about knee-high like a bench, inviting me for a sit. Thanking God for the words spoken over me by the group leader, I asked God what he thought of me in this moment.

Near my feet lay a piece of wood—a broken and crooked eight-inch remnant of Ponderosa pine, weathered by the sun and jagged on both ends.

Weathered, jagged, and broken, that's me, I thought.

The wood called to me. I responded and picked it up.

And the moment became a ceremony, the worthless wood transformed into an invitation to step into more. God spoke to my heart: "I see you—the journey we are on and the restoration we have made. Well done! Now let's do this together for others. You are weathered for sure, but also beautiful and strong. These men need you."

Tears. There is nothing else you can do in holy moments. God squeezes you, and all you can do is crack and leak. Maybe that's what Jesus had in mind when he said that living water would flow from us who believe (John 7:38). Tears remind us we are alive—that we can still feel, and there is something in our heart. That the deep well within us needs drawing out.

* * *

According to Dictionary.com, *initiation* is "formal admission or acceptance into . . . adult status in one's community or society. . . . [or] the act of initiating."[6] Let me expand on that with my own definition:

> Initiation is the ceremonies or the rites of passage that call someone up to more; it's any important act or event that serves to mark a passage from one stage of life to another.

Initiation and validation need some teasing apart, since the two can run together. Validations are the encouraging, inspiring, and strengthening moments in life, the "attaboys" that reassure us we're seen and loved for who we are, that we're worthwhile, and that we've got what it takes to grow and succeed. Validations occur, or should occur, throughout our lives.

Initiations, on the other hand, are rare, defining moments of calling, inaugural acts that bestow mission on a man. Initiation is a man's specific invitation —typically through communal affirmation, sometimes through a direct encounter with God—to a greater role, increased authority, and expanded impact in the kingdom.

Validation is not initiation. Initiation, however, when it occurs, is always a form of validation. It works something like this:

When you're . . .

> *eight years old*, your dad hears you singing and says, "Son, you can really carry a tune." (That's validation.)

> *twelve*, your guitar instructor tells you, "Another great lesson! Stick with it, kid. You've got talent." (More validation.)

> *seventeen*, a pretty girl at your school says, "I'm amazed at how beautifully you play guitar. You're so gifted!" (How validating is that!)

> *twenty*, you get a call from the leader of your town's hottest band. "We need a new guitarist," he says. "We've talked it over, and we'd like you to join us." (*Initiation*. Your time has arrived to step into something higher.)

That is how the masculine journey is supposed to go. Delivered through people you respect and whose opinions matter to you, initiation is the words, and perhaps the ceremony, that says, "You belong with us. Come up higher." Once stepped into, that new or expanded calling into which we are initiated is fortified with continued validation. We never outgrow the need to hear "Well done!"

* * *

The trick of those rare initiating moments in your life is to see God arranging and working on your behalf. The approval and applause of others are wonderful, but they're really the consolation prize; don't make them the source of your significance. Doing so leads to insecurity and striving, which in turn allows guilt, shame, and fear to enter the heart. Those are the key ingredients of bad kings.

That's why, while God partners with family, friends, and allies powerfully to validate us and initiate us, he may also sometimes skip the middlemen and deal with us one-on-one. Remember, God designed you to hear and receive from him Heart to heart, Spirit to spirit, Mind to mind. Every boy longs to be equipped, prepared for what life is going to throw at him. And when he is not . . . there is a loving Presence to show him the way.

I still have the eight-inch piece of pine from my Rocky Mountain encounter with the Father. It sits on a shelf in my home office among the many other trophies God has given me: rocks, knives, pictures, old key chains, a pipe, the bust of a cowboy, an empty shotgun shell, and more. Items of no value to others but priceless to me.

Each of them has a story to tell. I love it when someone sees my trophy case and asks, "What is this?" I share the stories of the times when God came for my heart, affirmed me, healed me, invited me, grew me, honored me, cherished me. Each article is a marker on the trail of God's love in my life, reminding me of what has been and that there is more yet to come. He's not done, and neither am I. There are more battles to fight. More ceremonies to experience. Pieces yet to be added as testimonies that I am my Father's and he is mine.

Playing Newly

In his second letter to the believers in Corinth, the apostle Paul wrote these remarkable words: "If anyone is in Christ, he is a new creation. The old has passed away; behold, the new has come" (2 Corinthians 5:17 ESV).

Think about that: a new creation. A clean slate, a fresh start. Is that good news or what! And it's exactly what it means to be "born again" (John 3:3–8).

But for a man to play newly, he has to recover his true heart—the one that has been pushed into the shadows by his false self (aka the imposter). His identity must be reclaimed if he is to expect different results and become entrusted with more, a good king in the kingdom of God.

By the time a young man turns twenty, the collective trauma to his soul—the episodes of guilt, shame, and fear in his life—have taken their toll. Reinforced through constant repetition over time, his failed strategies to make life work cause many a man either to put up walls so life won't hurt as badly or to put out a cup begging for love, panhandling from other image bearers who are as broken and needy as he is.

We may think of this fractured coping mechanism as just a part of our personality. But really? Is it a legitimate part—who we truly want to be? Is it what God created us to be?

Left unexamined, the reasons why we think the way we think, do the things we do, and believe our often questionable interpretation of the world give the enemy of our life with God more than a few buttons to push.

Of course there is good in us too, even if our story was bad from the word go. The enemy wants to capitalize on the bad in order to secure a diminished future. But the Trinity wants to call forth the best in us and bring healing and training to the wounding moments, redeeming the bad and setting us free.

God wants to work it all out for the good.

It's our choice. Because although God's love is unconditional, his healing, training, and entrusting us with more depends on our will. We can continue to be wounded by the enemy and to wound others in turn. Or, with God, we can revisit the wounding moments in our life and let him heal us in ways that transform the bad into powerful resources for good.

Left undealt with, your wounds will perpetuate more wounds. Healed, they become resources of healing for others. Either way, your life will have impact and influence. The question is, what kind?

Which way will you choose?

The odds that your heart was handled well in your youth are slim. You can't move through this life without making mistakes and having others make them. You are both a cause and a victim of collateral damage. No one is immune. That's how fallenness works. It is a game too many men play with little understanding of how it is to be played and what the objective is. Survival? Yes, but for what?

Your life and all it means is ultimately for the lives of others.

The Board Is Set

You are created to live in a Larger Story, called to play a vital role in an epic clash of kingdoms, a war between the light and the darkness. But most men will not graduate from a far smaller story in which they are the center, with all people and circumstances revolving around them. How can they do otherwise when so few men have experienced life-giving, life-changing ceremonies during the course of their lives? How can a man love and lead when he lacks the validation and initiation to prepare him, answer his core questions, settle his heart, guide him, and invite him upward into the larger story and the larger role that is his to play?

The ache and want for more doesn't go away as we journey from boyhood to manhood. The enemy seeks to pound it out of us through adversity, numb us to the feel of it, deafen us to its call. But somewhere deep within us, it lives—and beckons. What can we do about it? How should we respond?

We must seek. Jesus gave us this promise:

Ask and keep on asking, and it will be given to you; seek and keep on seeking, and you will find; knock and keep on knocking, and the door will be opened to you. For everyone who keeps on asking [persistently], receives; and he who keeps on seeking [persistently], finds; and to him who keeps on knocking [persistently], the door will be opened. (Luke 11:9–10 AMP)

For those who will seek, a crown of more awaits them on the far side of the checkerboard. If you have read this far and your heart exclaims, "I knew it!" then you are ready to make that journey: the excavation, reconstruction, and restoration of *you*.

Take courage! Proverbs 16:9 says, "A man's mind plans his way [as he journeys through life], but the Lord directs his steps and establishes them" (AMP).

Step in the direction of healing and of training your masculine heart for what it was created for—reigning and ruling—and watch what God does. You will need a lot of help. We all do. That is part of the joy of knowing God as Father. When you ask, seek, and knock, the Father *will* give, show, and answer through validation and initiation, healing and training.

This journey of transformation will take courage. It is an invitation to battle—to tangling with trying circumstances and challenging persons, to revisiting mistakes you've made and the sins inflicted on you by others. But exploring with God the good he is up to in your life, losing one life so you can gain a far better one—that is worth every step. Because good is what the Trinity is, and good is what the Trinity is up to in your life. There is nothing better!

The time is now and the board is set.

It's your move.

CHAPTER 2
Good Kings

Then God said, "Let us make mankind in our image, in our likeness, so that they may rule. . . . God blessed them and said to them, "Be fruitful and increase in number; fill the earth and subdue it. Rule . . ."
—*Genesis 1:26, 28*

There is no passion to be found playing small—in settling for a life that is less than the one you are capable of living.
—*Nelson Mandela*

I once heard author and pastor Graham Cooke pose this question: *Where has all the goodness gone? . . . We are behind. . . . Evil is winning. What if the problem is not crime, not terrorism, not poverty, not abortion, not drugs? . . . What if the problem is simply the lack of goodness? Scripture says we overcome evil with good. So where has all the goodness gone?*

The goodness of God is given to those who are ready to wield it and distribute it. That is the essence of a good king: the ability, the character, and the dedication to be a conduit for God's goodness in ways that deeply influence people's lives.

But good kings need regular, quality deposits of love in their own hearts. Then they can continually and deeply partner with God to offer love to the hearts of others. Love is the bedrock of goodness. The two are inextricably linked, and where the love is lacking or weak, you can bet the goodness is too. Conversely, when our hearts are settled in God's love for us, then we are able to impart that love to others in ways that are practical, insightful, wise, and powerful. Ways that shape and change the lives of men and women for the better. We help them gain a vision for how their stories fit into a Larger Story, and we help them actually take their place in that Larger Story. As beloved sons of our good Father, we reign in this life in the manner he intends.

What a King Does

So what does it mean to reign?

To *reign* over something—or rule over it; the words in this context are almost interchangeable—is to have authority over its development and to shape its destiny. We exercise our influence over something so it can grow fruit. By virtue of our experience, our position, our resources, our relationships, and our character, we have a significant impact. Whether it's good or bad is another matter, but either way, reign and rule are what a king does.

Used as a noun, *reign* signifies our reach, the time span of our reach, and most importantly, our influence on or authority over people and things, relationships and missions, circumstances and futures.

The instinct to reign is God-given.[1] When we're young, it may express itself in how we arrange our bedroom. I remember, as a boy, putting my bed in a different corner, moving my dresser along a different wall, and shuffling things around in my closet to improve the space. Posters went up and came down.

As we get older, our reign expands. From our room at home, to participation in our school class, to membership on a team, we increasingly exercise our influence to make more and more things prosper. We rule over our houses and cars, improving or maintaining them. We preside over our diet, sleep, workouts and physical fitness, our schedule, our overall well-being. We make choices and act in ways we hope will benefit our wife, our children, our friends and colleagues. All of these take an act of our will, and implementing our will exercises a God-like quality within us. This is important in a man's journey, caring for what is entrusted to him.

The Long Road to Mastery

Webster's defines *lord* as "one that has achieved mastery or that exercises leadership or great power in some area."[2] Unquestionably that describes Jesus during his earthly ministry. Demons cast out of people, vision restored to the blind, crippled limbs made whole, even dead people restored to life, all at a command from his mouth— that's the epitome of lordship.

Yet Jesus used his authority to serve others, to love them, and in doing so, he endured opposition, rejection, and incalculable suffering on their behalf. Jesus flipped lordship on its head when he made *descending* the way to influence rather than *ascending*.

I daresay a king without scars is not much of a king at all. And a king who hasn't caused some scars and heard from those he has wounded is a man who has either played it safe or has very few people in his life who love him enough that they are willing to be honest with him. Either that or everyone is afraid of him.

Growing to become a good king is a long and ongoing process of training; hence, ruling is a messy business, because while we are in training, so are the other image bearers in and around our domain. This means there will be more collisions and disruptions than steady growth and flow. We want training to be at least two steps forward and one step back, but more often it can feel like one step forward and two knocked back.

Solomon felt overwhelmed to find himself thrust into the role of king. He felt unqualified to inherit the throne of his father, David, and that humble self-assess-ment was the beginning of his wisdom. But young men today don't see it the same way. More often, they carry entitlement in one pocket and impatience in the other. This is one reason why it's rare to find a younger man leading and loving well.

Yet who can blame them? We boomers set the precedent. Our parents gave us better lives than their own parents gave them. Credit cards in the 1980s taught us we didn't have to wait—we'd still have to pay, but we could have what we wanted *now*. Later, along came Google and transformed research from trips to the library and a stack of books on a table to instant information on our laptop. Such advantages aren't bad per se. However, they foster an attitude of entitlement and impatience: *How fast can I get there, and how little do I need to do in order to arrive?* Men coming up in today's culture are conditioned not just to desire instant gratification but to expect it.

Contrast that mindset with the wisdom and stability of a man's whose character has been chiseled out of long experience rather than having too much handed him far too easily and quickly.

That's why I'm not much interested in hearing some twenty- or thirty-something preach or teach, or in reading his book on marriage, parenting, or leadership. It's not that we didn't know anything at that age. But what we knew came largely from our heads rather than a backlog of life experience. We hadn't yet walked far with God in the transformational life, persevering in the journey and finding out for ourselves how true something really is.

Where Your Will Is Done

A king presides over all that is placed under his charge. He oversees and attends to the people entrusted to him and the territory granted him. Over time his kingdom grows or shrinks, usually depending on how well he reigns.

Some men inherit kingdoms; others are tasked with building them. The late Dallas Willard taught that your *kingdom* as "where your will is done."[3] But *how* a man rules over his kingdom, how he exercises his will, how he chooses, these are a separate matter. And matter they do, greatly.

Good kings are meant to exercise fierce mastery, take affectionate responsibility, and do it for the good of others. It takes time to learn how, and time to *un*learn previous, unproductive thinking and ways. This is why receiving wealth and position at a young age, whether over a company or a church, often ends in catastrophe. Men in their twenties and thirties who have what it takes to rule well are the exception, as rare as unicorns.

Why? Not enough miles on the odometer of their hearts. Not enough guidance, validation, and initiation from older men. Not enough wisdom earned through the experiences of life. Not a thick enough file of "I'll never do that again."

Until a man has prioritized partnering with God to dismantle his false self, that creature largely calls the shots, and other people get wounded. But a younger man can hardly see his false self. It's not because the damage it inflicts is small—it's not; it's because his ability to justify it is great. It is an old story. The headlines are full of men who do not know how to reign well. A man is incapable of caring for and helping others when he himself hasn't yet learned who he really is and how to walk with God.

* * *

Those miles and that kind of wisdom don't come easily or quickly. They are hard-earned—so don't waste your pain. If you're still breathing, then you're still here, and if you're still here, then you're still needed. You are the only one who can play *your* part in the epic story of "Thy kingdom come."

Remember what God is up to. He is looking for men (and women) to whom he can entrust his power and authority. He wants seasoned men, experienced men. Men who can help others because they've been there in the place of struggle, battle, and uncertainty, and they've learned from the hard times until they became the good times. Men who know what it means to persevere and who are equipped, by their story and their character, to pass on what they know. You never know when it might be you. When the teacher is ready, the student will appear.

Wise Counsel and Good Friends

God's interest in training men isn't so their lives will be easier; it is so their lives will be good. That's what the Father showed me when he arranged for me to watch the 2006 movie *Rocky Balboa*, number six in the Rocky series.

By now the champ is old, yet he is determined to make another comeback. His son, Robert, embarrassed and scared of humiliation, opposes the move. The tension between them comes to a head one evening on a street corner in downtown Philadelphia when Robert confronts his father.

> This is only gonna end up bad for you and bad for me. . . . Is that what you want? . . . Doesn't it bother you that people are making you out to be a joke? Do you think that's right? *Do you?*

Rocky, a man who has learned many hard lessons, responds first with a story of love and affection of how, as a new father, he used to hold Robert in one hand. Then he continues,

> The time come for you to be your own man and take on the world, and you did. But somewhere along the line, you changed. You stopped being you. You let people stick a finger in your face and tell you you're no good. And when things got hard, you started looking for something to blame, like a big shadow.
>
> Let me tell you something you already know. The world ain't all sunshine and rainbows. It's a very mean and nasty place, and I don't care how tough you are, it will beat you to your knees and keep you there permanently if you let it. You, me, or nobody is gonna hit as hard as life.
>
> But it ain't about how hard you hit. It's about how hard you can get

hit and keep moving forward. How much you can take and keep moving forward. That's how winning is done! Now, if you know what you're worth, then go out and get what you're worth. But ya gotta be willing to take the hits and not pointing fingers saying you ain't where you wanna be because of him, or her, or anybody! Cowards do that, and that ain't you! You're better than that!

I'm always gonna love you no matter what. No matter what happens. You're my son and you're my blood. You're the best thing in my life.

But until you start believing in yourself, ya ain't gonna have a life![4]

The first time I took in this scene, it drew tears and a smile. At some point Rocky's voice gave way to the Father's. Every man needs a few of these speeches in his life. They're an invitation for him to look at his circumstances and see a higher point of view. Because it's so easy to succumb to the gravitational pull of a smaller story and trudge around in the weeds without even realizing it.

But few men receive such exhortations because there are few good kings to give them. And a man has to be willing to listen. Life-giving, life-changing admonishment doesn't happen in isolation. The invitation to more takes two.

* * *

"Love one another," Jesus told his friends. "As I have loved you, so you must love one another" (John 13:34). The disciples were nearing the culmination of a long, exhilarating, and difficult journey of learning who their Lord was, who they were, and how God's kingdom operates. Now, in a few words, Jesus tied it all together for them. *Love each other. Be present for each other. Believe in each other. Give the best of who you are.*

The first part of the journey was coming to an end. The second part, one they never imagined, was about to begin. And they were to do it together.

To recover your masculine heart, you will need friends, and you will need to be a friend. There are no lone rangers in the kingdom—Jesus made sure of that. Men who go it alone usually want it that way so their false self can operate unchecked. To become good kings, we need the clashing of iron, the kind that sharpens rather than wounds. The kind that invites us to lift away the masks of the false self so that, with the freedom and impact of who we really are and what we have to offer this fallen world, we can walk in our story and in the Larger Story.

Because there is a Larger Story: the epic Story of what God is up to in this world.

In it, all of history on every level—

> your own history and the history of the human race;
> friendships, family relationships, and international alliances;
> peace and conflict, from the interpersonal to the international;
> justice and injustice, from the microcosm to the macrocosm;
> prosperity and poverty, both individual and national;
> the advancement, use, and abuse of science and technology

—it *all* fits into a great metanarrative, a cosmic clash between the kingdom of darkness and the kingdom of light.

The Larger Story is a tale that is still being told, unfolding even as you read, and your own story has a place in that Larger Story. Don't minimize it. In God's eyes your story is of tremendous consequence, far more than you know—a story within *the* Story.

To see the Larger Story, you just have to ask. Jesus said he needed to leave in order to make way for the Holy Spirit—the one who takes up residence inside you to guide, teach, and comfort you, and more. The Holy Spirit is the ultimate friend, personal, intimate, and good. And he wants to restore your ability to choose.

Redemptive Brotherhood

> The glory of young men is their strength,
>> gray hair the splendor of the old.
>
> (Proverbs 20:29)

> I write to you, fathers,
>> because you know him who is from the beginning.
> I write to you, young men,
>> because you are strong,
>> and the word of God lives in you,
>> and you have overcome the evil one.
>
> (1 John 2:14)

We need one another. The young men need older men to show them the way, and older men need younger men with whom they can share their wisdom. If we are to see God's kingdom come and his will done "on earth as it is in heaven," we need meaningful and redemptive masculine relationships in which masculinity is bestowed upon masculinity. Where are those in their sixties and seventies who have earned their wisdom through hardship and mistakes? Where are the wise elder-sages who have been redeemed—not just theologically but experientially—to tell the stories of how to love deeply and fight courageously? Where are the seasoned men who can show how *not* to wound through either aggression or passivity?

Of *course* you have some regrets. Of *course* you didn't know then what you know now. That's a huge part of the value you bring. Because it's not just the victories that make a man great; it's also the mistakes, the things you would do over again if you could, the holy regrets, the failures that motivated you to go to God and trust him for healing and restoration. Failure is critical to sculpting kingly character and to defining your path, so that when you look back, you can see there *is* a path God has been loving and leading you on. Then, grounded in a relationship that privileges you to speak into another life, you can tell a fellow traveler, "I know the way."

These are the redemptive relationships every man needs and what redemptive brotherhood is all about. Friendships forged over time with oriented men—men both younger and older, living in the Larger Story together, moving in the same direction—are a powerful way for God to lovingly work to reclaim lost ground in men's hearts. If wounding happens in relationships, so does redemption and restoration.

Whether through oriented friendships or skipping the middlemen and speaking directly to your heart, the Father doesn't waste your pain, your suffering, or even your worst failings. You shouldn't either.

Kings Choose

In 1990, as a young man, a wounded warrior not yet a king, I stood before a man in front of me with a crowd behind me and a young woman beside me. That day when Robin and I publicly chose each other, I consented to make her my wife and promised her a whole list of things, and she consented and promised back. Best decision I ever made. Who knew what path was in front of us? We sure didn't, and yet here we are today, still beating the odds.

Kings make, execute, and live with choices. The older we become, the better we should get at it. As men, you and I choose from an internal grid that develops over time. This grid, also known as our *will*, triangulates the connection of our hearts, minds, and souls, the territory dividing our true self and our false self. Kingdom men have more of their heart, mind, and soul in alliance with God. Men who don't yet know God well live disoriented, with a simple system of morality and with more heart territory that belongs to the enemy than to God. As for men who don't yet know God at all . . . well, their will is compromised by a sin nature that renders them lost—spiritually dead until Christ makes them alive. They have no chance to reign and rule well. Only with God living and working inside us do you and I have a chance to make good choices. Not necessarily easy choices but good ones.

But some choices over our journey compromise rather than improve our choosing system. Every day our choices either bind or free us, including our choice of how we see our circumstances. The ways we respond influence, in turn, how we and others will be affected further along as one moment gives way to another. Individual choices may seem trivial, but not when you add them up. If I choose to overeat over a couple years, I'm going to live with the results in my clothes, doctor visits, drug prescriptions, and general health. It's all connected. Our choices are moving in either a good direction or a bad one.

This is why you must see and examine your internal grid. Why do you do the things you do, say the things you say, feel the way you feel? Who built you good? If you assume it was you, you are living in the disoriented group—not a good place for a king to be.

We are the one creature granted the ability to exercise a free will. Whether we're choosing between pizza or spaghetti or between weightier matters of good or evil, life or death, our ability to choose is one of the ways we image God's nature. God chooses:

God has *chosen* you from the beginning for salvation through the sanctifying work of the Spirit [that sets you apart for God's purpose] and by your faith in the truth [of God's word that leads you to spiritual maturity]. (2 Thessalonians 2:13 AMP; all emphases here and following are mine)

And as his image bearers, we also choose:

Choose for yourselves this day whom you will serve. . . . But as for me and my household, we will serve the Lord." (Joshua 24:15)

Anyone who *chooses* to do the will of God will find out whether my teaching comes from God or whether I speak on my own. (John 7:17)

* * *

A loving relationship is all about two hearts choosing to focus their attention and engage their thoughtfulness on each other's behalf. Love is a choice—*and* a feeling. Love is an emotion that settles our hearts and fuels our choices. Receiving God's love over and over again—seeing it, hearing it, experiencing it—this is the good stuff of which good kings are made.

Intimacy with God is essential. Choosing him over all other suitors, even the good, trustworthy ones—counselors, teachers, friends, even your wife—is an easy choice when you experience the reality of his love and the goodness it produces. You don't have to make this Life happen. Your primary job is simply to stay close to the One who does make Life happen. It's in closeness that you can hear him tell you how he sees you. It's through intimacy that he can show you what it is you need, where you can hold back, and where you can press forward. It's in being in love with God that he can remind you who you are in the kingdom.

Contrary to popular preaching, you're so much more than a sinner. You're an image bearer. That's the truth redeemed men need to be told: that they are saints and can be like their King. It's the truth our enemy fiercely opposes and our Father wants us to hear again, and again, and again, so it sinks ever more deeply into our hearts and settles us in his love, recalibrating our internal grid and freeing us to choose well. Set the bar low and we'll knock our heads on it every time. Set the bar high—show and tell us who we truly are, the beloved sons of God—and watch us come alive.

Six Lies That Hinder Kingship

God is up to nothing less than recovering what was lost: you and me, restoring us, remaking us into who we can become (Luke 19:10). It's what God wants for us and what we deeply want for ourselves. The last thing I want to do is believe less and therefore live less, don't you agree?

But if we are going to become who we are meant to be, we will need loving and caring instruction. And we won't trust or receive that instruction if we're believing lies about the One who offers it or about our relationship with him.

For so long, this was my problem. I believed lies of the enemy, especially those that commonly slip in as religious truth. Six in particular hampered my ability to hear God on my masculine journey—and if you can't hear the voice of God, you can't become. The six beliefs are:

God does not speak.
God is far away.
God is mad at me.
I am not good enough.
Every thought I have is my own.
If God did speak, it wouldn't be good.

Any of these sound familiar? Every man I've ever talked to about this has a few beliefs from the list. If you do, you can trade them in for something better. We'll talk in depth about *unsubscribing* in chapter 11, in the section "Agreements, Vows, and Their Antidote," but you don't have to wait. I invite you to jump ahead, read that section, then return here and do a self-inventory. Are any of the above lies active in you? Unsubscribe from them. That's how you get your heart back, and get your heart back you must. How else will you love and care for other hearts entrusted to you?

* * *

Maybe you've heard the old notion that God wants you to get out of the way. It's not true. God doesn't want you out of the way; he wants you as part of *his* way. He desires to grow you up so he can entrust you with more of the kingdom life for others to experience and receive through you. You are not in the way. Just the opposite. You are a vital player in God's redemptive work. It is a partnership—not equal partners, but partners nonetheless. And partners communicate to see something significant done.

Communication is a two-way affair. Yet while we talk to God, too few of us know how to listen. We must recover the voice of God in our lives so we can be instructed on how to reclaim the image we bear—the image of his Son, the "firstborn among many brethren" (Romans 8:29). Our spiritual ears need to be open so we can become who our Father tells us we are. We need to hear him speak to us so we can participate, as beloved sons and good kings under the great King, in the restoration of the world.

Our Father's Life-Giving Voice

To become good kings, we need validation and initiation. We need a kind and loving voice that tells us who we are and who we are to become. For with many of us, another voice has gotten there first. So we also need to see what the enemy has done to us to fashion our false self within us, and we need to shed that false self. Wounding experiences speak lies to a man's heart, and decades of listening to the voices of shame, guilt, fear, loss, and take their toll.

Thankfully, the enemy isn't the only voice in our life. God is the master communicator, and he speaks to us today as surely as he did to the ancients who wrote the Scriptures. The Bible, God's written revelation and the foundation and plumb line for our faith, reveals a God of ongoing dialogue, not a God who went mute after giving us a collection of divinely inspired writings.

In *Hearing God*, Dallas Willard wrote:

> The ideal for hearing from God is finally determined by who God is, what kind of beings we are and what a personal relationship between ourselves and God should be like. *Our failure to hear God has its deepest roots in a failure to understand, accept and grow into a conversational relationship with God*, the sort of relationship suited to friends who are mature personalities in a shared enterprise, no matter how different they may be in other respects. . . . "The sheep follow him because they know his voice" (Jn 10:4). . . .[5]
>
> In our attempts to understand how God speaks to us and guides us we must, above all, hold on to the fact that learning how to hear God is to be sought *only as a part of a certain kind of life*, a life of loving fellowship with the King and his other subjects within the kingdom of the heavens.[6]

The One who created communication in such variety—talking, singing, worship, a burning bush, stone tablets of the Ten Commandments, the prophets—clearly is a God who speaks. He certainly did when he walked among us in the flesh. Can you really not imagine Jesus laughing, crying, smiling, and maybe even occasionally winking? Don't the people you love do that? The meals Jesus ate with his friends—the miracle feeding of the five thousand, the intimacy of the Last Supper, and the countless other times of food and fellowship we know little or nothing about—were hardly like silent dinners in a monastery. When and why did we ever come to believe that the most loving Being in the universe—the *Word*, for goodness sake!—doesn't still speak to us intimately today? It just doesn't make sense.

God knows (oh, how he knows!) the rival voices that have dropped their lying suggestions over us like a net over a butterfly. Whispers to capture us. Taunts, accusations, and interrogations to make us doubt the love and intentions of God. That's why Jesus considered it utterly vital that he send the Holy Spirit to teach, counsel, and guide us. Hearing him, feeling him, is a key part of how we came into the kingdom. Once in, God continues to offer us intimate counsel about all kinds of things that pertain to Life. We just need to learn how to hear his voice.

Because there is still so much more to talk about. Jesus himself said so shortly before his crucifixion. In John 16:12, he told his friends, "I still have many things to say to you, but you cannot bear them now" (ESV).

Really? Jesus was about to die. If he had anything important left to say, it seems like then would have been a good time. But no, Jesus had a better idea:

> "When the Spirit of truth comes, he will guide you into all the truth, for he
> will not speak on his own authority, but whatever he hears, he will speak,
> and he will declare to you the things that are to come. He will glorify me,
> for he will take what is mine and declare it to you." (John: 13–14 ESV).

When he promised them—and us—"I'll never leave you nor forsake you," the thing he did *not* say is, "but I'm not going to talk to you anymore." He didn't purchase us for himself with his own life in order to give us the silent treatment. That's not what any healthy, vibrant relationship is about. Rather, God's intimate voice whispers guidance, reveals counsel, and shows and tells us for the purpose of restoring us into our true image.

All so we can walk with him as kings in the Larger Story.

A Warrior King

All the heroes of all the epic stories of all time speak a message our hearts resonate with. It is this: There is still *good* in this Larger Story, and it is worth fighting for. Eventually good triumphs over evil. And one hero stands above the rest: a Warrior King who loves, serves, sacrifices, and fiercely models what it is to be a man who walks with the Father. All other heroic figures, whether real-life or the stuff of novels, legend, and Hollywood, borrow their qualities from the one who has them all: Jesus, the God-Man—Son of God and Son of Man, the one true King.

Wildest of all, Jesus shares his qualities, power, and authority with you and me. As an image bearer, you—*you*—reflect the likeness of the hero of this Larger Story, and he has written you into a vital role. You are to play a part alongside him, with him. He in you and you in him (John 14:11, 20). *In*—you are that close to him. You can't be any closer. The word is *intimate.*

But experiencing intimacy is far different from reading about it. Having ongoing, personal experiences with God is what Life for an image bearer, the Life leading up to and of being a good king, is all about. It's what Jesus experienced and what, therefore, we are to experience.

Experiencing God is what you were created for, and it is your greatest happiness—being loved by your Father, seen by him, validated, initiated, invited, enjoyed for who and what you truly are: a beloved son of God. Psalm 34:8 stands as an open invitation: "Taste and see that the Lord is good."

If we can come to know Jesus for who he really is and enter into a life-giving apprenticeship with him, we will discover who we are as well, and what we have it in us to become. Through Jesus, the Father didn't just save us *from* something terrible; he also saved us *for* something glorious. His purpose is to heal us, validate us, initiate us, and restore us as image bearers so he can entrust us with his power and authority.

The King of kings wants to share his love and instruction with his men, his apprentices in the kingdom, who are willing to trust him with the recovery of their true hearts. Learn the heart of the King of kings and you will find your way to your own heart.

To be good kings, we need a good king after whom we can model our lives. A hero who inspires us to courage. One whose loving rulership over us shows us, frees us, and empowers us to rule with love in turn.

We have such a king: the Lamb of God. The Savior of the world. The Good Shepherd. The King of kings.

CHAPTER 3
The King of Kings

[They] twisted together a crown of thorns and set it on his head. They put a staff in his right hand. Then they knelt in front of him and mocked him.
"Hail, king of the Jews!" they said.
—Matthew 27:29

The most striking thing about our Lord is the union of great ferocity with extreme tenderness.
—C. S. Lewis

When I was little, I used to dress up as my heroes. Sometimes I was Superman. A towel or sheet would do for a cape. I'd stand with my fists on my hips, then jump off the couch and "fly" for a second. I'd leap over Lincoln Log buildings with a single bound and lift whatever rock or log I could to show my strength.

Other times I was one of my sports heroes, announcing my name as I swung a bat or dribbled a ball. The play-by-play always dramatically moved to two outs with bases loaded or to the countdown of the game clock: *three, two* . . . "Havlicek fakes, he shoots . . . Celtics WIN!"

Imitation is truly the greatest form of flattery. Who can forget the commercial in 1992 when Gatorade sold us more than a drink—they sold us a dream.

Sometimes I dream that he is me.
You've got to see that's how I dream to be.

The King of Kings

I dream I move, I dream I groove Like Mike.
If I could Be Like Mike.
Oh, if I could Be Like Mike

Tongues out and the number 23 on their shirts, many a boy and girl aspired to be like Michael Jordan.

Jesus had that same effect on young hearts. Children flocked to him. Jesus was their hero. Maybe it was because he healed them, or because he called them to be part of miracles like the feeding of thousands. Or maybe because he just listened to them.

Jesus said we would need a faith like theirs, like a child's, if we were ever going to come into the kingdom (Luke 18:16–17). I believe the children not only wanted to be *with* Jesus but they wanted to be *like* Jesus.

Dallas Willard put it this way in his book *The Great Omission*:

In the heart of a disciple there is a *desire*, and there is a *decision* or settled intent. Having come to some understanding of what it means, and thus having "counted up the costs," the disciple of Christ desires above all else to be like him. . . . The disciple is one who, intent upon becoming Christ-like and so dwelling in *his* "faith and practice," systematically and progressively rearranges his affairs to that end.[1]

I wonder why most men don't see Jesus that way today, as someone to be like? How has Jesus lost his status in the world, in our hearts, lost the position of who we want to be? It is one of the greatest spells Satan has ever cast over the world and reinforces daily: making Jesus seem irrelevant, or making our becoming like him seem unrealistic, unwanted or both.

Too often, whom we are told we need to be as Christian men is very different from the person we dreamed of becoming. We need to reclaim an accurate image of Jesus in all his goodness, kindness, generosity, and strength, his fierce strength. If he isn't inviting enough, or his life attractive enough, or his way engaging enough, then we are in trouble.

In the face of oppression, injustice, suffering, and an ever-lurking distorted religiosity in which service to God replaces intimacy with God, the authentic Jesus must be recovered. In order to be good kings we need to experience a Good King. The apostle Paul wrote,

Those whom He foreknew [and loved and chose beforehand], He also pre-

ned to be conformed to the image of His Son [and ultimately share in His complete sanctification], so that He would be the firstborn [the most beloved and honored] among many believers. (Romans 8:29 AMP)

If I get Jesus back, if I recover the one true King, then I've got a real shot at recovering who I myself am—who I have it in me to be, my true self who bears the image of the King. And that is exactly what God has arranged. Jesus became like me so I could become like him.

This is what Romans 8 is all about: Jesus became like us sinful men by clothing himself in flesh so we could become glorious men like him. What has the prince of darkness done to our hearts to blunt us to this truth? What spell has dimmed our perception of Jesus so that we don't intensely desire to be like him?

Willard again:

The central point lies in a fact noted by Henri Nouwen: *nothing conflicts with the love of Christ like service to Christ.* What a strange thing to say! Perhaps it is an overstatement. But it is true that well-meaning service *to* God has a very strong tendency to undermine the kind of vision of God that fuels greatness *for* God in the human scene."[2]

What the Father wants to do in us, and what the Spirit is joyfully committed to working out inside our heart, mind, will, and soul, is a *renovation* where the blueprint is gloriously and simply Jesus. My prayer is, "Remake me to be like the Son."

This renovating process is called *sanctification.* It's another word for being transformed from the inside out into who you and I truly are as each of us bears God's image uniquely. It won't happen in a moment, renovation; it's going to take some time. All great works of art do. But make no mistake, *this* is the reason God saved us in the first place, to see us remade.

The growth process will be stunted, though, if we don't have a hero we want to be like. Knowing Jesus by name—*all* his names—is a good place to start. Exploring his identity can help us discover ours, since he is the one whose image we are being conformed to (Romans 8:29).

What if we could truly feel and think that way, believe in our bones that nothing could be wilder or greater than to be like the real Superman, the God-Man, the Son of God and Son of Man? After all, that's his purpose in redeeming us. As C. S. Lewis aptly wrote, "The Son of God became a man to enable men to become sons of God."[3]

The King of Kings

Jesus is called many things: Messiah, Lord, the Christ, Son of Man, Son of David, Son of God, Teacher, Savior and Shepherd . . . and King. In Revelation 19:16, John declares that Jesus is the King of kings and Lord of lords. A *king* reigns over a territory and its people; a *lord* exercises his will over all that is under his care and control. *How* a king reigns and rules, whether well or badly, depends on his heart. Jesus loves fiercely; takes responsibility for those under his care; gives, not depletes; focuses on others; and is life inviting and life producing.

As New Testament scholar N. T. Wright has said, "If you want to know who God is, look at Jesus. If you want to know what it means to be human, look at Jesus. If you want to know what love is, look at Jesus. If you want to know what grief is, look at Jesus. And go on looking until you're not just a spectator, but you're actually part of the drama which has him as the central character."[4]

Jesus doesn't call us sidekicks. He calls us friends. That's what he is after with us: not usefulness or servitude but intimacy. Because "useful" produces one kind of relationship while "intimate friends" makes for something quite different.

How I see Jesus and what he wants from me directly relates to how I interact with him. To believe lies about him is detrimental to my personal *becoming*, the evolution of me into me. But to grasp the truth—wow. No telling where that can lead, but you can bet it'll be good.

Born to Make Trouble

Jesus was the most popular figure of his day. Twice the Jewish people tried to make him king (John 6:15; Luke 19:28–38). And that was a huge problem, not only for Jesus's enemies but for Jesus himself. He was destined for the office of King of kings— but on his terms, not the people's. His kingdom would be established not by a rise to political power but by descent, becoming the Savior of all.

Taking the lead in his Father's story of redemption, Jesus reestablished God's kingdom and freed us, his believing image bearers, from sin's domain. Similar to the TV series *Undercover Boss*, the Son entered humanity incognito in order "to seek and to save that which was lost" (Luke 19:10 KJV) and reclaim, as the "last Adam," what the first Adam gave away.* His kingdom is one of power and authority, love

---

* For the apostle Paul's comparison and contrast between Adam and Jesus as the "last Adam," see 1 Corinthians 15:45 and Romans 5.

and Life. That is why, when Pilate asked him, "Are you the king of the Jews?" Jesus replied, "It is as you say" (Matthew 27:11 AMP). Jesus knew who he was and why he came. It wasn't to be a nice guy. It was to be a warrior-king whose truth speaking, radical commitment to his Father's agenda, and wild love for you and me rocked the religious and political status quo.

Nice guys don't get crucified; troublemakers do. Jesus was a one-man wrecking enterprise against the oppressive Pharisaical system that Judaism had become. He also made trouble for Rome, whose corrupt government and brutal military occupied the Holy Land. Rome was not fond of mountainside picnic gatherings of five thousand, or of seashore sermons that taught any way other than the Roman way.

"Do not think that I have come to bring peace on the earth," Jesus told his disciples. "I have not come to bring peace, but a sword [of division between belief and unbelief]" (Matthew 10:34 AMP).

Beyond the Jewish leaders and Roman governors, Jesus came to make trouble for the greatest troublemaker of all: Satan, the reigning spiritual authority in the world. The existing religious operating system only enabled him by empowering sin. It was time for an upgrade. No more lambs and bulls, altars and blood. Instead, one Lamb, one cross, and one ultimate sacrifice to usher in a new, flawless system. Amazing!

Oswald Chambers wrote, "Jesus Christ became Incarnate for one purpose, to make a way back to God that man might stand before Him as He was created to do, the friend and lover of God Himself."[5]

* * *

Why go on and on about Jesus—who he is and why he came? Because with the empowerment of the Spirit, the Father is inviting *us* to become like the Son. As God's image bearers, we have Trinity DNA in us.

But *do we want to become the sons of God?* Really?

Sit in this a moment and search your heart. There was a time when my own heart responded, "Yeah, I guess so." It was the churchy answer, the "right" answer. The ought-to answer.

Today, though, my answer is like fireworks inside me. "*Yes!* Nothing would be better. I'm in!"

If I can't answer that way, then something is wrong—not *with* me but *in* me. Something is in the way. Because, for anyone who has encountered Jesus again and again for who he really, *yes* will come automatically and straight from the heart.

Until we've experienced him that way, up close and intimate, I'm afraid Jesus will seem more like a mere historical character and less than who he truly is. And instead of jumping at the opportunity to be like him, we will continue to nod politely and miss the goodness and wildness of not only his life but our own.

In his brilliant book *Beautiful Outlaw*, John Eldredge writes,

> We need Jesus like we need oxygen. Like we need water. Like the branch needs the vine. Jesus is not merely a figure for devotions. He is the missing essence of your existence. Whether we know it or not, we are desperate for Jesus. . . . The purpose of his life, death, and resurrection was to ransom you from your sin, deliver you from the clutches of evil, restore you to God—*so that* his personality and his life could heal and fill your personality, your humanity, and your life. This is the reason he came.[6]

To miss Jesus or misunderstand him is to miss everything, including ourselves and who we can become. Knowing *who* Jesus is, is the secret to solving the mystery of who *you* are, because that is exactly what the Father is up to—redeeming you and restoring you to the unique expression of Jesus you have deep within you.

To understand *why* Jesus came just might raise the bar of your expectations. It could show you the true desires of your heart, propel you to be close to him, and allow him to be close to you. *That's* how you become like him—through intimacy. And that is why he came: to get close to you. It's through that closeness that a man experiences what it is to become wholehearted, for his masculine heart to be truly free, at home, unencumbered and uncompromised.

Why did Jesus come? To bring us home.

Why Jesus Came

The Father's purposes for sending his Son were many. "To save us from our sins" is paramount—but having been saved *from*, what are we saved *for*? To restrict why Jesus came to a single answer is like taking one bite of a gourmet meal, or standing on the rim of the Grand Canyon only long enough to snap a selfie and get a five-second glimpse of its glory, or opening just one Christmas present in a lifetime of Christmases.

Jesus's different names alone speak to the multifaceted nature of his mission: Rabbi, Master, Christ, Son of David, Son of God, Son of Man, Savior,

Shepherd, King . . . just to mention a few. And consider what he said he came to do:

> *Seek* and *save* what was lost. (Luke 19:10)
> Give us *Life* to the full. (John 10:10)
> Give his life as our *ransom*. (Matthew 20:28)

. . . and what his friends, those who knew him best, said he came to do:

> Peter—*Restore* us and *strengthen* us. (1 Peter 5:10)
> John—Solve the sin problem so we could *live in the light*. (1 John 2)
> Paul—Give himself for our sins to *rescue* us from evil. (Galatians 1:4)
> Bring us into God's *kingdom*. (Colossians 1:13)
> Set us *free* from sin and its consequences. (Romans 6:18)

Jesus seeks us, rescues us, saves us, gives us Life, establishes his kingdom in us, invites us to be his beloved, and then sets out to partner with us to restore our heart. He carries us from bondage to freedom, all the while teaching us so he can entrust us with more. That is a heck of a mission statement—and yet there is so much more.

If this is what Jesus has done and is doing, then by implication it's something we desperately need and can't do for ourselves. For instance, as prisoners of sin, we didn't need an elaborate escape—we needed to be ransomed, paid for. So instead of tunneling us out, Jesus decided he would walk us right out the prison gates. But it would cost him something.

Ransom is what a person pays to regain someone they love who is held captive. It ascribes value to the loved one; it declares their worth in terms of what one is willing to pay. Jesus paid for us with his life so we ourselves could have Life. That is our value to God. That is what we are worth to the Father.

I don't have to try to matter—I *do* matter. I was expensive; you were expensive. Jesus didn't just pay the price; he *was* the price. "He endured the cross" for one reason: "the joy set before him" (Hebrews 12:2). That's you and me. We are that joy. And he was *glad* to pay.

How Kingly!

The first unofficial glimpse of why Jesus came occurred at a party, a wedding reception. A bit of a preview, actually, of things to come. You know the story—water into wine.

After a few elbows and nods from his mother, Jesus, with a grin, tells her that now is not the time. But Mary, the once-teenage mom, knew who her son was then, and you can bet she knows now. Just as Jesus was waiting for the time, so was she.

There's nothing like a mother's light push to get her son onstage. Maybe Mary has had a little liquid courage—remember, they were out of wine. Just saying. Regardless, it's at a party that Jesus, at his mother's urging, pulls back the veil just for a moment to save the day and give a peek at what is waiting behind the curtain for humanity: the Father's affectionate goodness and the Son's gracious heart.

Later in John's gospel, Jesus said, "The Son can do nothing by himself; he can do only what he sees his Father doing, because whatever the Father does the Son also does." (John 5:19). On this festive occasion, the Father is glad to honor Mary's request, and the result is a party-saving batch of primo vino. The Father is good, and Jesus came to show the goodness of the Father.

* * *

Jesus's "official" inauguration into his larger mission came at his baptism and the forty days that followed. Right after major validation by his Father, right after toweling off, came his initiation as the Spirit led him into battle in the Judean wilderness.

After being called up by the Father ("You are my Son, whom I love") the Messiah is called out by the enemy ("If you are the Son of God . . .").[7] It is an ancient tactic of Satan's, going after our identity. He did so with the Son of God, and he does so with all the sons of God.

Finally, like a last-second half-court shot, Satan tries another approach: "If you worship me, I will give you all the kingdoms of the land."[8] Do you see what's in his offer? The prince of this dark world is offering Christ power and authority. But Jesus blocks the devil's desperation shot. The King of kings is determined to take back power and authority on another hill at another time.

And from that moment, it is on. Jesus came to take back, by force, the power and authority of the world. The King of kings reveals that he can both go forty rounds with his adversary *and* provision a dinner party. How kingly! Some days the Larger Story will invite us to domestic chores; other times we will be summoned, led by the Spirit into battle.

Battle Is the Backdrop

From the fall in the garden till this moment, the entire story has been war. That should be obvious. It was a cherubim with a flaming sword that God posted outside Eden, for crying out loud, not just a "Keep Out" sign. That ought to tell you something.

What is going on in the spiritual realm plays out in the physical realm, not the other way around. A spiritual battle is in progress for your affection, attention, and allegiance. Add a few billion people to the mix, and the war over one heart will directly impact the war of dozens if not hundreds of other hearts.

A man will need to learn how to fight—learn how to take care of his own heart, mind, body, and soul—long before he comes into caring for the hearts of others. Otherwise the results will be catastrophic. We are to experience being loved as sons and then trained as warriors first. Then we can be entrusted, as good kings, with protecting and providing for others.

The Biggest Reason Jesus Came (Mic Drop!)

After healing up a bit from his wilderness fight with Satan, Jesus rolls back into town—Nazareth, to be exact. His hometown (Luke 4:14–16). It's the Sabbath, so what does a good Jewish man do? He goes to church.

There at the local synagogue, standing in the midst of the townspeople he has grown up with, Jesus is given the scroll of Isaiah to read. He unrolls it to this passage:

> "The Spirit of the Lord is on me,
> because he has anointed me
> to proclaim good news to the poor.
> He has sent me to proclaim freedom for the prisoners
> and recovery of sight for the blind,
> to set the oppressed free,
> to proclaim the year of the Lord's favor."
>
> (Luke 4:18–19; cf. Isaiah 61:1–2)

Jesus rolls up the scroll, hands it back to the attendant, and sits down. It's a reading like any other reading, like a thousand before.

But then, with the eyes of the congregation fastened on him, Jesus continues with a line they don't expect: "Today this scripture is fulfilled in your hearing" (Luke 4:21).

In other words, "It's talking about me. I'm the one. This is what I am going to do."

There it is: the heartbeat of Jesus's mission. The biggest reason why he has come. And to make sure his listeners feel the weight of what he is proposing, Jesus adds, in essence, "And I'm not going to be doing it here."[9]

Mic drop.

The disruption sucks the air right out of the room. No prophet is accepted in his hometown, he tells them. But guess what? He is about something bigger, something that will take his message beyond Nazareth to the whole Jewish conference and then farther, much, much farther.

To drive his point home, Jesus brings up the stories of Elijah and Elisha and God's goodness through them to a foreign widow and a pagan leper. To two people outside the Hebrew home team (vv. 24–27).

The implication is clear: God's empowering grace will reach the outcasts and unapproved while the "in" crowd will miss out because of their unreceptiveness.

Provocative words! Who does this carpenter's kid whom everyone knows think he is, anyway?

As they heard these things [about God's grace to these two Gentiles], the people in the synagogue were filled with a great rage (v. 28 AMP)

Jesus is making it plain that God's plan of redemption involves far more than Israel, and his Jewish townies don't like the sound of that at all. Yet it is *why* Jesus came.

C. S. Lewis writes in *Mere Christianity*, "Enemy-occupied territory—that is what this world is. Christianity is the story of how the rightful king has landed, you might say landed in disguise, and is calling us all to take part in a great campaign of sabotage."[10]

The larger mission of Jesus gives us a larger gospel of the kingdom and invites us to words and themes like

Life

Heart

Kingdom

Ransom

Redemption

Restoration

FREEDOM

"It is for freedom that Christ has set us free" (Galatians 5:1).

As Dallas Willard put it, "If our gospel does not free the individual up for a unique life of spiritual adventure in living with God daily, we simply have not entered fully into the good news that Jesus brought."[11]

But when freedom is the goal, there is going to be a fight. One we are invited up and into. One we must enter and participate in. We are spiritual beings on a physical journey, finding and fighting our way home.

So, Who Do You Say He Is?

Have you ever noticed the power of a good and timely question? It stays with you. It demands something. It invites. It disrupts and can provoke a response.

Who are you?

What do you want?

Why are you here?

How can I help you?

Do you know who I am?

Who do you say that I am?

Jesus, the main character and hero in the Larger Story—a true story, *our* story—knew the power of asking questions. They expose lies. They reveal truths about God and about ourselves. And, if we will let them, they invite us into a deeper revelation of and intimacy with God.

Matthew's gospel takes us inside the moment when Jesus asked his disciples a turning-point question:

"Who do people say that the Son of Man is?" And they answered, "Some say John the Baptist; others, Elijah; and still others, Jeremiah, or [just] one of the prophets." He said to them, "But who do you say that I am?" Simon Peter replied, "You are the Christ (the Messiah, the

Anointed), the Son of the living God." Then Jesus answered him, "Blessed [happy, spiritually secure, favored by God] are you, Simon son of Jonah, because flesh and blood (mortal man) did not reveal this to you, but My Father who is in heaven. (Matthew 16:13–17 AMP)

How about you? Who do *you* say Jesus is? It's a crucial question, because how you see him determines whether you'll want to become like him. To see Jesus for who he truly is, is to glimpse your own possibilities as an image bearer crafted after the Son. Remember, he became like you so you could become like him.

Jesus continues with this remarkable validation for Peter:

I say to you that you are Peter, and on this rock I will build My church; and the gates of Hades (death) will not overpower it [by preventing the resurrection of the Christ]. I will give you the keys (authority) of the kingdom of heaven; and whatever you bind [forbid, declare to be improper and unlawful] on earth will have [already] been bound in heaven, and whatever you loose [permit, declare lawful] on earth will have [already] been loosed in heaven. (vv. 18–19 AMP)

To be entrusted with more depends on whether we will entrust our lives to Jesus. When we do, we are given a new identity and new authority in the kingdom that gives us both privileges and responsibilities. This has been the plan of the Trinity all along: to make "little Christs" of us (that's what the word *Christian* means). But "little" hardly describes the weight or magnitude of the role God has in mind for his sons and daughters.

C. S. Lewis writes, "The more we let God take us over, the more truly ourselves we become—because He made us. He invented us. He invented all the different people that you and I were intended to be. . . . It is when I turn to Christ, when I give up myself to His personality, that I first begin to have a real personality of my own."[12]

God is all about reshaping and restoring you and me, remaking us from the inside out to reign like Jesus in our own spheres of influence with goodness and grace, love and strength. As George MacDonald wrote, "To follow him [Jesus] is to be learning of him, to think his thoughts, to use his judgments, to see things as he sees them, to feel things as he feels them, to be of the same heart, soul, and mind, as he is—that we also may be of the same mind with his Father." And further on,

"'I and the Father are one,' is the center-truth of the universe. And the encircling truth is, 'That they also may be one in us.'"[13]

This is the very Large Story of which you are a part. It is moving to an end that will release the final beginning. To understand its Author is to understand his invitation to play your part, and play it well. Who do you say he is?

He is coming after you for your answer.

Experiencing Him

When I was thirty-eight years old, the King of kings came after me. For far too long, I had Jesus wrong. But, as John Eldredge put it, "an intimate encounter with Jesus is the most transforming experience of human existence."[14]

The most significant conversion in my life came to me in a quiet moment sitting on the side of a mountain, disrupted by the sense of my own futility. "God, how do you see me?" I asked him. "Who am I to you?"

You are my son in whom I am well pleased.

That was the next thought that entered my mind. More was to come.

I see you, and I love what I see. You are mine. You are enough.

Through tears, I said, "That's what I wanted."

I know. And, as if with a wink, *There's more. I'll show you. Stay close to me and I'll show you.*

For thirty-some years I had been a Christian. But that day I became his, and he, mine. He lifted the weights of performance off me and overwhelmed me with his attention and affection. And ever since, his training for me hasn't been about *doing* more; it has been about *becoming* more—about being entrusted with more, without the pressure, striving, or proving, but from a settled heart. Unfinished, yes, but not unsettled. And that has made all the difference.

I can tell you from experience, if you have Jesus wrong, you can't get right.

* * *

More such deeply personal encounters followed that first one in the ensuing weeks and months. And my Father's agenda became clear: more of his love for me to experience. More Life. More freedom. Honestly, I didn't know those things existed. Now I know.

God has big plans for me—and for you. The early years of our restoration mostly involve healing from the past and getting things out of the way that are in the way of receiving his love. That healing doesn't just alter a man's relationship with God; it begins to alter every relationship.

In my own life today, most days now are about training—training for reigning. I also still need healing, both from a long and treacherous past and from the daily attempted woundings that are par for life's course. The difference is, now I know how to defend myself. I know how to respond and, very importantly, how *not* to respond when someone sins against me or otherwise hurts me. The King is teaching and training me to be like him, showing me how to be a good king. It's a lot of work, but it's the best kind.

He's looking for other recruits as well. Other apprentices. Are you ready to be found and to become?

The King of kings wants you. He wants to give you the Life you have always wanted but can never earn or provide for yourself. What have you got to lose, other than all that stands in the way of your becoming whom you were made to be?

The One who created you wants to walk with you into more. More than you can imagine, down a path only he can make, in a direction only he knows. Healing and training, validation and initiation, the maturation of a kingly heart within—these await you. And other hearts await your experience and wisdom as your personal kingdom expands within that of the great, all-governing King of kings.

So tell God you're willing, if indeed you are. Willing to walk with the King—to know him, learn from him, experience his love, his correction, his guidance, his encouragement, his provision, his companionship. Consent, declare, say it out loud:

I'm willing to learn how to wield your power and authority on behalf of others.
I'm willing to lose my preconceptions and church-speak and gain the mind and language of a heart settled in the Father's love.

In the words of Dallas Willard, "The most important thing in your life . . . is not what you do; it's who you become. That's what you will take into eternity."[15]

What say you? You in?

CHAPTER 4
The Larger Story

Then God said, "Let us make mankind in our image, in our likeness, so that they may rule. . . . God blessed them and said to them, "Be fruitful and increase in number; fill the earth and subdue it. Rule . . ."
—Genesis 1:26, 28

This is the heart of Camelot. Not these stones, not these timbers, these palaces and towers. Burn them all and Camelot lives on, because it lives in us. Camelot is a belief that we hold in our hearts.
—King Arthur, *First Knight*

We were all just standing around in our upland hunting garb, waiting. A couple dozen men with a handful of dogs and a bunch of shotguns—we were all waiting for the outfitter to pick us up and take us into the fields of South Dakota to hunt pheasant. Some men had their sons with them. A few, like me, brought their dads. We had made this an annual hunting retreat, mixing a conference for men with the beauty and fun of hunting together in the landscape of *Dances with Wolves*. I've found the prairie is an incredible place to encounter God.

As the troops grew impatient, Jesus gave me an idea for how to redeem the increasingly painful wait. I whistled everyone to circle together and asked a question: "If your shotgun could talk, what story would it tell?"

I wish I had hit the record button. For the next hour, almost every story involved family and the validating or initiating that went with passing down or handing over these sentimental heirlooms. Many of the men told of their favorite hunt, whom they were with, and precious moments of past adventures. Sharing each story from the perspective of the shotgun made the telling all the more fun and the listening all the more enjoyable. And the experience was having such an impact on us that when the outfitters finally did arrive, the holy moment continued as our guides took a place in the circle of honor.

The great modern author and poet Madeleine L'Engle had it right when she wrote, "Stories make us more alive, more human, more courageous, more loving."[1]

Life is a story.

You are a story. Your parents are a story.

Everyone has a story, and everyone is also a character living as a part of a much larger story.

The Gospels are all stories—stories of God coming near, making it known that we are wanted and that Love wins.

The Bible's sixty-six books and hundreds of characters tell a grand and important history, filled both with clues to a current, hard reality and with hope for a future featuring everyone's favorite line: "And they lived happily ever after." It is a very LARGE story, the story of God and the invitation to see our story in the light of his story.

It was author Sue Kidd who wrote, "Stories have to be told or they die, and when they die, we can't remember who we are or why we're here."[2] When we were little, many of us looked forward to bedtime not because we were going to bed but because someone was going to read or tell us a story. Stories feed us, and in stories we find the characters and qualities we long for and hope to someday be. Facts are always important, but it's the story that gives them weight and purpose, color and context, and that awakens our heart to what is most real and true.

Missing Your Story

A good story moves the heart more deeply than a good algebra class. Narrative always trumps academics. It is the *story* that makes science, math, and theology come alive. A man's kingdom, a man's fall, a man's ascent, and a man's reign are far more than facts or fill-in-the-blank answers on some quiz. They are a story.

"Miracles," wrote C. S. Lewis, "are a retelling in small letters of the very same story which is written across the whole world in letters too large for some of us to see."[3]

Miss the Larger Story and you will miss your story.

In the film *Dead Poets Society*, Professor Keating (played by Robin Williams) put it like this:

> I read from Whitman.
> "O me, O life! of the questions of these recurring,
> of the endless trains of the faithless, of cities fill'd with the foolish . . ."
> Skipping . . .
> "What good amid these, O me, O life?
> *Answer*
> That you are here—that life exists, and identity.
> That the powerful play goes on, and you may contribute a verse."
> "That the powerful play goes on, and you may contribute a verse."
> Incredible. . . .
> What will your verse be?

Our stories intersect, our contributions collide, and together we either become more or retreat into less. History is full of the wild collisions of characters that stepped onto the grand stage to play a part in time in a much Larger Story. A story they were born into that was already in motion, and one that will carry on after they are gone and continue until God brings the curtain down on these chapters and opens up the new beginning that has no ending, the restoration of all things new (Revelation 21:5).

Until then, be assured, your life matters. Your story matters. It matters a great deal. Every choice and every word, every action and every interaction, matters. Every man and woman will have an effect on the lives of others. In different roles, many often at the same time—husband, father, grandfather, son, brother, stepfather, stepson—each of us is integral to the grand story. There are no minor roles. Every man has an impact, and every man is also impacted along his masculine journey.

From infancy to the grave, boyhood to old age, every man will both be marked and leave his mark. The question is, to what end? Wounded hearts wound hearts, and free hearts free hearts, and therefore there is always much more going on from day to day than meets the eye. There is always "the rest of the story." Learning what is real and true along the way is a hazardous enterprise. What are the odds you have interpreted your life accurately?

* * *

Having worked with men for thirty years, and in walking with a small team of men devoted to fighting for the hearts of tens of thousands of men collectively, I am certain of two things: Every man is one of the walking wounded. And God is in the business of healing men and redeeming their stories.

God has been and is redeeming my story for both my good and his. Whatever you think you might know of God and your own heart, I promise you there is more. With God, there is *always* more. And friend, the great news is, you were made for more.

God will recast the story of your life in a whole new light, like a before-and-after picture. If you don't see it, then you aren't paying attention—but that's all right, because God specializes in that too, in getting our attention. He wakes us up at the right time in our stories so we can participate in his rewriting us, editing us, reconstructing us so he can entrust us with more.

God doesn't want you to miss your story and his work in it, because that is what you have to offer the world—your story. Then when the world asks, "What happened to you?" you can respond with a story about how God has been loving you and is at work in your life.

Middle-earth

In J. R. R. Tolkien's classic *Lord of the Rings* trilogy, Middle-earth was a place in which two realms, spiritual and physical, intersected. The veil between those realms was lifted, and the conflict between good and evil was constantly on display.

It is the same with the Scriptures. When we peer into the Bible's collection of stories, we see them bound together in one grand tale that invites us to see our lives in the context of war between good and evil—the Larger Story.

The man who lives small because he fails to discern that Larger Story is a dangerous man—dangerous to himself, to those entrusted to his care, and to all around him. Such men, disoriented kings, predominate in the landscape of the Larger Story. To be under their rule is more than unpleasant. It is costly.

Costly because life is overwhelming most of the time. It's supposed to be.

If it wasn't more than we can handle, we might fall into the idea that we are in control. That notion is a spell cast over kings that deceives them into playing small. We are *not* in control. And it is the overwhelming that often brings us to the One who is, so we can present our hearts to God.

In book 2 of Tolkien's epic, as discouragement creeps in during his perilous journey with Frodo, the ring-bearer, the hobbit Sam sees the Larger Story and is reminded it is all going somewhere.

> We shouldn't be here at all, if we'd known more about it before we started. But I suppose it's often that way. The brave things in the old tales and songs, Mr. Frodo: adventures, as I used to call them. I used to think that they were things the wonderful folk of the stories went out and looked for. . . . But that's not the way of it with the tales that really mattered, or the ones that stay in the mind. Folk seem to have been just landed in them, usually—their paths were laid that way, as you put it. But I expect they had lots of chances, like us, of turning back, only they didn't. And if they had, we shouldn't know, because they'd have been forgotten. . . . I wonder what sort of a tale we've fallen into?[4]

In order to recover Who We Are, we too must wonder what sort of tale we've fallen into. We need to see our days in this world as part of, as an important contribution to, the chapters to come. Tolkien's Middle-earth represents the Larger Story our own story is in—the context of our days, the Where We Are. Only when we grasp this can we align with the Author and the story he is writing. Then, and only then, can we join him in the great redemption and restoration of all things. Then, and only then, can we be kings who provide and who protect against evil. Kings who are well-equipped, well-informed, and well-trained—or, as my friend Bart Hansen of Wild at Heart put it, "men who are dangerous for good."

The context of our story is a tale first of woe, of terrible fallenness, and then of a comeback, of enormous restoration. We know how it began in Genesis and where it ends in Revelation, when this present story will give way to the next. Until then, we live in the middle—exposed, outside the garden. And the serpent, who was also in the garden, now has an army outside it where we are. Here in Middle-earth we encounter his forces every moment of every day. Whether we perceive it or not, in this fallen place, the kingdom of darkness is at work all around us.

Have you ever wondered why there is always a war somewhere across the globe? Why there is continued oppression, strife, bondage, painful injustices, hatred between image bearers, disregard for the planet, indifference among people toward one another, discord in marriages and the breakdown of families? It's because there is a war . . . and we are in it.

We live in the middle, the now-but-not-yet of redemption that lies between the promise and its fulfillment.

The Two Realms

A *realm* is an area ruled or characterized by a particular kind of influence and activity. You have a realm—your reign, your sphere of influence that expands or contracts in relation to your life experiences. It's where your smaller story plays out within the Larger Story. And that Larger Story encompasses two great realms: the spiritual realm and the physical realm.

We are invited to see life and our stories through the realm that matters most: the spiritual realm. Like an airport observation deck or a lofty hilltop, the spiritual perspective allows us to see the whole wide landscape of capital-*L* Life spread out before us. God invites us to view and interpret everything—*everything*—from that standpoint.

> "Do not store up for yourselves treasures on earth, where moths and vermin destroy, and where thieves break in and steal. But store up for yourselves treasures in heaven, where moths and vermin do not destroy, and where thieves do not break in and steal. For where your treasure is, there your heart will be also." (Matthew 6:19–21)

> "Seek first the kingdom of God." (Matthew 6:33 ESV)

> "What good will it be for someone to gain the whole world [physical realm], yet forfeit their soul?" (Matthew 16:26)

> Since, then, you have been raised with Christ, set your hearts on things above. (Colossians 3:1)

> Our struggle is not against flesh and blood, but against the rulers, against the authorities, against the powers of this dark world and against the spiritual forces of evil in the heavenly realms. (Ephesians 6:12)

Our citizenship is in heaven. And we eagerly await a Savior from there, the
Lord Jesus Christ. (Philippians 3:20)

God sovereignly rules over it all. The creator of the universe is also its sustainer,
often covertly. Not that it's God's intention to be hidden; he wants to be known. But
those who don't believe in him are unequipped to discern him. And, sadly, even many
who do believe may know the cross but not God's intimate presence.

* * *

Some things in the spiritual realm are for you, and others are very much against you
and what you may become—a good king. The enemy knows what God will heal and
train you to do: love people *into* his kingdom, and love those *within* his kingdom.
Satan would rather that not happen. He wants to use you to wound others, thus
discrediting and diminishing God's relevance in their lives. God wants you to understand how it all works and what you're up against.

Our struggle is not against flesh and blood, but against the rulers, against
the authorities, against the powers of this dark world and against the spiritual forces of evil in the heavenly realms. (Ephesians 6:12)

In the realm that matters most, the spiritual realm, there are two kingdoms: the
kingdom of darkness and the kingdom of light. The first is governed by Satan, the
prince of this dark world (John 12:31). The second, God's kingdom of light, is ruled
by Jesus, the Prince of Peace, the King of kings and Lord of lords (Isaiah 9:6; Revelation 17:14). These two kingdoms are at war with each other—and you, as a son of
the Light (1 Thessalonians 5:5), are caught up in the conflict. The dark kingdom is
pitted against you; the kingdom of light—God's kingdom—is fighting for you; and
both are recruiting you to fight for them.

Let's look more closely at each of these kingdoms.

The Kingdom of God

The first-century Jews, well aware of God's promises, looked forward to the coming
of the Messiah, who would step into the shoes of the covenant God made with King
David.

"Your house and your kingdom will endure forever before me; your throne will be established forever." (2 Samuel 7:16)

I will declare that your love stands firm forever,
> that you have established your faithfulness in heaven itself.
You said, "I have made a covenant with my chosen one,
> I have sworn to David my servant,
'I will establish your line forever
> and make your throne firm through all generations.'"
>
> (Psalm 89:2–4)

The priests of Jesus's day believed strongly in a promised king, the Messiah, who would return the Jews to their glory days. But those religious leaders were so misled in their expectations of what the Messiah would be like, look like, that they didn't recognize the reality when he stood in their midst. Jesus, the Son of God—right there before their eyes, and they missed him.

The people *almost* got it. That is what the original Palm Sunday was all about: a parade during Passover in honor of the new king. And right they were: the King had come. But the nature of the King and his kingdom were nothing like what the Jewish people envisioned. They anticipated a political conqueror, they thought he had arrived, and they were excited. The Romans were not so happy. And the Pharisees and Sadducees, who lived like lawyers and politicians, the "official" representatives to Rome in a dirty political system . . . they weren't havin' it.

These religious leaders were determined to enforce the Jewish law of Sabbaths, rituals, and rules. Jesus, who in their eyes broke their law regularly, wasn't who or what they wanted as a king. They wanted a heavyweight political deliverer who would free them from Roman oppression and restore Israel to its rightful place in the world. But Jesus was aiming at a much higher weight class to secure a far greater deliverance and a freedom those religious minds couldn't fathom.

They really believed they could prevent the Prince of Heaven from becoming the King of the Jews, and they were determined that Jesus had to die. But the Father, in ages past, had already decided that would happen. The cross was God's plan, and Jesus, the sacrificial "lamb without blemish or defect" (1 Peter 1:19), had come to fulfill it. Those religious leaders, under the influence of the kingdom of darkness and their own false-self ways, unwittingly played right into the Father's design.

The cross was Love's secret weapon, obtaining God's forgiveness for us and destroying the grip of sin through the Messiah's death and resurrection. The Father wrote the Son into our story to teach us the Larger Story and to knock out death and win us back. Through God's power and authority, the cross and resurrection made Life available to us once again. Wildly, the Trinity has cut the keys to the kingdom and handed them to us, and now Father, Son, and Holy Spirit invite us to join them in using their shared power and authority to see all things restored.

Amazing! Yet also, so sad. Sad in that we have too long underachieved, continuing to live small and to lose more than we win. But that can change. It *must* change.

* * *

Jesus taught more about the kingdom of God and how it works than he did anything else. For just a few examples, he compared the kingdom to . . .

"a man who sowed good seed in his field. But while he was sleeping, his enemy came and sowed weeds among the wheat." (Matthew 13:24)

"yeast that a woman took and mixed into about sixty pounds of flour until it worked all through the dough." (Matthew 13:33)

"a mustard seed, which is the smallest of all seeds on earth. Yet when planted, it becomes the largest of all garden plants." (Mark 4:31–32)

"a farmer [who] went out to sow his seed. As he was scattering the seed, some fell along the path . . . [and some] on rocky ground . . . among thorns . . . on good soil." (Luke 8:5–8)

The kingdom belongs, Jesus said, to the poor in spirit (Matthew 5:3) and to little children and people who come to God like a child (Mark 10:14–15). It's to the child-hearted, he said, not the worldly wise, that God reveals his kingdom secrets (Luke 10:21–22).

Even Pontius Pilate was given a powerful glimpse into the nature of God's kingdom, though he didn't at all understand:

Jesus replied, "My kingdom is not of this world [nor does it have its origin in this world]. If My kingdom were of this world, My servants would be fighting [hard] to keep Me from being handed over to the Jews; but as it is, My kingdom is not of this world." So Pilate said to Him, "Then You are a King?" Jesus answered, "You say [correctly] that I am a King. This is why I was born, and for this I have come into the world, to testify to the truth. Everyone who is of the truth [who is a friend of the truth and belongs to the truth] hears and listens carefully to My voice." (John 18:36–37 AMP)

Yet for as much as Jesus had to say about the kingdom, it is not often that we talk about it in the Christianity of today. We haven't evolved. Actually, we've regressed, lost ground. We play small, right into our enemy's plan. The spiritual stalkers, predators, and bullies have the upper hand for now—because we've allowed it. Like the first Adam, we've given away our power and authority as image bearers, truth tellers, sons of the Father and men of his kingdom.

But that can change in a moment, and the enemy hordes know it. Their own power and authority hangs by a thread of lies that, once brought into the light, can be broken. That's what it takes, in a single life, to set a prisoner free. To set *us* free—you and me.

By "free," I'm not talking about salvation in the sense of getting saved from judgment and hell. That's a great gift, but I'm talking about still more, about Life in all its facets: living fully with a whole heart, walking intimately with God and others, experiencing the Father's love as a daily reality, taking our place in the battle, and loving courageously until Jesus returns.

Make no mistake, our enemy has power and authority—but only as much as we give them. And we have given them way too much. Now is the time for us, as warrior kings in our Father's kingdom, to take back what we've relinquished.

Dragons and Lions on the Loose

Given how often the Scriptures talk of Satan, his demons, and their effect on both individuals and all of humanity, it's amazing how seldom we speak in the church about the kingdom of darkness.

There are wars in the physical realm because there is a war in the spiritual realm. Love and hatred permeate the earth because Love and hatred battle in the spirit. The spiritual and physical are not parallel universes; they are intertwined, mixed together, existing inside one another in the same universe. And right now you are in both realms at the same time—a dangerous place to live.

Though unseen, the spiritual realm isn't unfelt or undetected. The question is, do we have eyes to see, ears to hear, and hearts that are awake to what is really going on? Are you aware, even as you read these words, that you are wanted and being watched, both by God and by the enemy? Do you know there are heroes, holy and good, who are for you? And villains who are against you?

Being awake to, oriented to, the Larger Story you're living in—a story that encompasses both the physical and spiritual realms—makes the difference between being a casualty versus a rescuer of casualties.

* * *

In the book of Revelation, the apostle John tells of a war in the spiritual realm. Led by the archangel Michael, the forces of heaven defeat a mutiny by Satan and his rebel angels, even as events play out in the physical realm with the birth of Christ. John then describes what follows:

> [Satan,] who continually deceives and seduces the entire inhabited world
> . . . was thrown down to the earth, and his angels were thrown down with
> him. . . . he who accuses [believers] and keeps bringing charges [of sin-
> ful behavior] against them before our God day and night. (Revelation 12:
> AMP)[5]

Our enemy invites us to agree with him over a myriad of deceptions—to consent to his lies and false suggestions about God, others, and especially ourselves. Then, based on those agreements, Satan goes to God and accuses us of being unfaithful. That's how our adversary operates. First he invites us to think or do; then he goes and tells on us.

Why would we want to help him in his work? And how do we do so? I'll tell you why and how: because we don't know the devil's methods and motives and we are naïve to our own glorious role in the Larger Story. Our enemy is in it for more than tempting us to sin. Darkness wants to claim us and subsequently have claim to and influence on our kingdoms.

In every wounding moment when a person says or does something unloving to someone else, our enemy uses one image bearer against another image bearer. Instead of loving one another as Christ commanded, we join the efforts of the other side by wounding one another. We aid the enemy in delivering fiery arrows of hurt, pain, and assault on each other. And in so doing, we keep the enemy's fallen world system in play.

Powerful Lies

We desperately need to be trained to see and hear with eyes and ears of the heart to reclaim what has been stolen or lost. The enemy forces want your kingdom, and they get it if and when their long, sustained assault pays off. It's a covert operation; they whisper in the first person, masking as your own inner voice to suggest, *We're not here. This is just you.*

Satan's number one lie, the thing he wants planted deep in every image bearer's heart, is, *You are on your own.* As early in your masculine journey as possible, he wants to get "inside" so that one day he can go to work on the outside.

That's how lies and sin work. It's not what a man does; it's all the dark messages programmed into him—how he thinks, what he believes—that drive his actions. Like default settings filed away and operating undetected, the programming drives the operation. Proverbs 23:7 says, "For as [a man] thinks in his heart, so is he" (NKJV).

The day when a boy's heart is wounded, and a lie is believed, and an agreement is made, and a vow is declared that *I'm on my own*, that is the day when the loss begins. The foundation of belovedness is shaken with fear, guilt, or shame, and the construction begins of a false self which guarantees that, years later, the grown man will live with something to hide, something to fear, and something to prove. What happens in a moment in youth will be reinforced over years by the enemy in the hope of one day cashing it in. Counselor and author John Eldredge observes, "Every man carries a wound. I have never met a man without one. No matter how good your life may have seemed to you, you live in a broken world full of broken people."[6]

* * *

The second most powerful lie I hear from the hearts of men is "Something is wrong with me." That's the voice of shame, and it often leads to the vow "I'm OK" when a man is not OK. The forces of darkness will do their best to keep an image bearer in a state of ignorance and naiveté, a false sense of security. Minimizing what happened to you is an indirect but powerful way to diminish your story and your worth.

There are things that happen to a young boy, to a teenager, to a grown man, that are *not* OK, not at all. And until you've faced the reality and impact of their not-OK-ness, *you* won't be OK. To think otherwise is denial. Any diminishment of those things and their negative effect on your heart is like a room without windows: it closes your heart to the light, and the voices of lies are your roommates.

It matters. Your story and all that happened to you in this war matters. One way or another you have been wounded on your masculine journey. Many times, actually. That's what happens in wars. And that's what happens when a boy has no one to fight for him or teach him how to fight the lies with the truth. But for many men, it's very hard to see and admit the ways the enemy delivered terrible blows, arrows to their younger heart. And they carry the wounds and lies into manhood.

So they remain disoriented, their ability to grasp their place in the Larger Story blocked until they experience healing encounters with God.

The Healing of Kings

Healing is part of every man's journey toward becoming a good king. And the good news is, healing is what God has for us. The things that impede our ability to see and walk with power and authority in the Larger Story—our

issues with anger, trust, anxiety, intimacy, and other insecurities
false expectations, deficits and fears, self-centeredness and controls,
depression, codependency, and narcissism,
addictions to food, alcohol, pornography, and so on

—all these and more are what our Father wants to transform, by his grace, from crippling liabilities into powerful assets to wield in his kingdom.

Healing is one of the big ways our small story fits into the Larger Story as we learn, step by step, how to offer our broken places to the Father and receive his words of love and affection, his insight into what is true, and his encouragement to trust him. What we gain in the process then multiplies outward as the healing we receive becomes the healing we in turn help others find.

In chapters to come, we'll look more closely at the healing journey. Our Father invites us to partner with him in dismantling our false self, constructed by the enemy with the help of his wounders. Something far better awaits you and me—the ability to see our place in the Larger Story and move in it with a settled heart that will impact the world for good. God's intention is to initiate and validate us individually into the role he created for each of us as a good king.

There are times when you can take back a lot of ground in a single moment. But in general, after twenty, thirty, forty years of living with a wounded and compromised operating system, recovery and restoration won't happen overnight. It's going to take a few years. That's how God operates. But that, friend, is the beauty of healing, because it's where intimacy with the Father lies: walking with him in the restoration of you.

In order to go forward, you'll need to go back. What happened to you? Both the questions and the answers are in your story. And so are the clues, and the keys, to your place in the Larger Story.

What You Believe Matters

This world isn't right—not yet. It's certainly not a place where an image bearer can afford to walk in ignorance with a bad case of naiveté.

You can very much be a Christian and still walk around like a zombie. So here is the truth: Jesus came to show us who God is, what the kingdom of heaven is really like, and how it all works. Religion and its ruler have been replaced with a new covenant and a new King.* But what we have received and continue to pass down is the old way based on performance. A system of service has crept back in and replaced intimacy.

If you are not experiencing intimacy with God—unconditional love, the very thing you were created for—then something is wrong, gravely wrong. It is critical that you and I experience God's love for us, for it is our greatest joy and our greatest weapon. God moves first, he moves most, and he wants to move us by his love to respond in love. "We love him, because he first loved us" (1 John 4:19 KJV).

* * *

A disoriented man will embrace what he should let go of and let go of what he should embrace. In the words of the great eighteenth-century theologian Jonathan Edwards, "The devil can counterfeit all the saving operations and graces of the Spirit of God."[7] That is how the Father of Lies works. He counterfeits the truth, disguising the untrue as another possibility, a reasonable conclusion, and we believe it and take it in. It's a trick as old as the fall—but it still works.

Because what you believe matters; it has power and authority in your life.

---

* The Bible uses the word *religion* in a neutral sense, as something that can be either good or bad (see James 1:26–27). But modern believers have come to view religion negatively, as dry theology and traditions disengaged from the heart—going through the motions without any real relationship with God. Since that's the meaning I intend, and since it's how most readers understand religion, it's how I'm using the word in this book.

If believing the truth in your heart can set you free, and if believing a lie can shackle you with fear, guilt, and shame, then *belief* is where the battle rages and the war for the heart is fought. I ask you again: What are the odds you have interpreted your life accurately?

The negative files stored up in the heart take time to see and clean out. But take courage—God is with you and will partner with you in the renovation and restoration of *you*. You cannot make it happen, any more than I can, but we sure can cooperate and collaborate with God to see lies exposed and to take back ground. And we must. If we are going to be good kings entrusted with more and more of his kingdom here on earth, we need to submit to God's internal remodeling.

George MacDonald wrote, "Foolish is the man, and there are many such men, who would set the world right by waging war on the evils around him, while he neglects that integral part of the world where lies his business, his first business— namely his own character and conduct."[8]

A man's character and conduct lie deep in the core of his being, forged through years of experience. Our attitudes, perspectives, conclusions—the things we believe and live by—come from all the many things we've been through. We hold those beliefs in our heart. It's time they were unearthed, brought to the surface and examined with God. Our prayer is King David's prayer of invitation:

Search me, God, and know my heart;
> test me and know my anxious thoughts.
See if there is any offensive way in me,
> and lead me in the way everlasting.
> (Psalm 139:23–24)

CHAPTER 5
The Heart of a King

*I pray that the eyes of your heart may be enlightened in order that you may know the
hope to which he has called you, the riches of his glorious inheritance in his holy people,
and his incomparably great power for us who believe.*
—Ephesians 1:18–19

*He who reigns within himself and rules passions, desires,
and fears is more than a king.*
—John Milton

W hen we were on a road trip as kids, my brothers and I would ask our parents
two questions from the back seat of the family car: "Where are we going?
How long till we get there?"

You asked them too—remember? Every kid wants to know.

Grown men aren't all that different. We still want a general idea of what to expect
and what to keep in mind when we head into something new. This chapter will give
you that. It's your prep for the chapters to come. Those are something like a road trip
on which you explore different scenic outlooks along the highway. The difference
is, on the masculine journey, each outlook is part of a stage, and once you arrive at
a given stage, you never really leave it—or, better put, what happened to you there,
what is formed in you, doesn't leave you. It becomes a part of you as you travel the
road from boyhood to king, and beyond to elder-sage. So, what do you need to know
before you embark?

The first part of this chapter is foundational because it addresses the thing that matters most to God: your heart. Your core identity, your deepest you, who you are when everything else is stripped away.

What is the heart's significance? What does the Bible really teach about it? Why is there such a battle waged against it? Vital questions, because the heart and its journey eventually determines the nature of a man's kingship—how he will reign and rule, whether well or poorly. In order to make sense of the chapters to come, you need to first understand what God has done for your heart through his Son, and what he will yet do for you in partnership with him.

Then in the latter part of this chapter, four charts and their descriptions will equip you with some important perspectives you will need to keep in mind as we consider each stage of the masculine journey.

* * *

Let's start with why it's important to deeply explore this journey in the first place: The only way to know if the story you are telling yourself is true—the story you have believed for many years; the story you are living today—is to go back with God and examine each stage. With his help, you need to remember those stages, sort out the truth from the lies you internalized, and invite God to free your heart, redeem the stages, and restore you to the man he created you to be.

You must go back in order to go forward.

You must remember in order to recover.

And you must see anything and everything that is in the way of receiving love.

Why? So you can become a king who loves well because you know from experience how well you yourself are loved by your Father.

The enemy knows what happens when a man gets his heart back whole, fully functional, and empowered to love powerfully. He knows that the healing experience equips a man to partner with God in healing others, and this the enemy dreads more than anything.

Getting Your Heart Back

I know a lot of men who put in sixty hours a week and yet are passive. Passivity doesn't mean a man is lazy or inactive. Passivity is the inability to engage —in current circumstances; in relationships that need a man's strong and kind presence, his discerning and helpful words, his strength against anything that is untrue.

You have to know your strength to offer it, and you have to have earned your wisdom and learned the way of love in order to bring the weight of who you are into the arena of life and people. And even still, to engage takes courage. Because engagement doesn't mean we fight the battles we can win; it means we fight the battles that need fighting.

Many of the moments when a man forges his identity will not be in his Google calendar. To the man who cannot see what God is up to in his life, those moments will often appear as inconveniences. God wants to partner with a good man to bring good to current relationships and circumstances. Any movement against passivity and toward engaging is a holy step in the right direction, toward a man's strength and away from the curse of Adam, a movement toward being entrusted with more and away from shrinking into less.

L. Frank Baum's *Wonderful Wizard of Oz* taught us that, for our journey, we need courage, wisdom and heart. The Tin Man character declared, "I shall take the heart . . . for brains do not make one happy, and happiness is the best thing in the world."[1] Yet later, in the famous 1939 film adaptation of the book, the Tin Man also said, "Now I know I've got a heart—'cause it's breaking." The part of us that experiences happiness and joy, the heart, is the riskiest part because it also knows grief. Joy and sorrow: in this life, you don't get the one without the other. That's the privilege and the cost of love.

"To love at all is to be vulnerable," wrote C. S. Lewis in *The Four Loves*.

> Love anything and your heart will certainly be wrung and possibly be broken. If you want to make sure of keeping it intact, you must give your heart to no one, not even to an animal. Wrap it carefully round with hobbies and little luxuries; avoid all entanglements; lock it up safe in the casket or coffin of your selfishness. But in that casket—safe, dark, motionless, airless—it will change. It will not be broken; it will become unbreakable, impenetrable, irredeemable.[2]

That's why it's essential for men to get their heart back. We can't love without it. And without love, we cannot be good kings.

The Heart Is Crucial

"Get your heart back"? Does that line up with your inherited theology? It sure didn't with mine. The first time I heard that the heart is central and that the redeemed heart is good, everything I had learned growing up pushed back. All my life I had been taught that "the heart is deceitful above all things, and desperately wicked" (Jeremiah 17:9 KJV; cf. Genesis 6:5).

How like the enemy to twist the Scriptures! If we accept his interpretation of them, the result is never good. If you believe your heart is wicked, you will live that way. If you're convinced it is untrustworthy, you will shut it down. One of Satan's great, diabolical accomplishments is to turn us into Tin Men, attempting to do life without a heart.

The power of a lie is that you believe it, and what you believe has authority in your life. But the devil's accusation that you are wicked at your core—that *you* are the problem—couldn't be further from the truth. Not if you're a believer, "born again, not of perishable seed, but of imperishable, through the living and enduring word of God" (1 Peter 1:23). Beloved son of God, it is impossible for the Spirit of God to birth something that is unrighteous. He speaks far better of you than what you were taught—and possibly better than you often speak of yourself.

We are the ones Jesus left the right hand of the Father to rescue and redeem. We are the glorious ones who bear God's image. In this life we struggle with our sins, limitations, and lies of the false self. But deeper than these, who we really are—our core, our heart, our true identity—is stamped with our Father's nature, havingbeen given new life through the Son and inhabited by the Holy Spirit. We have Trinity DNA and therefore share in God's glory (much more on that in chapter 14).

The enemy knows better than we do how all this works. He'll break all hell loose to prevent a man or woman from discovering who they truly are, growing into their true identity, experiencing life and love, and then offering life and love to the world around them.

Friend, you don't have to *try* to matter. You matter by right of birth. Your heart matters. It is the treasure of the kingdom.

* * *

Not only is the heart central, but the heart can be *good*. Jesus himself made that plain:

A *good* man brings good things out of the good stored up in his heart, and an evil man brings evil things out of the evil stored up in his heart. For the mouth speaks what the heart is full of. (Luke 6:45)*

So the question is, What is stored up there? Answer: What has been collected over the journey. Jesus taught how this works and what it leads to:

The seed on good soil stands for those with a *noble and good heart*, who hear the word, retain it, and by persevering produce a crop. (Luke 8:15)

Jesus understands the significance of the heart and is coming after your heart. Yes, the heart can be hard, assaulted, used, wicked, and wounded. But Jesus came to change all that. He wants your heart so you can experience "Blessed are the pure in heart, for they will see God (Matthew 5:8) and enjoy God from a whole heart.

"Flee the evil desires of youth," Paul exhorted his friend and apprentice Timothy, "and pursue righteousness, faith, love and peace, along with those who call on the Lord out of a *pure heart*" (2 Timothy 2:22).

What? The heart can be pure? Apparently it can. The heart God moves into and resides in is the new holy of holies. How can it then be wicked? It is the territory God occupies and is going to lovingly renovate and redecorate. A work from the inside out. He is jealous and fierce in his care of it, and he will continue his good work in it (Philippians 1:6), transforming us from within. That is how good kings are made—or might I say, remade.

The enemy has long prevailed in twisting the definition and importance of the heart. Is the redeemed heart good? Yes! And God wants to teach us how to live from it. Speaking from personal experience, that changes everything.

Nothing Tame or Safe

God has an agenda. He is working all things to the good for those who love him (Romans 8:28). So if things aren't good yet, he isn't done yet—not in your story and not in the frontier of the Larger Story. That is a wild idea, to be sure, but you and I were made for the wild. There is nothing tame or safe or predictable or controllable about God, the Larger Story, or your story. It's high time we quit trying to make it so.

Life outside the garden is war, and in that war, love is the most powerful weapon. God is love, and therefore love can't be dethroned. There is a mystery to it all, truly,

---

* My emphases in the three Scripture quotes in this section.

and that is the way it is supposed to be. None of us want a God we can figure out or predict. Rather, we need one who lives beyond the borders of our comprehension, theology, and current experience. With God, there is always more!

God is not a personal genie we use to manage our small stories. We can't make him in our image, and to think otherwise is to fool ourselves and live very small. No, we need a God who is more mystery than certainty. One who will work in mysterious ways. There is nothing tame or safe about that God—the true God, the Living God. Nothing manageable or simple. Everything about walking with him is adventure, always frontier. As my good friend and teammate Gary Barkalow has said, "Don't confuse mystery with disorientation. . . . Mystery is an invitation into intimacy with God. . . . Do you want to solve God or enjoy him?"

Having the Right Perspective

Just as we cannot control God, God did not make us to be controlled. That's what robots or servants are for, but God didn't make us either of those. He made us sons (and daughters) bearing his image. He wants lovers, choosers, intimate allies, beings who desire relationship with him as much as he does with us. So God made us free-willed, able to choose to love and to want him back.

God makes the first move and invites us to move in return. It is a responsive relationship, not a controlling one, and emulating him as his image bearers enlarges our lives. We were not created to live small. We were made to live big lives, glorious because they express the glory of God. But whenever we attempt to control, in all the unhealthy ways the word *control* can play out, we are choosing to live in the center of our story. And that is when the story gets really, really small. You, king in training, were not created to be in the center of the story. But that does not mean you were not created to have an important part to play—a powerful role, large and significant, with good desires that come standard within the heart of every image bearer. We long to matter and want to belong because we were made to matter and made to belong.

Look at your story and the desires of your heart. They are telling you something about who you are and what you were made for. Author Dan Allender wrote, "Stories don't give answers, but they do offer perspective."[3] And oh, how we need a good dose of perspective if we are going to take our place in the Larger Story and share in the life, *live* the life, that God created us to live.

The Battle for the Heart

The promise of God is life abundant, life to the full. Anyone feel a little gypped? I hope it is becoming clearer why you might feel shortchanged. Life outside the garden is hard, and we live in constant danger of settling for less. Most men exist dazed and confused because of everything that has happened to them. Fallenness has that effect on the heart, and sin drives it all home.

If the garden is what we were created for, then the garden and the Tree of Life are what we will one day see restored (Revelation 22). But until then we live in the in-between, between the first and second coming of Christ our King. We live in the middle, where there is a great battle for the heart. And if we do not see what is really going on, we will be casualties of that conflict again and again, victims of our own ignorance and, even worse, prisoners of war.

You matter that much. Your heart matters that much. Solomon knew this when he wrote Proverbs 4:23:

> Above all else, guard your heart, for everything you do flows from it. (NIV)

> Keep vigilant watch over your heart; that's where life starts. (MSG)

> Above everything else guard your heart, because from it flow the springs of life. (ISV)

The Old Testament is full of passages and stories concerning the heart. After God's people gave themselves to things other than him, the prophet Ezekiel knew how God would intervene for their hearts:

> I'll remove the stone heart from your body and replace it with a heart that's God-willed, not self-willed. I'll put my Spirit in you and make it possible for you to do what I tell you and live by my commands. (Ezekiel 36:26 MSG)

Paul the apostle knew the significance of the battle for the heart:

> If you declare with your mouth, "Jesus is Lord," and believe in your heart that God raised him from the dead, you will be saved. For it is with your heart that you believe and are justified, and it is with your mouth that you profess your faith and are saved. (Romans 10:9–10)

We need an act of the heart to enter into the kingdom of God.

The heart is the center of the great conflict. It is the subject of hundreds of Scriptures. And the mission of the kingdom of God is to rescue the heart, redeem it, and restore it to glory. All because we matter that much to God. All so we can be reinstated to our place in the Larger Story as co-heirs, reigning and ruling with Christ in what he has reclaimed for us: life *abundant* and *full*.

Life that is available here and now.

Why, then, are so few men experiencing it? Why does it seem there are so few good kings?

It's because most men are unfathered and unfinished. They are living with unanswered questions as to who they are and why they are here. And they have believed lies about who they are, and especially who their heavenly Father is, because their earthly fathers didn't know and couldn't show and tell them.

God wants to remedy this in your life. But he's not going to just swoop in and magically fix you all on his own. He wants you involved and experiencing firsthand his love that transforms you. He's not remote like some secret admirer; he's present, a proud and engaged Father who takes joy in seeing you become who you have it in you to be. The Father has an agenda for your good and, eventually, the good of many others to whom you will show the way once you yourself have experienced the way of the heart.

Learning by Living: *Ginosko*

Remember how, when you were a kid, your parents would mark your height with a pencil on the kitchen doorway to show how you were growing over time? Those lines of growth tell a story—and more than a story. They tell of a journey. For just as your body grew when you were a boy, so your heart has been growing up, maturing into more. Yet sadly, if mistreated, it can retreat into less.

Here's the thing: Reading about adult heroes when you were a kid didn't make you six feet tall and bulging with muscles, any more than reading a marriage book as a man will automatically make you a good husband, or watching a video series on parenting will make you a good father. So it is with becoming a good king: It takes experience and practice, on-the-job training, in order to truly learn and understand the ways of the kingdom and who you are in it.

Trials and errors on the field of battle, rightly understood: That's how learning is done. Doing it wrong, and doing it right, and coming to know what is true and what isn't: That's how wisdom is earned. In between all the quarter- and half-inch marks are hundreds of moments, experiences, that all add up. The chance we have interpreted them all accurately is slim. But I have learned over the years that it's never too late to come to know what really happened, and why—what marks were left on our heart and what new marks can be made.

* * *

The Greek word for "know," *ginosko*, refers to experiential knowledge. Not book learning but life learning, the kind of knowledge that comes not from written texts or classrooms but from doing and experiencing; from playing the violin, not just reading about how to play it.

It is one thing to know that freezing occurs at 32 degrees Fahrenheit; it is another thing to be caught outside in the frigid air, exposed and shivering, experiencing what freezing is all about. Academic truth is wonderful, but even more wonderful is when we become aware and notice, "Here is what this feels like." Then truth has meaning; it ceases to be merely intellectual and becomes personal property. That is when the truth becomes *more true*. And when it's more true, it can do what it is supposed to do—set us free.

That is *ginosko*: when we experience a truth in such a way that it becomes real to us.

From marriage to friendships to our interaction with God, the *ginosko* kind of knowing is very much a part of our deepest relationships. For instance, *ginosko* is the biblical Greek translation of the original Hebrew expression for sexual intercourse between a man and women: "Adam knew [*ginosko*] his wife" (Genesis 4:1 ESV). It describes an intimate knowing through the deeply interpersonal experience of love-making.

And in friendships, you could almost expect that John, the friend who knew Jesus best—in his own words, "the disciple whom Jesus loved" (John 21:20)—would use the word *ginosko* more than seventy-five times in his gospel. For John, Jesus's words "I am the way, the truth, and the life" went beyond just a factual statement. They were also a knowing that burned in John's heart because he had walked with, talked with, eaten with, done life with the man who made that claim. For John—and for you and me—those words were, and are, an invitation to *ginosko* Jesus by *experiencing* him as the way, the truth, and the life. Until we do, the fact remains true and good, but it has yet to profoundly change us.

Until we experience the love of Jesus for ourselves, other experiences and characters will influence our lives more powerfully, shape our beliefs more subtly and deeply, and therefore play out in our decisions and behaviors more dangerously. And the wounding moments, in which we endure pain and which create their own kind of *ginosko*, will, as they long have done, exert a bad influence on our hearts.

But they are exactly what the Father wants to get his hands on to remedy and redeem. So take heart, friend! You are here, and he is coming after you. You are his beloved son. You are on his heart and mind, and your glory and destiny are what he wants to fiercely recover and lovingly introduce you to. And then he wants to turn you loose on behalf of the hearts of others.

The Architect of Your Heart

Every masculine heart *evolves*, and with life's gauntlet of trials, it's understandable why most men don't evolve well. They've been deprived of blessing, validation, initiation, the offering of encouraging words, and the training their hearts needed.

The critical moments and materials needed to reconstruct a good man happen on a journey of becoming, on which we can either become more or retreat into less. Thankfully, God, the architect of your heart and the master craftsman of intimate relationships, is walking with you. His plan all along was, and is, for you to become like Jesus (Romans 6:5; 8:28–30). He wants to build you into the version of you that is most like himself. And that journey of reconstruction starts with this foundational truth:

> *You are an image bearer, made with God qualities.*
> *You possess your heavenly Father's DNA.*
> *And you carry within you the reality of immortality.*

Remember that, image bearer. *Remember it.* Your heart is good. In Christ we were reborn and given what we need to become who we were made to be. Our problem isn't that we think too much of ourselves but too little. We have become convinced we are less than who we really are, and so we live there, in that less. For some reason, the bad stuff is easier to believe. But God has other plans. C. S. Lewis writes,

Imagine yourself as a living house. God comes in to rebuild that house. At first, perhaps, you can understand what He is doing. He is getting the drains right and stopping the leaks in the roof and so on; you knew that those jobs needed doing and so you are not surprised. But presently He starts knocking the house about in a way that hurts abominably and does not seem to make any sense. What on earth is He up to? The explanation is that He is building quite a different house from the one you thought of—throwing out a new wing here, putting on an extra floor there, running up towers, making courtyards. You thought you were being made into a decent little cottage: but He is building a palace. He intends to come and live in it Himself.[4]

It is time we started replacing the enemy's lies about our identity with a far better reality: the truth of sonship and belovedness. That's the foundation for what God wants to make of our lives. Reconstruction is about to commence as, in the next chapters, we start looking closely at the blueprint—the stages of a man's life—and begin replacing the history of losses with invitations to explore again.

The Six Stages of a Man's Life

The masculine journey is anything but simple, but we need to somehow make sense of it, especially our past. One way is to take inventory of our personal journey in stages, each stage being about a decade. This isn't an exact science, of course, but it's a helpful way to break down the journey into its significant mile markers. Rather than attempting to consider our life as a whole, it's less overwhelming and more realistic to go back with God and explore the details stage by stage and decade by decade.

So we come at last to the six stages of the journey toward becoming a king and beyond.[5] They are

Boyhood
Explorer
Warrior
Lover

King
Elder-Sage

The stages are not all neat and tidy, with easy transitions and clear guidelines. Rather, they overlap, and at times the cart gets ahead of the horse, often with damaging results.

In the chapters that follow, we'll cover territory that many authors have written whole books about. We'll follow God through the mountains and valleys of masculinity down the path into what he meant when he meant a *man*, and we'll compare that path with our own. Be forewarned: Parts of it may seem overwhelming. Overwhelmed is how I sure felt when I first saw my story in the context of the Larger Story. But it's only when we feel as daunted as we should that we turn to the One—the only one—who can help us recover and heal. Only God can restore us, train us, and then turn us loose, free to love others back to life because, from personal experience, we *ginosko* the power of his love in our own life.

* * *

Before you can connect the dots, you have to collect the dots. The significant moments of good and of bad, of wounding and of validation. The Dad stories, the Mom stories, the impact on your heart of family, teachers, coaches, pastors, priests, babysitters, peers, friends, even total strangers. Collecting and connecting all the different key dots is critical, so you can treasure the good and give the wounding moments, their messages, and even their messengers to God.

Every man, every masculine heart, has been wounded in boyhood. Few, very precious few, have recovered. And much of what we call our personality is an elaborate disguise, a way of coping, a way of covering up our injuries so we can soldier on under the lies we've believed. God wants to free us from those lies. He is the one, ultimately, who brings healing to our heart. But he does so in partnership with us. As we revisit each stage of our life with God, he will help us identify the key dots and reveal how to connect this one with that. With his help and a process for healing, our false self will diminish and our true self will emerge.

Four Views on the Six Stages

At the beginning of this chapter I mentioned four charts that will give you perspective on the masculine journey, how it works, and what lies ahead. It's time now to present them as visual aids that can help you connect the journey's six stages.

The stages need definition, and the following chapters will provide it. But in personal experience, the borders can get fuzzy. There's overlap. There's layering. And that's where these charts and their descriptions come in handy. No, more than handy —essential. Keep them very much in mind as you proceed through the book. They'll help you square each stage, as you read about it, with your personal experience. Because your path is *your* path. It's unique, and while the stages lay out a roadmap, I'll bet my bottom dollar your life has involved plenty of bushwhacking. It's amazing you're still here, amazing you're still standing—perhaps just barely, but *standing*. Bravo for you, and praise God! Now let's move forward.

Linear Timeline

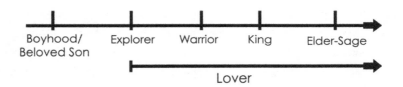

We all are living on a timeline. Day after day, the accumulation of days makes something, forms something—a life. The masculine journey is the story of a man moving through the various stages on such a timeline. While the stages aren't boxed in, as the next charts show, they can and often do get out of order in a way that creates a train wreck.

Because the process overall is linear, it can be observed chronologically. One stage leads to another, and, like the ticking crocodile in *Peter Pan*, time is chasing us all. As Søren Kierkegaard wrote, "Life must be understood backward. But . . . it must be lived forwards."[6]

Building on the Foundation

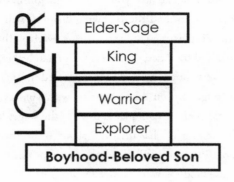

Every builder and every architect will tell you the most critical part of any construction is its foundation, and so it is with the masculine heart. If poor materials are used, it doesn't matter how solid the plan is. The building will one day need repair, and usually a very expensive one. Every floor is at risk of being "off," endangering all who reside on it. Restoration and reconstruction are a big business; people in that profession make their living on worn-out or just plain bad construction.

The masculine heart is no different. God has provided some ancient blueprints for its sound construction. But over time, qualified architects left the drafting tables, and the ensuing generations of builders have been far from building men of integrity. Because we build from experience, even bad experience, Satan and this fallen world have made it hard to construct a good man. But to see what God intended us to be is to feel the weight of what the second-century church leader Iranaeus meant when he wrote, "The glory of God is man fully alive."

The Parts Form a Whole

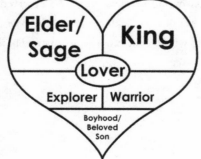

Have you ever heard a boy say something beyond his years? Or witnessed him do something noble? Have you ever heard a man in his seventies tell a silly joke or watched him learn a new skill? Have you ever seen a young man tenderly care for an injured animal or write a song or poem, something of beauty and romance?

It's all in there—all the pieces and parts that make up a man.

Certainly, on a timeline there is to be an emphasis on the appropriate stage, but at any time a boy can be sagely, a warrior can be a lover, and a sage can be youthful. As with a puzzle from the manufacturer, the pieces are all there; it's just that when it gets dumped out and many hands try to put it together, pieces get lost or misplaced.

The masculine journey is one with many parts and pieces, and each one needs some initiation and validation in order for all the parts to connect smoothly, one part to another. A man plays many roles in his life, and having the equipment to play each role is critical.

What Is and Is Becoming

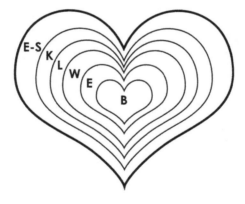

Surely you remember Dr. Suess's beloved Christmas story, *How the Grinch Stole Christmas!* At the end of the tale, the sourpuss of a Grinch has a shocking revelation about what Christmas is really about, and his shriveled, miserly heart grows into something big, good, and giving.

This is what God wants to do in a man's life, growing, expanding, loving him so that his heart swells. Being loved comes first; then, with that deep center established, living water can flow from it into the hearts of others. This is what it means to be a good king. We allow God to love us at each and every stage of our journey. We go back in order to go forward. We grieve with God the losses, turn to God to repair what is broken, and trust God to restore and secure each stage—every floor, each piece and part—so we can become *more*.

More, entrusted with the most valuable things of the kingdom . . .

> its ways,
>
> its resources,
>
> and its greatest treasure: the hearts of others.

* * *

The question remains: *What happened to you?*

Proverbs 25:2 responds:

> It is the glory of God to conceal a matter;
>> to search out a matter is the glory of kings.

Beloved son, king in the making, be of good courage. The King of kings is with you, and the search is about to begin.

PART TWO
The Journey of a King

God will meet you where you are in order to
take you where he wants you to go.
—*Tony Evans*

Common to all the stories we love to tell, the hero or heroine must take a journey. A journey forward, outward into the unknown, yet also back, inward into the all too familiar. Whatever other destiny the story may entail, the adventurer always is in pursuit of one vital thing that has been lost: themselves.

Whether in galaxies far, far away, or in the dirt streets of Dodge City, or in a land of old with its castles and Round Table, the battle between good and evil can be told in a hundred different settings, but the characters, the hearts caught up in such stories, are always finding their way to who they truly are and what they have it in themselves to become, and to a greater destiny that is waiting to find them. Courage and hope are always required for epic journeys, for without those qualities, characters stay at home amid the familiar and comfortable—and, sadly, they just stay the same. Every character, every image bearer, is playing a part in the Larger Story. Just one person can sabotage your own part by underestimating it, and that's you.

There is good reason why you underestimate who you are and your significant role in the story God is unfolding. Jesus made this clear when he spoke of a thief who comes only to steal, kill, and destroy (John 10:10). Part 1 began to expose and tear down that thief's lies with some foundational, life-giving truths: You bear God's image. Your masculine heart is the treasure of the kingdom. And your heart has been under siege from the day you arrived, the day God ordained for your life to be written into the Larger Story.

Now, in part 2, you are invited to explore, with courage and hope, your story through the stages of the masculine journey, and to ask the critical questions all great characters eventually must ask:

Who am I?
Where am I?
How did I get here?
What is the way home?

CHAPTER 6
Boyhood
Where the Masculine Journey Begins

And Jesus matured, growing up in both body and spirit,
blessed by both God and people.
—*Luke 2:52 (MSG)*

No one gets to adulthood without a wound.
—Robert Bly, *Iron John*

DO YOU SEE ME?

DO YOU LOVE WHAT YOU SEE?

Turning the corner and stepping onto Jersey Street, I was getting closer. My eyes did their best to take in the panoramic views and all that was going on around me. Three months earlier the arrangements had been made, and the count-down added to the moment. I was somewhere I had never been before, and yet it was familiar. My heart knew, and I was letting it have free rein.

When I was five, my family lived in Southern California, and that is where I was introduced to baseball stadiums and big league games. My dad took me to see the Dodgers and to Angel games, always in the cheap seats but also always to games that had bat night or helmet night. Baseball was a generous game.

Now, decades later here in Boston, standing in line three hours before the game, I felt young. Inside, I walked past concession stands and souvenir shops beginning to buzz with activity. I could see where I was going, through the tunnel into the inner sanctuary of the field.

Earlier that day I had toured a good bit of the city with Robin. One brochure said thirty-two churches were official historical landmarks. I'm pretty sure Fenway Park, built in 1912, was at the top of the list of the town's holy sites. It felt holy to me, anyway. My official Fenway guide led me and my tour group to some seats down the first base line, behind the home team dugout. Beyond our guide, out on the field, we could see batting practice underway. Crack! Crack! Crack!

After sharing several of the special moments in Red Sox history with our group, the guide led us onto the field. Less than ten yards away, Red Sox players were taking swings in the batting cage. We stood in silence and listened.

Crack! Crack! Crack! Nothing like that sound, echoing over and over again. And baseball has a smell too, just like a garden or a garage, the ocean or the woods. My senses, awake to the moment, were inviting me back into my personal history as well as that of the Red Sox. I started to remember when my own bat, ball, and glove never laid idle for long.

And then, at last, it was time.

Time to be escorted to one of baseball's holiest views: the Big Green Monster. Here, atop Fenway's one-of-a-kind left field wall, many of the balls from batting practice were now heading at me rather than away from me. With every swing, the dream of one coming directly my way increased. The boy in me was fully alive.

We finished the pregame tour and walked the beautiful old stadium at our leisure. Along the old brick walls were pictures and plaques of all sizes and shapes memorializing the heroes, commemorating the players, teams, and moments that meant something to this place. I remembered my shoe boxes of baseball cards, especially the All Star set from my birth year, 1964. Brooks Robinson, Mickey Mantle, Hank Aaron, Willie Mays, Carl Yastrzemski . . . they had played in this stadium. It was a *Field of Dreams* moment.

Days later, as I prayed and journaled, part of my heart felt as if it had been pulled out from the back of a closet, like the "kid's table" that only comes out once a year when family comes around. I was sitting at that table, remembering a life larger than just me and asking God, *What is it that can move a heart so?*

A few days later the Father brought this quote from *The Little Prince* across my path: "All grown-ups were children once—although few of them remember it."[1]

There it was—the answer to my question. God was inviting me to recover something I needed to be a good king. He was prompting fifty-six-year-old me to remember the simple happiness of *wonder* and the importance of being young.

Serious as life can become, it is still faith like that of a child that inherits the kingdom (Matthew 18:3–5). Recovering wonder and youthfulness of heart as we walk with God allows us, as men, to love those in their early stages of life, inviting them to wonder, innocence, and play. And it's vital that we do. For our children's sake, our own, and that of the kingdom, we need to claim for ourselves today what far too many of us never knew as kids.

Tales of Our Fathers

"I was asked by a counselor a few years back, 'Tell me about your dad,'" said my friend Steve. "I remember the first thing out of my mouth: 'Well, he didn't beat me.'"

He stared down at our coffee, paused, then looked me in the eye and said, "What kind of answer is that?"

We were telling Dad stories, a circle of six men in our fifties sharing what we remembered about growing up. Some of our fathers were still alive; others had passed on.

Jim spoke up. "My dad never hugged me or physically engaged. We never wrestled or played together—nothing. I wonder if that is why I crave affection so much now?"

I wonder too.

Another man shared, "My dad taught me how to work. Ever since I can remember, he was always working. If I was going to spend any time with him, we were working on something. I wonder if that is why I can't sit still and relax, why I always have to be doing?"

I wonder.

Jeff weighed in. "My dad left when I was three. We saw him maybe once a year, and when we did, it was awful. He couldn't engage. Every birthday and every event in school, every one, I thought, *Maybe he will show up*. It never happened. That's why I never miss my kids' stuff. I'm going to be there no matter what."

I wonder if Jeff's kids can appreciate his presence. I also wonder if, with every event Jeff attends, it softens his dad's absence and proves he is a better man than his dad ever was.

I wonder.

Then Craig shared, and Craig doesn't often share. "Well, my dad was constantly present, telling me what I should and shouldn't do. Nothing was ever good enough. *I* was never good enough. After my games, he would go over every mistake. I got to where I dreaded his presence."

Could that be why Craig often seems so defensive? Why it's hard to have a conversation with him that doesn't turn into a debate to be won or lost?

I wonder.

For many of us, our dads loomed large in our lives—for some of us, beneficially; for others, not so much. For still others, Dad wasn't there at all. In this and the following chapters, we'll look at how our fathers—and our mothers, our siblings, and others—shaped our heart, whether for good or bad. Much has conspired against us through the years, as we grew from boyhood to manhood, to steal our wholesome childlike qualities. In the face of wounds, youthful hearts grow tough, armor plated with never-agains. Cynicism leaks in and clouds out the wonder. That's how our enemy operates.

But our heavenly Father is also at work, and his intention for us is Life with a capital *L*. He has a way forward toward reclaiming the wonder. The young-at-heartedness. All the best qualities of a child, guided by the wisdom and experience of a grown man and equipped by the Spirit with the power and authority of kings.

Let's look at what that journey forward entails.

The Stories You Were Born Into

When you were born, you were born into a story that had been unfolding for decades. Your mom and your dad are both a story. Each of your grandparents is a story, and their stories came together to make new chapters and set new courses. And through the generations, you and I were finally written in. The way our hearts were handled by those we were given to has shaped not only our own stories but many others as well, far more than many of us will ever know this side of heaven.

Whether you were planned by your earthly parents, or were a pleasant surprise, or were something of an inconvenience, you were and have always been known, planned, and wanted by God. It's amazing how often the Bible speaks to our value and worth *before* we were even born. Take, as a sampler, these four passages from the Amplified Bible:

> You formed my innermost parts;
> You knit me [together] in my mother's womb.
> I will give thanks and praise to You,
> for I am fearfully and wonderfully made;
> Wonderful are Your works,
> And my soul knows it very well.
>
> (Psalm 139:12–14)

> When Elizabeth heard Mary's greeting, her baby leaped in her womb; and Elizabeth was filled with the Holy Spirit and empowered by Him. (Luke 1:41)

> At the end of eight days, when He was to be circumcised, He was named Jesus, the name given [to Him] by the angel [Gabriel] before He was conceived in the womb. (Luke 2:21)

> "Before I formed you in the womb I knew you [and approved of you as My chosen instrument],
> And before you were born I consecrated you [to Myself as My own];
> I have appointed you as a prophet to the nations."
>
> (Jeremiah 1:5)

But since you were born into a broken world, how your heart was handled from the day you were conceived is as important as your first steps and first words. Were your days in the womb surrounded by blessing, anticipation, and preparation, or were they subject to strife, fear, and sadness? The difference matters, because what your mom and dad were going through, you went through too.

Since being loved is core to how we were created and receiving love is what we were created for, our experience of being a *beloved son* is the foundation from which all other stages in our development are built. Whether you were born in the newest birthing facility or in a manger, the environment that matters most is how your parents welcomed you into their lives. The way you were nurtured, protected, and provided for in the womb and in the early days of infancy lays the foundation for how you receive, how you interpret, and how you pursue being loved.

Did your parents make you the center of their universe, welcomed and cherished? Did they hold you and sing over you, hug you, provide, protect, and pray blessings over you? Those two image bearers weren't perfect, but they didn't need to be; what matters is whether they were *good*. Because a father and mother whose loving hearts were most concerned about loving your own heart are the foundation to demonstrating what is already true in the spiritual realm: that you are loved.

Author Henri Nouwen wrote in *The Life of the Beloved*, "Being the Beloved expresses the core truth of our existence. We are the Beloved. We are intimately loved long before our parents, teachers, spouses, children and friends loved or wounded us. That's the truth of our lives. That's the truth spoken by the voice of our God that says, 'You are my Beloved. . . . On you my favor rests.'"[2]

Unfortunately, not all of us had a safe passage into this world. That "core truth of our existence" wasn't what we experienced at the hands of those to whom our hearts were entrusted, who were supposed to show us love's meaning. But that time of our life isn't a matter we usually consider or a question we think to explore: *What kind of story was I born into?*

Boyhood Stage

My boyhood years were spent first in Southern California from ages four to six; then in Salt Lake City from six to nine; then in Seattle from nine through twelve. The West in the 1970s was a great exploration for my parents: "Load the boys up and let's go."

I'm the oldest of three brothers within five years and a "surprise" little sister ten years my younger. My parents were adventurers, so vacations to the Grand Canyon, Tetons, redwood forests, and shores of the Pacific Ocean were regular events in our loaded-down, some-kind-of-yellow Opel station wagon. Some expeditions offered miles of waves and sand for running and building castles; others invited boulder climbing and stone skipping along calmer shores. Fishing poles and hiking sticks, bathing suits and binoculars—we kids were raised exploring.

When my family wasn't on the trail, the cities we lived in hosted professional and college teams. Since my dad had played football and basketball in college, the bleachers also became a place to explore, cheering on our teams and enjoying those great meals of hotdogs, sodas, and popcorn. When we were little, my two brothers and I had our dad's time. We had his presence. As I reflect back and compare what I got to what most boys experienced, I realize I was given a rare gift indeed.

The boyhood stage of the masculine journey is, or should be, a time of being seen, wanted, and affirmed, a time of play and wonder, a time when a boy experiences that he is the joy of his father and has the attention of his mother. Fundamental questions he is asking are

Do you see me?
Do you love what you see?

He yearns to know he is prized and delighted in.

The father creates a world that is safe, and he is often the leader of play, present and engaged. He brings surprises for his son, places to look into and things to learn hands-on, gifts that speak to the boy's heart. "Hands-on" often describes the relationship itself: walking hand in hand with Dad, being carried close to his chest, getting rides on his shoulders. This is the time for the boy to experience that someone is looking out for him, that the world is not up to him, that "Dad's got things under control."

In all of it, the main job of Dad is to answer the deep questions of his boy's heart—*Do you see me? Do you love what you see?*—hundreds of times over with strong and tender replies, *Yes, and yes!*

Jesus himself navigated through this stage, moving from the manger to Egypt and then back. His earthly father, Joseph, protected him, thanks to the prompting of heaven, moving him away from the threat of death at the hands of the jealous King Herod. Jesus was probably close to two at the time. After three and a half years, when it was safe to return from Egypt, Joseph brought Jesus and Mary back to Nazareth, together with any siblings who may have been born abroad.

What were your own early years like? How did your father relate to you and answer your questions? What expeditions, adventures and events do you remember that spoke to your heart either positively or negatively? As you look back at the foundational years, what experiences told you that you were special and that you mattered—or what circumstances and encounters communicated that somehow you weren't special or didn't matter?

Initiating and Validating: Raising the Beloved Son

During boyhood, being a beloved son—having a foundation as someone seen, wanted, and dearly loved—is the ideal bedrock on which to construct a man. Boyhood is when, for a time, we are bigger than the world, and we *are* the center of the universe. It is a time of receiving attention, provision, and a safe environment in which to play and to learn.

Yet parents walk a fine line between engaging versus spoiling on the one hand or ignoring on the other. Parents' world may revolve around their son, but that doesn't mean he gets everything he wants. Don't confuse spoiling with providing. This is the stage when the young masculine heart is first given choices: what to wear, which vegetable he wants, what chores he should do before he goes out to play. He hears and processes the answer *no* and learns the first stages of trust.

The entire geography of a boy's life at this time often consists of upstairs and downstairs, his room and other rooms, the backyard and front yard, home and school. Hearts at this stage don't need world travel—they have their imaginations to transport them all kinds of places. A loved boy feels that life is where he is, and where he is, that's life!

Boyhood should be a time of little responsibility and lots of play, exploration, wonder, dirt, building things, and breaking things. And superheroes! As John Eldredge once said, "When boys dress up like superheroes, they aren't pretending. They're rehearsing."[3] It is in a boy to be brave, courageous, and daring, and also kind, caring, and helpful. One day he will need to be all those things for the hearts of others.

During these wonder years of books and balls, music lessons and bikes, forts and dogs, chores and privileges, Mom and Dad's job is to provide, protect, and preserve their boy's innocence as long as possible. Sooner or later it will give way to life's harsh realities—it isn't a matter of if but when. Meanwhile, to a boy who is *safe*, his entire world feels like a great adventure. Being the beloved son pours deep, strong foundational footings in this stage. And that good foundation, and what is built upon it, will in turn be able to withstand the storms and battles in the stages to come.

A father's presence is paramount. It is his presence that assures a boy he is being watched over, cared for, and seen. Though he'd probably not know how to express it, his heart knows, "I'm safe, wanted, and loved." When a boy is invited to go places with Dad, it's a very good thing. I remember just going to the grocery store with my dad. He would always walk us by the Brach's candy bins at the front of the store. Man, that was a lot of candy! He would reach into one of the bins and pull out a couple pieces, one for him and one for me. (It was a few years later when I realized the candy wasn't complimentary.)

* * *

Bedtime is a sacred time for validating and initiating the boy. It's when he needs to be tucked in, read to, asked questions of, and taught how to pray by hearing his father pray. When the lights in the world dim, intimate conversations can happen. Time slows down and connections are possible, physical, emotional, and spiritual. Tuck-in is a time for storytelling, when a son hears his father tell of when he himself was a boy—stories of adventure, of learning, and even of mischief and trouble Dad got into. Tucking in can be a time to sing or maybe recite a poem together, all the while feeling the arms of Dad, his presence in words and facial expressions, physical strength and emotional tenderness.

It is important for a boy to be introduced to other men—to see men being men in the company of other men, observing them and being introduced to Dad's friends, learning a handshake, the importance of looking someone in the eye, and how to honor others with good manners.

The boy also becomes acquainted with physical strength. He wrestles with Dad and discovers the feel of a five-o'clock shadow. He learns about hitting, kicking, throwing a ball, and punching a bag. Lifting and moving stuff with Dad is as important as playing with other boys. Garages, workbenches, and gardens, places the kid sweats a little with Dad while helping with a project around the house, are food for the boy's soul.

Outdoor play is huge. We live in a day of computer screens, but as wonderful as the virtual world can be, it's not a substitute for interacting with the creation, seeing, smelling, touching, experiencing all it has to offer a young heart. Think of David in the fields with his sheep, learning so much about the natural world around him—the moon and stars, sun and storms, wildflowers and wild beasts—and seeing in all of it the heart and ways of God. So many of David's great psalms were shaped by his outdoor boyhood.

The Wounded Boy

The late sixties and early seventies, when I was a boy, were a time when people rang the doorbell and called each other on phones with long tangled cords that attached to the kitchen wall. My brother and I would jump up to see which one of us could answer first, shouting, "I got it! I got it." We lived in very trusting days.

Things changed, though, as more and more light got shed on the darkness of even those decades. I remember the "Don't Talk to Strangers" campaigns in elementary school. Folks never used to discuss such things, but as crimes against children appeared in the evening news and in daily newspapers, what became increasingly clear wasn't that the world was *getting* more unsafe but that it was *already* unsafe, and it was time to talk about it. Since the garden, this fallen world has been a dangerous place, full of wounded, struggling people and an enemy roaming about. Darkness uses people to use people. It's through humans that evil is able to steal, kill, and destroy with no regard to age, color, status, or gender.

All hearts have been sinned against, so every heart has been wounded. Even those assigned to protect us, and especially they, have at one time or another wounded us. It cannot be avoided; there are too many opportunities for it to happen. Even the best of parents are imperfect, and our enemy is that good at capitalizing on even the smallest opportunities. Parents may be getting better as they learn to walk with God, but they could also be getting worse, as people often get stuck in their ways. In any case, whether intentionally or unintentionally, aggressively or passively, your mom and dad wounded you, guaranteed.

You would think that seeing this and recognizing it in our lives would help us avoid wounding others. But often it's just the opposite. There is a major reason to get healing: not just for our own sake, but also so we don't do to others what was done to us. You know the maxim, and it bears repeating: Wounded hearts wound hearts.

* * *

What's going on in you right now as you read this? Chances are you're wrestling with two questions that connect your boyhood with your fatherhood: *What happened to me?* and *What am I doing to my own kids?* The way your heart was handled back then plays into how you handle the hearts entrusted to you today. But there's good news: The damage to your heart can be treated and healed, and the restoration you experience can have a life-giving impact, not only on you but also, wonderfully and significantly, on your children. In order for that to happen, though, you've first got to explore the damage—not just the wounds but also the ways you responded to them that have shaped your false self.

Many of our fathers operated in our stories out of their own woundedness. Instead of being a good king, their false self made them something else: a man who abdicated his reign and rule altogether. An MIA. But every king wounds, whether he's a good king, a bad king, or no king at all. And our fathers were by no means the only wounder. Through a multitude of voices—Dad, Mom, aunts, uncles, teachers, coaches, clergy, other kids' parents, and more—the enemy delivers harsh messages to a boy's heart:

> *Why can't you get it right?* (Guilt)
>
> *Something is wrong with you.* (Shame and Rejection)
>
> *You are unprotected and on your own.* (Fear)
>
> *If you had done more, your mom (or dad) would have stayed and loved you.* (Conditional Love)

All of us have been touched by experiences with lying implications, judged for what we did, judged for what we didn't do, branded for our disobedience, labeled for our gullibility, and on, and on. The wounds of performance cut deep when we were young, and they can be difficult to revisit. Why go back to explore something we've spent a lifetime trying to forget?

The enemy desperately wants us to believe love is conditional. Even our drawings and coloring book pictures on the refrigerator are things he can eventually twist into lying whispers: *You are applauded, encouraged, and seen—loved—for what you do, not for who you are.** A boy's future kingdom is always subject to enemy infiltration, decades before he becomes a king.

---

* Please don't misunderstand me. I'm not saying it's wrong for parents to post their children's artwork on the refrigerator. Of course it's OK! It's one of the ways Mom and Dad validate their kids, and that's a good thing. My point is simply that the enemy can twist even the most loving validations, from displaying drawings to celebrating good grades or sports achievements, into the lie that love is performance based. A boy whose pictures don't get hung on the refrigerator art gallery can easily get the same ugly message.

How Conditional Love Enters

Boyhood is very much about observing and taking notes. It's the time when we begin to shape beliefs about who we are, how life works, and whether or not we are safe. When a boy grows up *not* feeling he is the beloved son—if instead he experiences abandonment, loss, betrayal, shaming, and even violence—his innocence is stolen, his heart learns to hide, and the compulsion to somehow prove his value or protect himself is driven deep inside him. The wounds are profound, and they can camouflage themselves well.

Wounding happens in a multitude of ways.

- When a heart is missed, ignored, or shunned, that's a wound.
- Death, disease, disability, financial hardship, any kind of tragedy and loss in the family, can inflict trauma on a boy's heart.
- Anger, accusation, or diminishment by a parent, grandparent, or another person leave in their wake confusion, unrest, and fear.
- Shaming messages that cause a young heart to feel not merely "I did something wrong" but "Something is wrong with me"—these lies cut and pierce and leave long-lasting wounds.

And so it goes, in endless and heartbreaking variety.

As boys, we didn't fully understand what was going on around us. All we knew was, Dad is mad, or Mom is frustrated. And kids blame themselves way too easily. We couldn't separate our parents' behavior from ourselves. From *their* words, attitudes, and actions, we inferred whether *we* were either good or bad. Many of us learned along the way that it's better to be a "good boy" than a loved boy.

Awful as wounding moments may be, the lying messages we derive from them are even worse. Such lies hit hard, and when we agree with them, they have the power to shape our beliefs and control our lives. In response, we make vows about how we will carry on: "I will never _____," or "I will always _____." That's how it works: Whether consciously or subconsciously, we make an *agreement* that the lie is true, and we *vow* how we will act or think in response to prove ourselves right or protect ourselves henceforth. That combination of agreements and vows, internalized, makes up the system of the false self that is so powerful and operational in a man's life. It explains why, left undealt with, what happened to us when we were four years old can remain fully operational in us when we're fifty-four.

When Dad's Not There

A boy needs to live in a world made safe by his father—a world in which he's free to explore, free to dare, to make messes, to try things, to fail and succeed while simply being a boy. What he *doesn't* need is to grow up too soon. Wounding is almost guaranteed when a boy is left to figure things out on his own instead of being led, taught, validated, and initiated by a father who cares for him.

The death of a father or the divorce of parents takes a boy out by removing the father from the boy's story. The wonder years become the wondering years: "Why did Dad leave? What did I do wrong? What will I do now?" Such questions translate into rejection and abandonment. They speak loudly to the boy's core, foundational questions: *No, I don't see you. And what I do see, I don't love. If I did, I would have stayed and been your father. Something is wrong with you.*

For that matter, a father doesn't have to leave physically to be missing in action. Whether it's because he's overwhelmed, clinically depressed, trapped in an addiction, or just perpetually running busy in order to provide, a father can live under the same roof as his son and still be a functional no-show. In any case, the earlier in the masculine journey a boy experiences the absence of his dad, the deeper that boy's sadness will go, and as he grows, he'll try to fill the hole with performance, work, women, anything for comfort. If that doesn't work, then the buses of drug addiction, alcoholism, and porn run all day, every day, waiting to meet him at the all-too-familiar stops. If divorce occurs later in the boy's masculine journey, in the explorer or warrior stages, anger is likelier to be his response. Hatred will brood in his heart, and insecurity will invite him to vow, "I'll show you. I didn't need you anyway."

* * *

When a father leaves, two foundational cracks occur in a boy's heart. The enemy drives home the message "You are alone," and in response, the boy may isolate. Or worse, he may feel responsible for the happiness and well-being of Mom and his siblings, if any. He's now the "man of the house"—a king far, far too soon, skipping several stages of development. A boy's heart isn't made to carry such a load, to care for others when he himself is supposed to be cared for and invited to play, not provide.

This is often the reason a man in his forties will shuck responsibility as a warrior and king in favor of play and irresponsibility. We call it a "midlife crisis," and so it is. The man is attempting to return to an undeveloped stage to soothe unhealed wounds.

* * *

Ironically, a parent who overprotects can bring the end of innocence through heavy-handed control. Yes, kids can get hurt—it's inevitable. But the greater, unseen injury can come through a parent's reaction. Boys, when they get hurt, easily believe their father is mad at them, not mad at the circumstances. Unable to make the distinction, a boy feels Dad's anger and wrongly thinks, "He's mad at *me*" rather than "He's reacting because I got hurt." What else is his little heart going to conclude? The enemy then expands on the lie and secures it: *Dad's mad at you and doesn't love you because*

> *you make mistakes*
> *you aren't careful*
> *you don't pay attention*
> *you're stupid*
> *you always/never _____ (fill in the blank)*

In these volatile moments, the kingdom of darkness is after the boy's trust. Distrust, once established, will be a weapon used against the father and the son, and against the son in his relationship with God, for years and years to come. It only takes a few such moments to sabotage a man's foundation.

But here's the crazy-good news: Regardless of what you did or didn't get as a boy, your heart can be healed. Remember, we are all unfinished and unfathered to some degree. This is what the Trinity wants to walk you through as a man so you can reclaim what was taken from you. God's unconditional love is the remedy that heals all wounds and transforms you from false-self-dominant to true.

Pornography and Sexual Abuse

The worst wounding to any masculine heart, especially during the foundational time of boyhood and belovedness, is sexual wounding. Whether through overt physical abuse or through word or image, any kind of inappropriate exposure to sex is a traumatic assault on a boy's heart.

The average age today for introduction to pornography is ten years old. Things haven't changed much from three decades ago; the average age then was just about the same. The enemy knows there's something about that age. Porn at any age traumatizes the masculine heart and soul, but boys in particular do not know what to do with such visual stimulation. Few are prepared for this beast when it first comes calling. It holds both the allure of forbidden fruit and the promise of one day getting close to that fruit. Pornography takes something God made for an appropriate time and circumstance and delivers it way too soon into a masculine heart's story. The enemy's intention is to sabotage *every* relationship a boy will have, especially with a girl and, eventually, with his wife.

None of us who encountered porn in our youth went out looking for it—it found us. Whether another boy introduced us to it, or we found a magazine in the woods or in a box in Dad's closet, the result is always the same: Innocence was stolen.

That's a huge reason why, as a boy approaches his transition from boyhood into the explorer stage and his ability to understand increases, he needs the "sex talk." He needs a trusted father to talk with him about the male and female bodies, what sex is, what it is for, and how it works. Yet of the thousands of men I have talked to over the years, an astonishing majority—I estimate 90 percent—never had that talk with their dad. The 10 percent who did tell either a funny story or a sad one about how it went.

Sexual headlines glare at boys in the media, littering their hearts with messages about a powerful subject through which very few are ever guided by their dads. The enemy, who thrives on confusion and experimentation, seizes that advantage in order to disrupt the vital order of stages in the masculine journey. By introducing the lover stage before explorer and warrior, he seeks to sabotage a man's future kingdom. It will take many conversations to settle and impart courage to a young masculine heart.

How did your father engage you in this area of sex and sexuality? Who tutored you—other boys, magazines, videos, girls, the overt messages of the world? If those were your teachers, then you get what you paid for—or maybe more accurately, you paid for what you got, and you are very likely still paying.

Recently a mother asked me what I thought about the effects of pornography on boys. "I trust my son [age nine], and we have security on his screens," she told me. *She has no idea*, I thought, and asked, "Do you know if he has been exposed?" He had, through another boy at school.

Like a virus, pornography is transmitted through exposure. The woman's son wasn't just already infected—he was contagious. But I knew the mom wasn't ready to hear that. So I asked instead, "Does the other boy have 'security' on his screens?" She wasn't sure; I was. Plenty of third-graders are delighted to share what passes to them unfiltered through the internet.

* * *

Worse yet than pornography is sexual abuse. Roughly one in six men in America were sexually abused as children. In this physical and emotional type of abuse, the perpetrator, usually a trusted adult, sins by taking advantage of a youth. Foul spirits of guilt and shame attach to these dark encounters, and like parasites, they stay along for the journey into manhood.

Whether through pornography or physical sexual abuse, and often through both, the shipwrecks of sexual assault leave us all wet, cold, half drowned, and battered, with a part of our heart marooned. The heart doesn't measure trauma, just experiences it. I can't compare what happened to me with what happened to you. What I'm certain of is, we're all in this together. Every man of us needs to learn how to heal from sexual assault on our heart in whatever form, or forms, it took. We need Jesus to restore the broken, marooned places as part of our healing. We'll engage with him in that process further along in the book.

* * *

Inevitably the first stage of the masculine journey, boyhood, draws to a close. However we were or weren't fathered; whatever wounds we incurred through the words and actions of others; whatever impacts our heart experienced from influences beyond our control, both good and evil, protective and damaging—all of this will carry with us into the next stage: the explorer stage, where a boy embarks on the great adventure.

It's a stage where the world becomes larger, a place of expanding possibilities, fascination, and growth. But the dangers increase as well, and the enemy often uses reinforcements to halt the boy's progress across the checkerboard. Who will be there to protect him, to teach him how life works and how, when he is hurt or wounded, to get back in the game? Who will validate and initiate him and cheer him on as he learns how to play, how to explore . . . and, eventually, how to fight?

CHAPTER 7
Explorer and Warrior
Discovering the World and Engaging in Battle

The Lord is a warrior; the Lord is his name
—Exodus 15:3

Truth may be vital, but without love it is unbearable.
—Pope Francis

EXPLORER

DO I HAVE STRENGTH?
CAN I COME THROUGH—DO I HAVE WHAT IT TAKES?

WARRIOR

HOW DO I DISCERN BETWEEN GOOD AND EVIL?
AND IN A DANGEROUS WORLD, HOW DO I OFFER MY
STRENGTH FOR GOOD?

A few months ago at my parents' home, I asked to see the family photos. The old albums with their yellow stains, the vintage Kodak pictures and even a few Polaroids, tell a story of me. Long before the age of instant, downloadable digital images, pictures were captured on film and developed through a time-consuming process of darkrooms and chemical baths. You went to the Kodak Shack, dropped off your film, and returned a week later to claim your treasures.

The photos, captured in a moment, always had a larger story to tell. There's a familiar, yellowed Polaroid picture of three-year-old me back in 1967 with our dog, a large Corkie named Lady. We're on the back patio on a summer day. I'm standing in a little plastic kiddie pool, holding a water hose, and the two of us are soaking wet.

Every turn of the page moves the clock forward just a bit until a year transpires. At one point the dog is gone and there are two boys, my younger brother and me, sitting on the floor holding Popsicle sticks, mouths stained cherry red. My brother, in diapers, is propped up and leaning back on my chest. He looks uncomfortable, probably because I'm holding him with a half nelson. I'm grinning; he looks terrified.

Next page, it's Christmas. I am wearing my new Roy Rogers cowboy hat, vest, holsters with two authentic cap gun six-shooters, and an oh-boy! look on my face.

The pages go on, as do the stories they captured and the memories they hold. If those pictures could talk, they'd tell bits and pieces of a story written in moments in time—the story of me.

* * *

For some of us, the wonder years of boyhood were truly wonder-full; for others, not so much. Psychology calls the first decade of our lives the "formative years." Some of us are fortunate to tell stories of being loved, protected, and provided for. Others are either trying to forget or else are still wondering, when we look back, "What the hell was that?" We know now what we didn't know then: Something was wrong.

Questions are often invitations to intimacy, to a conversation that can eventually lead to something better than answers: understanding. Answers that come before questions are not helpful. Being told what to feel, or lectured on what to think, is far less helpful than the freedom to gain understanding. But most of us experienced the opposite. Growing up, we were told what to think and feel rather than encouraged to share what we thought or felt. Few of us were invited to explore life's effect on our heart by someone who wanted to help us through, as opposed to pushing and pulling us through, life's difficult moments. Exploration is how perspective and wisdom are gained. If your story didn't allow for you to think and feel, to question and explore, then the explorer stage is a place God will want to work with you on in recovering your masculine heart.

Have you noticed that Jesus asked questions all the time? The King of kings' style was to ask questions and, many times, to answer a question with a question. Pastor and author Martin B. Copenhaven observed that in the Gospels, Jesus was asked 183 questions but directly answered only three. Three! What do you make of that? It's unfathomable to think the Messiah didn't know the answer or at least have a strong opinion. But maybe he valued the dialog. Maybe he wanted a heart to discover the truth for itself, feel it, take it in.

In order to go with God into your story, you need to be ready for inquiry and dialog. For invitations to intimacy that lead to perspective and understanding—and likely, to repentance, confession, and forgiveness. This is how stories are redeemed, men are restored, and the glory of their lives is uncovered.

Not Yet Men

We often call fourteen-year-old boys, and even eight-year-old boys, "young men." I recommend that we not—because they are not. It is a hopeful forecast, maybe even a compliment, and I get it; it sounds validating and encouraging. But it is more misleading than helpful. Seeing masculinity restored requires that we be clear not only on what it is but also on *when* it is. Ten-year-old boys are not young men; they have quite a way to go. And while seventeen-year-olds can drive, age has little to do with maturity. Having hair grow in new places is not the same as having character grow in new places. The one will happen just because it does; the other may never happen unless it's taught, modeled, and received.

Think of all the cultures that bring ritual and ceremony to the transition from boyhood to manhood, marking the date and time for a rite of passage. We have lost that in the West. So I recommend we warriors and kings point young masculine hearts, kindly and with great intention, to *what a man is* and invite boys of all ages to aspire to become good men.

We in our culture have lost our ability to get out in front of boys and call them up—to know when to do so, to determine what birthdays, graduations, and seasons of their lives are key. Ceremonies and rites of passage are critical to this stage of the masculine journey. They won't happen every weekend, but we dare not allow them never to happen at all. Some should be scheduled on the calendar, planned events to which others are invited. Other moments need to be just a father and son stepping into adventure together. Whether the occasion involves hitting a ball, playing a musical instrument, learning how to use a power saw, or passing down the shotgun our own dad handed down to us on a hunting trip, the words shared from father to son are what matter most. Ceremonies with powerful words are like rain to a desert. They make an oasis for good things to grow in a hostile environment.

So when the moment is there, square your shoulders, put your hands on your son, look him in the eye, and share the words that are appropriate.

How do you find those words, though? Most men didn't receive such validating and initiating moments themselves, so they are off their maps pioneering a new course and setting a new trajectory not only for another heart but also for their own. Maybe that's you. When and how were you initiated? Ask yourself, "What would I have loved to hear from my father or from a good king when I was growing up?" Whatever those words are—and your heart knows—those are the words for you to speak to your son's heart (or daughter, friend, or wife, any heart, masculine or feminine, young or old; no one ever grows out of wanting to be seen).

Explorer Stage

The most important piece to be installed in our heart during the earliest stage of the masculine journey, boyhood, is that we are seen and loved. For a boy to know he is the beloved son of a good father is foundational. During the ensuing stages, in countless ways, the enemy will attempt to convince him otherwise. That's the battle every boy faces as he transitions from adolescence to puberty and from the safety of the yard to the adventures of a much larger world.

Jesus went through the explorer stage. He grew up about fifteen miles from the Sea of Galilee, or half a day's walk. Mount Tabor, where years later Jesus would bring his closest friends to witness his transfiguration, was about five miles away. Jesus experienced life in a Jewish family in a Jewish neighborhood with a Jewish synagogue. He knew his way around a carpenter's shop and around the tense political climate of a Roman-occupied land. There in the region of Galilee, the young Jewish boy Jesus "grew in wisdom and stature, and in favor with God and man" (Luke 2:52). What better compliment could be paid a boy and his journey to becoming a man?

* * *

The explorer stage is a time of adventure and testing, of learning through trial and error how things work. During this stage, the questions asked by the young heart evolve from *Do you see me? Do you love what you see?* to become:

Do I have strength?
Can I come through—do I have what it takes?

This is a season of safety goggles and helmets, tools and equipment, a time of finding out how fast a thing can go, how high it can fly, how far it can travel. Far more is involved than physical strength alone, for strength comes in many ways: through risking, trying and testing, stepping out with courage into anything—sports, certainly, but also music, art, debate, creative writing, or a part in a play.

Now is when a boy's world expands from the safety of his bedroom, front yard, and backyard and becomes both more beautiful and more dangerous. Explorer is a time of pulling away from Mom and all the glorious ways she bears God's image in nurture and care. Good mothering isn't smothering mothering. The boy needs to make his own bed if he isn't doing so already. He can choose his clothes for the day himself. The lawnmower and household chores await him, along with other new ways to enter into the world of men, and invitations from Dad to do so. This stage should be marked with lessons and talks of "Son, God made you a male. You have a masculine heart. Let me show you what it's for."

Initiating and Validating the Explorer

The explorer stage tests a boy's strength so he can discover it and learn what it is for. When challenges come—and they will; this stage is the beginning of hard tests and important trials—the boy will succeed when he is surrounded with affirmation and encouragement, not criticism and sarcasm.

Disappointments are inevitable. The boy doesn't make first string on the basketball team. Not even an honorable mention in the science fair. But that's OK. Winning is wonderful and deserves celebrating, but it's not the main point. There is incredible value in training, competing, trying and failing, learning both to win and to lose graciously. Often the explorer gains more than we realize from experiencing the love, support, and encouragement of others who help him process a loss. (Who helped *you* process striking out, missing the shot, messing up at a recital?) Silence during failures—no one present to speak good words and listen with care, no one who asks and answers questions, no one with whom to share and compare experiences—will always be a win in the enemy's column.

This stage involves *increasing challenges*—harder chores, greater responsibility, and supervised opportunities. In a monumental shift from the boyhood stage, the boy must learn and understand that he is *not* the center of the universe. Experiencing belovedness—being seen and wanted—was critical in those earlier years, providing the foundation for stages to come. In boyhood, the boy was large and the world small. But now the next stage has arrived. In explorer, the world becomes larger, with invitations for the boy to see how it works and embrace new roles that await him.

* * *

Money and the value of things earned through chores, along with an allowance, are important at the explorer stage. Not everything a boy wants should be bought for him. The answer shouldn't always be no, but besides receiving an allowance, earning money through chores teaches the value of work and the cost of things.

The days of paperboys are long gone, but that was one of the jobs I had at thirteen. And at fifteen, I convinced my dad to buy me a mower so I could earn money mowing lawns. He agreed and set up an arrangement for me to pay him back from my earnings. Dad sat me down, and we made some fliers for the neighbors' mailboxes, and he showed me the basics of creating a little business plan that helped me think ahead about my expenses and profits. He didn't leave me alone to figure things out for myself, yet neither did he do my thinking for me or the work required. Instead, he summoned me to the kitchen table, asked me questions, and invited me to engage with him. He did it *with* me.

With my own kids, this is the stage when I introduced them to "halfsies." If they really wanted something, I told them I'd go half with them. Amazing how many things went back on the shelves at stores! But the principle was the same: I partnered with my children, showing them my support financially but also by helping them to think and decide for themselves what they were willing to do for themselves.

* * *

The outdoors is a great catalyst for the transition from being the center of the universe to being a part of it. Nature is large, and a boy will learn much from experiencing it. From watching insects instead of stomping them. From hearing a whippoorwill call in the distance as, with Dad's supervision, he builds and tends a campfire. From learning about native plants and birds and how to identify them from field guides. From discovering how to use the Big Dipper to locate the North Star.

Dad needs to raise his game when it comes to his words, particularly in asking good questions. It is also critical for him to bring his son into a circle of good kings. The explorer needs to be around other oriented men besides his father, who include him intentionally in their kingdoms and therefore are able to lovingly speak into his life. If you have an explorer to tend, this can be a great stage for both of you to learn together, a time when you yourself get from God what you didn't get from your dad when you were in this stage.

Several years ago some friends and I hosted a pheasant hunt in South Dakota. Men from around the country came, and a few took the opportunity to bring their son or daughter. The twenty in our group were circled up one afternoon, sharing stories from the day. Dads took the occasion to speak into their children's lives. My friend Tom turned to his son and said, "Son, these are the good guys. These are the type of men you want to seek out, and when you find them, invite them into your circle of friends." I'll always remember that moment and Tom's words. He was speaking to more than his son alone; he was speaking to all of us. My heart knew, and the nods and tear-filled eyes of the other men told me they did too: This was a holy moment, good for the hearts of many.

* * *

Inevitably, puberty arrives in the explorer stage. Whether a boy is an early or late bloomer, putting on height, growing hair, breaking out, and seeing his feet, ears, and nose increase in size is all a bit awkward. The boy needs a man more than a woman to guide him through the changes and help him navigate the geeky, gawky moments.

More is evolving than just the boy's body. His spiritual life also needs attention. The rote childhood prayers of Sunday school provided a foundation, but now he needs something deeper. It's time to introduce him to prayer as heart-to-heart conversation with God. Pilgrimages are needed in which a father arranges for his son to explore spiritual truths. These are times for the boy to discover, with Dad at his side, how the kingdom works and what his place is in it. They're not times to give a boy over to a youth minister or high school ministry, wonderful as they are. Imagine having so many good dads, so many good kings on the job, that there is no need to rely on the sub-contractors.

During the explorer stage, there is a jungle a boy must enter: middle school and high school. He can't be sheltered from it, but he must be prepared and protected as much as possible through many conversations with a watchful, caring father. In our own day, a lot of us were just dropped off and left to fend for ourselves. Imagine how different things might have been if our fathers had taken a more proactive approach. Dads first need good training themselves, in order to lay out strategies with their sons and have good things to say when bad things happen. In no way should a boy be pulled from the dangers of a fallen world; rather, he needs to be guided and coached in the ways of the two realms and two kingdoms. If evil forces have somehow been held at bay, this is the stage of their great invasion, and a boy needs to start learning what he is up against, how to guard his heart.

It was C. S. Lewis who wrote, "Since it is so likely that children will meet cruel enemies, let them at least have heard of brave knights and heroic courage. Otherwise you are making their destiny not brighter but darker."[1] Fathers who can tell good stories of their own trials and errors to their son or daughter will be serving and loving their young explorer's heart. In order to tell such post- or pregame stories, a father must watch for opportunities to create, with the help of the Holy Spirit, the best questions, validations, and experiences of love that fuel his explorer for another day. What did your father do to prepare you for, or help you recover from, the opportunities and dangers of your own explorer stage?

The Wounded Explorer

Exploring has its hazards. What found us was often more costly than what we found. By the time a boy is ten, the fallen world and other boys, most of whom have not been fathered well and are on their way to being disoriented men, are the "teachers" who tell a young explorer's heart what to do, what not to do, how to fit in, and how to use others in order to receive love, or at least how not to get hurt. But the rules of the jungle are not the rules of the kingdom.

Conditional love—acceptance, worth, and belonging through invitation (or rejection through exclusion)—is a powerful system that thrives in the wild of middle school and high school. Even the best guides are going to lose their young to that jungle. The trick, Dad, is to know when your son has wandered off path and how to go after him. There's a twofold training in it for you: You need to see how you yourself were wounded at this stage and go to God for healing; and you've also got to learn what it will take to support and encourage your kid.

In the explorer stage, peers have as much or more influence than the home front. Unsettled and unloved boys and girls can be used by the enemy to wield teasing, insults, and worse. This is why it's so crucial for a son to be grounded in his father's unconditional love during the earlier boyhood stage: For a boy to know his strength, it must first be instilled through belovedness so it can one day withstand the enemy's challenges. With that foundation in place, the challenges then become important. Because for true character and strength of heart to be forged within him, an explorer must be exposed to the evils of this world.

The explorer stage and the ensuing warrior stage overlap. Lessons learned well in explorer, and losses redeemed, can serve a young man in his warrior stage. On the other hand, if someone or something can take away the explorer's foundational sense of belovedness, then that deep wound will play forward badly in the warrior stage.

* * *

The explorer years are the years of teams and clubs, of applications and try-outs. Boy Scouts earn their merit badges on the challenging path to becoming an Eagle Scout. Joining a sports team is no longer as easy as "whoever signs up, plays"; now a young athlete has to practice and practice and practice some more. In all of it, from football to music to the debate team, a boy must learn that discipline is essential if he's going to do well. But there's another lesson that's just as important: Practicing and applying himself won't necessarily guarantee the boy gets what he's after—that spot on the team, that place in the choir, first chair in the trumpet section.

A father or a trusted father figure is key to framing the losses in a positive light and encouraging the boy to get up and try again. If a boy only hears through silence or words of rejection that he doesn't have what it takes—when no one is there to take him past the failure, no father and no fellowship of men to guide him in the way or explain how to recover from his failures—the result is a deep wound. Every failure is in fact an opportunity to grow; a boy can learn from it if he's shown how. But he needs a father, a mentor, or a coach to help him redeem the disappointment and gain from the loss. The same also holds true for the wins. Someone must be there to help the explorer celebrate and interpret his successes, so he can both enjoy them and know how to handle them appropriately.

Lack of validation and initiation into manhood strikes hard at a boy's heart in this stage. If everything is done for him, handed to him, it can later make for a spoiled, entitled king. But if nothing is ever done for the boy, if he experiences no help, guidance, or celebration of jobs well done, he may grow to become an over-achieving king, driven to prove his worth and living in the chaos of "winning" rather than loving. Either way, the result will be a king who is all about himself, and his kingdom will not be a good place for other hearts to live.

* * *

It's just a matter of time before innocence is stolen and shame bites and infects, creating distance between a boy and his father and his world. Shame ensures he won't talk to his father about whatever happened to cause it. We come by it through Adam: "I was afraid and so I hid." The spirit of shame wants to answer the boy's questions—

Do you see me?
Do you love what you see?
Do you want to be with me?
Do I have strength?
Can I come through?

—with no, no, no, no, and no.

We first discussed the "sex talk" in chapter 6. The explorer is done a great disservice when there isn't one, because this is the stage when girls enter a boy's story. Now the world and the kingdom of darkness work together in a new way, tempting the boy to explore, then shaming him for doing so, knocking him hard both coming and going. He needs a trusted father to promise him, "Son, shame will not come between us." And he needs Dad's reassurance that what is going on in him physically is normal, even though what is going on around him may not be.

A *series* of sex talks is actually a better idea than "*the* sex talk." To think a dad can cover so broad and important a subject between a few commercials on TV or on a drive to the store . . . no, this subject needs much more attention. The worst thing that can happen is for a father to give it no attention at all because his own fear, guilt, and shame keep him from stepping into this area of his boy's life. When Dad checks out at a time when his son so badly needs him to check in is in itself terribly wounding.

* * *

How were you taught that you had a strength and were helped to understand what it was for? How did you learn that you "have what it takes?" What were the tests and trials of initiation in your life during your explorer stage? Who stood beside you and helped you interpret those tests and trials, looking to validate you, warn you, coach you, and love you through the adventures and battles? Were you shielded from life's hard lessons and pain, or was your father present not to spare you from them but to guide you through them?

Further along, in part 3, we'll look at how we can go with God to explore answers to questions like these. Doing so can shine light on things that, if kept in the dark, enslave a man and compromise his kingdom. One of them, and quite possibly more, may be keeping you in a cycle of bondage today, weighed down by addictions or "medicating" yourself with expensive hobbies. Looking for life while still unhealed from trauma of years past isn't sustainable and doesn't work. Unresolved wounds block the way of receiving what you were made for and long for—love. Time to learn how to go back and fight for that lost ground. Time to recover your explorer and walk with God into adventure unhindered, uncompromised, and unashamed.

This is where your warrior begins to bravely step up and in to recover, with Jesus, what was lost in the past when you began exploring this dangerous world. Then you can go forward courageously with the Spirit to learn how to reign and rule well. Because—and yes, I've already said it; I'm saying it again—if wounded hearts wound hearts, then free hearts can free hearts.

Warrior Stage

There comes a time in one's journey when the masculine heart learns to *fight*. Not necessarily physically—that may be a part of it, but fighting can take many forms. Regardless, once entered into, battle will always be a part of the masculine journey. As the warrior matures, he will enter later stages as well, but he remains a warrior till the end of his days.

The warrior stage is when the transferring of will takes place. The will of the parents diminishes (though in the spiritual realm, parents always retain special authority in the battle for their child's heart), while the will of the young masculine heart takes on new force. More choices are to be exercised by the young warrior. In both the spiritual and natural realms, the burden of responsibility begins to transfer from parent to child. Mom and Dad cease to do for the warrior the things he must learn to do himself.

The transition from explorer to warrior is a critical one, and it can be a bit rough. Not handled well, it can produce a twenty-five-year-old who acts more like a whiny, entitled five-year-old than a grown man. On the other hand, what do you make of a fifteen-year-old who is responsible, hardworking, and wise beyond his years? He may still be a boy, but he's well on the road to maturity in his character.

Ready or not, like it or not, we all come of age. We become old enough to be held to a standard of behavior, held responsible for our choices, even tried as an adult in a court of law. It falls on us to choose between right and wrong, practice a morality, and fashion a character that has an impact for good or not good. This is the warrior stage. The questions now become

How do I discern between good and evil?
And in a dangerous world, how do I offer my strength for good?

In this stage, we will need a moral compass and strength of character to learn how to engage the real enemy of our heart, mind, body, and soul. Those are the components with which we are to love and be loved by God; they will need training, guarding, and advancing.

It is in this stage that a masculine heart moves from inheritance to ownership. Whatever he was given by his parents, whether right or wrong, good or bad, doesn't change it. A boy slowly becomes a man, and it's in the warrior stage that a masculine heart begins to take responsibility for his own life. If he was wounded in his past, then as a man he will need to go back with Jesus and fight for what was lost. Because a vital lesson of being a warrior is this: *Life is hard. There is good and evil in the world and within me as well. The fight over my will and beliefs is real, evil has a voice, and all my choices, words, and actions matter.*

* * *

Cultivating discipline of body, mind, heart, and spirit will serve and protect the young warrior well. The days are coming, if they haven't already arrived, when he must learn to guard his heart (Proverbs 4:23)—for that is a learning proposition.

The warrior's heart is strengthened every time he does not yield to fear or shame in the face of a fight. Learning comes in the school of hard knocks, experiences that require more of a young man—for while we were made for Eden, not war, yet war is the current reality and context of our days, all day and every day until our King returns. This cannot be understated or ignored; otherwise, the result will be a naïve king who can't guard his own heart, much less the hearts of others.

It bears repeating: Once a warrior, always a warrior—because life is a war between two kingdoms, darkness and light. As a man transitions to the later stages of lover, king, and elder-sage, he will always have the ability to offer who he is, his inner strength, to the hearts of others, because he knows through experience who he is. His father, and his Father, have shown and told him.

The older a warrior becomes, passing through the ensuing stages, the more impact he will have in the fight. He may not forever be the man in the ring; he may become the coach in the corner who counsels and encourages the man in the ring. But he is still a warrior—he just fights from a different position. It's not retirement, just repositioning.

Initiating and Validating the Warrior

Chief Sitting Bull said, "For us, warriors are not what you think of as warriors. The warrior is not someone who fights, because no one has the right to take another life. The warrior, for us, is one who sacrifices himself for the good of others."[2]

A warrior is a peacekeeper, and to become a warrior is to awaken to the evil in the world—to injustice, to pain, suffering, and oppression, to the forces that work against the kingdom of God and a man's true self. There are lots of ways for a warrior to fight without ever throwing a physical punch. And now is the time when a young man learns there are things worth fighting for, things that need a strong presence and voice:

A Cause—the advancing of God's kingdom, kindness, fairness, care for the less fortunate, and a voice and presence for the poor, marginalized, or abused. A cause always involves people.

People—siblings, parents, and friends, as well as those a man may not know but who need an advocate or new friend.

Principles and Character—the opportunities and challenges of learning how to care. The warrior's weapons are honesty, integrity, kindness, courage, and above all else, love.

It's during the warrior stage that a masculine heart comes to see what is really going on—to discern the devices of the unholy trinity: Satan, the false self (aka the flesh, aka the imposter), and this fallen world. So begins the man's training to wield his strength for others.

This, I'm convinced, is why so many men love epic movies such as *Braveheart, Gladiator, A River Runs Through It, The Lord of the Rings, The Chronicles of Narnia, The Matrix, Open Range,* and *Star Wars.* These stories move men because there is something set deep within men that *can* be moved. Again, it's not about swinging fists per se. Mr. Rogers was a warrior, fighting for the worth and value of every human life, specializing in young hearts.

However, if someone broke into your home and was threatening to harm your wife or daughter, I'm pretty sure the pacifist in you would give way to the aggressor. That part of who you are as a man would act to defend those precious to you. As G. K. Chesterton puts it, "The true soldier fights not because he hates what is in front of him, but because he loves what is behind him."[3]

* * *

In addition to a cause, every warrior needs a good king to fight under. Someone to teach him mission, vision, and strategy in the spiritual realm. Someone who is caring and kind and can take the beloved son and explorer and provide a relationship and environment in which to learn to fight. Jesus did this with his disciples. Not until well into year two of his ministry did he teach his friends how to confront the darkness in the world (see Luke 10). The first two years were about healing for their own hearts: how to see themselves, who they were, and how to see God and his kingdom—how it all worked, so they could eventually step up and in and play their part.

Today, Jesus wants the job as *your* King, and he has placed lesser kings, both good and bad, on your path to show you how, and how not, to one day care for the hearts in your kingdom. Good kings will validate a warrior's heart when he does well and coach him when he struggles or fails. One of my favorite things to do as a king is look for opportunities to validate younger hearts ("Well done! I'm proud of you") or initiate them ("Come with us. You belong"). I firmly believe it's because of our shortage of good kings that our warriors and explorers are struggling.

Wounded Warrior

The spring of 2017 was a tough few months for me and Zoweh's mission. Finances were a struggle (again). Doubt and fear, even dread, made regular house calls to my heart at the most inconvenient times. Sometimes they'd wake me in the middle of the night; other times they'd hit the pillow with me, keeping me awake, assailing me with questions about my good heart and tempting me to question the heart of God. These thoughts were flaming arrows shot into the fortress of me, igniting my mind. Up I'd go in flames—sweats, panic, forebodings of desolation . . . my, how fast fear and diminishment would escalate! I would have to get up and battle, pray it off, lean in.

It was one of the hardest times of my life, this testing of my faith. And the spiritual conflict my marriage, my team, and I personally were encountering came through some people who had entered our lives and brought their battle into our camp. That is how it works. We wrestle not only with our own false self and with false spirits attached to that imposter, but we also have to encounter the false selves of others and the spirits that attend them. The kingdom of darkness *uses* others to use and wound us.

When you encounter another person, another heart, you're dealing with far more than what is immediately before you. You're encountering the whole of that person's story. All its contributors, good and bad. That man or woman's wounding and its deep messages, and also the glory that resides there—usually the tangling of the two. You are encountering an image bearer of God who is fiercely opposed. In the words of the old saying, "Be kind, for everyone you meet is fighting a hard battle."

Most people don't know what they are carrying deep within them. The false self is a sinister creature. It isn't that other person, and it isn't you, but left unchecked, it will run the show, attempting to direct your world and everyone else's. So yes, it's true that everyone is going through something, but be careful. A warrior must learn that someone else's warfare is not necessarily his responsibility.

* * *

A man's warrior heart is wounded when he is told that all aggression, passion, or intensity is wrong. A man must learn to fight, and that lesson must come from other men. Moms and women have their own warrior hearts and can offer a boy some good things. But without a man to validate and initiate him, a boy will feel uncomfortable in the company of men and gravitate to comfort in the company of women. It's hard to blame him; disoriented men have made it clear to younger hearts, "Me aren't safe, nor are they good." A boy who learns from both parents how to fight for his own heart receives the training he needs to fight for the hearts of others later as a warrior.

The heart of a young man is wounded when he attempts to be a warrior and is shamed for trying. Or when he is overcome by fear, pushed around by guilt, or freezes in a moment that invites him to step up and in, and then lives with the regret of not engaging.

When his attempt to intervene in a situation does not go well, he may keenly feel that "No!" is the answer to his questions "Do I have what it takes? Can I come through? Am I strong?" He needs someone to tell him about first times and how they often don't go well, and that failures are just part of the journey.

With no one to follow up, ask the young heart questions, and invite his own questions . . .

Without someone to help him explore and interpret the battles of life . . .

Lacking a good king to mentor him . . .

a young warrior feels the sting of isolation, and a curse sets in, or a lie from an earlier stage is reinforced: "There is no one to help you. You are alone."

This sense of defeat is brutal to the warrior heart, and helplessness can haunt a man from as early as boyhood. Never winning at anything, being bullied, pushed around, and embarrassed—these experiences have crushed many a masculine heart and therefore stunt the warrior's heart. In the book *Iron John*, Robert Bly wrote: "Most American men today do not have enough awakened or living warriors inside to defend their soul houses. And most people, men or women, do not know what genuine outward or inward warriors would look like, or feel like."[4]

The warrior heart is wounded when there is no battle to fight—when we're told that to be assertive is bad, that to be passive is godly, and that there is never a time to rock the boat or confront others in love, fierce love if necessary. That's not how Jesus lived; he rocked boats, redrew lines, and confronted others redemptively.

Most wounding of all is when we encounter spiritual warfare and we don't know how to beat it. Fear, confusion, and resignation build as the enemy rushes in early with fierce assaults, often through other people used to deceive us and convince us we cannot be good, loved, or strong. Warriors need to be trained how to fight! The warrior spirit in you and me is good and is placed in us for noble and valiant purposes. We must learn how to be dangerous, wielding fierce, loving kindness. Jesus fought and still fights for you; he wants you to join him in the fight for others.

There are practical, commonsense aspects of being a warrior. The young masculine heart needs to be taught inner discipline, how to fight battles of the will in his own self-government. Sleeping and waking at reasonable hours, eating well, exercising . . . simple, essential disciplines from the explorer stage need to carry forward. Otherwise, what a warrior lacks the resolve to do for himself will show up in what he's unable to do for others. His dearth of inner disciplines will play out badly and will need to be recovered; otherwise, as a man enters the king stage, the people in his kingdom will suffer.

* * *

What events have shaped your warrior stage? Who was there to teach you as you entered it? Who helped you accurately interpret the battles of life and instructed you in them? When did you learn—when did you observe or experience firsthand, or even secondhand—how to fight for your own heart or the heart of another? Where was your father in this stage? Was anyone there to fight for you? To love, lead, and encourage you by showing you how to fight? To answer "Yes!" to your warrior questions: *Am I strong? Can I come through? Who will show me how?*

Questions like these are so important. Prayerfully consider them, and circle back to them in part 3, where you'll be invited to go with God to revisit some of the battles you have faced. And be confident of this: Someone is most surely here for you now—the wise, knowing, fiercely loving King of kings. He wants to take you back and fight for you and with you in the realm that matters most, to recover what matters most to him.

You.

CHAPTER 8

Lover
Pursuing and Protecting Beauty

"Arise, my darling, my beautiful one, come with me. See! The winter is past; the rains are over and gone. Flowers appear on the earth; the season of singing has come, the cooing of doves is heard in our land. The fig tree forms its early fruit; the blossoming vines spread their fragrance. Arise, come, my darling; my beautiful one, come with me."
—*Song of Songs 2:10–13*

The most striking thing about our Lord is the union of great ferocity with extreme tenderness.
—*C. S. Lewis*

> TO LOVE BEAUTY.
> TO ENTER INTO MYSTERY.
> TO KNOW AND BE KNOWN.
> THIS IS WHAT MY LOVER'S HEART
> WAS CREATED FOR.

The first time I saw the Broadway musical *Les Miserables*, I was twenty-three years old. The play was at the Shubert Theater in Los Angeles, and from beginning to end, I was transfixed. The stage, the voices, every song and every element of the story . . . my heart was captivated.

Written by French novelist Victor Hugo in 1862, *Les Miserables* was adapted for the theater stage in 1980 and has been loved worldwide ever since. The story is set in the midst of the late 1700s, when the oppressive French government, poverty, and disease are leading to the French Revolution. The main character, Jean Valjean, is a paroled convict who encounters God, breaks parole, changes his identity, and becomes a new man, the mayor of a small town and a successful factory owner.

When Fantine, a woman in his employ, is mistreated by her coworkers and unjustly fired by her supervisor, turning to prostitution in order to provide for her young daughter, Valjean eventually finds out. Grieved, he cares for her when she is sick and, upon her death, takes in Fantine's daughter, Cosette, as his own. All the while, he is being relentlessly pursued by a suspicious police inspector who is eager to put the former convict back in prison.

Valjean, desiring to protect his adopted daughter from his tainted past and the brutal outside world, flees with her from the small town to hide in the bustle and fragility of Paris. But several years later, as the revolution begins to break out, Cosette falls in love with Marius, a young warrior with outspoken ideals, whose romantic heart invades hers.

Marius and his revolutionary brothers move to the streets to make their stand behind strategic blockades. The first shots are fired, confusion ensues, young Marius's fate is uncertain . . .

And for the first time, there in the Shubert Theater, I heard Valjean sing the song "Bring Him Home":

God on high, hear my prayer
In my need you have always been there
He is young, he's afraid
Let him rest heaven blessed
Bring him home
Bring him home
Bring him home[1]

I was undone. It was as if God the Father were singing those words over me, about me, and to me, all at the same time. Tears at row 38, aisle D, seat 9.

Tears are typical when the heart witnesses love through the invitation of beauty. Beauty in any form has the capacity to woo our hearts to the sacred. Because a part of our heart has been so assaulted, so arrested, and so shut down, we all too often don't see beauty's invitation in the darkness. Beauty is an invitation to the light, a summons to love. St. Augustine wrote, "He who is always beautiful has loved us first. . . . How shall we be beautiful? By loving him who is always beautiful. Beauty grows in you to the extent that love grows, because charity [love] itself is the soul's beauty."

Beauty resurrects. Beauty inspires. Beauty provokes and stirs, nourishes and fuels the soul. And therefore, beauty can be badly misunderstood and even gravely corrupted. Our enemy uses beauty to lure. Possibly the greatest mistake many men make in the masculine journey is to see beauty as something to consume. In particular, through his lies, the enemy twists our understanding of what the beauty of women is for and extinguishes the goodness of why God created them. One of Satan's most successful tactics, perhaps his best, is to get boys and young men to reach for girls and young women too soon. Get the cart before the horse and the driver, cart, and horse are in trouble every time. Hearts are bound to get hurt. Put dozens of these carts on the road at a time and you can count on a demolition derby. You can almost hear the sounds and crashes when the false selves of enough men get tangled too soon with the lover stage.

More Than Feminine Beauty

Ah, the lover stage. Inevitably it arrives—the chemistry, the spark, the mystery of the connection between a man and a woman. From boyhood onward we are moving toward it. Even in our very earliest years, its raw material exists in us—we could call it the lover part of our heart. It is core to our being and central to our development as image bearers. The lover stage is simply the coming of age of something that has always been there. As it awakens to beauty, so we truly awaken as lovers. For we are made for love, made to long for it, receive it, and give it. God created you and me to enjoy loving relationships with others and with God himself. When we were young, the lover part of us was primarily wired to receive. But as we mature, the lover part adds a new posture: *romance*, the ability to pursue.

God created us to seek and enjoy beauty and romance in all their forms. For the two go together, and they are not limited to the attraction between a man and a woman. The Creator himself woos us with affectionate words he wants us to hear, from his heart to ours, and pursues us through the beauty of his creation. Beauty and romance converge in a sunset, a piece of music, a work of art, the flicker and smell of a campfire, the spread of the landscape far below from atop a mountain.

Romance, our soul's enraptured response to beauty, is a facet and an expression of love intimately shared between two hearts. For above all, we live in a love story. Throughout our lives, our joy, our glory, and the battle we wage are all about love.

The lover stage slumbers restlessly in every second-grade boy who thinks the girl sitting next to him is pretty. It awakens in puberty's flush of hormones and physical changes and steps awkwardly through adolescence. It matures in romantic love and marriage. And it stays with us the rest of our lives.

* * *

The danger for every masculine heart moved at the discovery of feminine beauty is to misinterpret it. Beauty in all its forms is not for our gratification. It is a quality to be marveled at and loved, not a commodity to be exploited. God created beauty in women, and in the world at large, in order to display a part of his glory in a way that says, "Come and see." Men are to protect that beauty. Our protectiveness is another aspect of God's glory, and it is crucial when our quest for beauty combines with the sex drive.

Here's where things typically get gnarly. You see, in a perfect world, the warrior stage will precede the lover stage. But puberty happens when it happens, and hormones can be pretty insistent, right? The juncture between these two stages is a tension zone; it isn't neatly defined, and when the ideal order gets flipped, as happens far too often, the result is never good. Because it's the warrior who brings security and self-control to the lover stage. The warrior is the one who recognizes there is evil that wants to corrupt all that is good. And it is the warrior that invites a younger man into the battle for the heart. A man must learn to protect both his heart and the heart of women from misapprehending what beauty—*all* beauty—is for.

Beauty is intended to point us to God as its ultimate source, thus helping us to know him better and deepening our ability to experience his love and love him in return. Beauty intensifies our awe of God and enriches our romance and friendship with him. For God is not only beautiful—he is beauty. And he is more than fond of you—he is in love with you.

Romance is to start with God, *then* move toward the feminine. That is what a man must understand as he awakens to desire, to the power and the pull of womanly beauty. Never underestimate the potency of that awakening. For in woman, beauty comes to us in the form most like ourselves—as another image bearer uniquely designed to partner with us, bone of our bones and flesh of our flesh (Genesis 2:23). And so, God's invitation for a man to navigate the uncharted waters of beauty and romance involves fragile, powerful, and volatile moments. Only after he has been trained in the difference between good and evil can he handle the weight and expanse of female beauty.

God invites the man to protect a woman while pursuing a romance with her. He will need to make himself vulnerable often as he learns how to love her, in the hope that she will honor him with her own love in return. This is why nothing is more beautiful than two people walking with God together, and why few things are more fragile than two hearts pursuing the thing they were created for: romance with God and romance with each other. It is what we were made for—and so it is what the enemy violently opposes.

The Great Romancer

When you look at creation, you are gazing upon art at its most foundational and transcendent. And where there is art, there is an artist.

When God created the world, he held nothing back. Can you imagine what it was all like when the first strokes of paint were drying, when the sculptures were taking shape, and the Artist stepped back from everything he had created and, with deep satisfaction, declared, "It is good"? Picture it—the earth and sky spoken as landscape onto the canvas of creation. Oceans and mountains crafted into shape and placed just so. Daisies and redwoods, hummingbirds and whales, horses and monkeys, otters and elephants, all shimmering and dripping with dew and awaiting their names.

It was beyond words. The most beautiful things always are.

And then God created his masterpiece: humankind. Man and woman, set in creation as more than just two additional creatures. Far, far more. These were the Artist's image bearers, a son and daughter, friends of God, imbued with the dignity of colaborers with God. Man and woman were created to be caretakers of the planet he had created for them and, one day, co-heirs of it all. It is a love story—a world made for romance by Love himself.

God is Love, and we are invited to see through creation to the Love behind it. To God, the Great Romancer.

But what we see and experience now is fallen creation—a beautiful world still, but marred and scarred by the presence of sin. Like a priceless masterpiece covered by a drop cloth or, worse, defaced by someone drawing over it with crayons, creation was, and still is, compromised. And humanity lives lost. It is as if something of creation was extracted, eliminated, pulled away, leaving us less for now. Incomplete.

Eden was forfeited. For now, it is like a lost city, uninhabited, waiting for the return of those for whom it was created.

This is our present condition. No matter how hard we try to make this world our home, something vital has been lost. Something that must be found, must be restored. But what?

Our relationship with the Great Romancer. That is what must be found.

Simon Tugwell, a late nineteenth-century Dominican monk and church historian, wrote, "So long as we imagine it is we who have to look for God, we must often lose heart. But it is the other way about: he is looking for us."

This is where our freedom can be found: in *our* being found, again and again.

One day all will be made new. The Artist and his creation will be fully recovered, living happily ever after. Paul tells us this in Romans:

> For the creation waits in eager expectation for the children of God to be revealed. For the creation was subjected to frustration, not by its own choice, but by the will of the one who subjected it, in hope that the creation itself will be liberated from its bondage to decay and brought into the freedom and glory of the children of God. (Romans 8:19–21)

One day we will get the garden back, with upgrades. Our King is presently preparing a place for each of us (John 14:2–3)—quite a gift for his sons and daughters, his intimate allies. Meanwhile, we need to be healed up, trained up, and shown what true beauty is and how the sacred romance works.

The lover stage is what glues all the other stages together and will make a man after God's own heart—if and when that stage is reclaimed. In the boyhood stage, we were to experience what it is to be loved; in the lover stage, we are to experience and learn how to love. Being loved is what God intends as the rock-solid foundation on which we construct a life of loving others.

* * *

How often have you been told that love is not a feeling and that feelings and emotions have nothing to do with God's love?

Horse hockey! That is the craziest thing I've ever heard.

Experiencing God's love, enjoying the beauty of the Trinity, being caught up in romance, is tasting and seeing that God is good. An intimate relationship *feels* like something. Being loved by God is what transforms you. Not just reading about being loved by God but experiencing the love of God. Hearing him say to you—to *you*— "I love you. You are mine, and I am yours."

A man can read about God's love all his life, like reading a brochure for the Grand Canyon. The brochure will invite him there. But only when the man actually stands on the rim of the canyon can he be transformed by beauty and romanced to the Creator's affection. When a man moves from the study of the theological to the experience of the theological, something significant happens. And you won't have to pry his experience out of him, because he'll be bursting with it. He can't help trying to share with you what he's found, because he feels the love and pleasure of his creator.

We talk about the person we are in love with because we experience them. And a relationship with God is, above all else, an invitation to an experience. It is a love story about you and the One who loved you first, loves you most, and, wild as it sounds, is love itself.

Love Stories

When I was growing up in the 1970s, Evel Knievel was jumping over things on his motorcycle, Farah Facet was an Angel, Apple Jacks were for breakfast, and only four channels played on TV.

Back then, just like today, television was an unofficial "authority" on life and culture. If you were home sick and stuck on the couch, your only options were game shows, talk shows, and soap operas. My mom had her favorites, *All My Children* and *General Hospital*. For a nine-year-old trapped into watching *All My Children*, even a few moments left an impression. Relationships seemed to be either aboutkissing or arguing. One moment, the good guy was rescuing someone; the next, the bad guy was plotting revenge.

But it wasn't just those morning soap operas that glorified the shallow end of the relational pool. Shallow was everywhere. *Knots Landing, Dallas, 90210,* even *Happy*

Days . . . shallow is what the unofficial authorities taught: a lifestyle of how to be users and consumers. And that is where most people lived then and live today.

On the other hand . . .

* * *

Gladiator, The Matrix, Braveheart . . . I couldn't have told you, when I first watched those movies, why I loved them. I just did. They're films men know by heart, with characters that inspire us. *The Last of the Mohicans, The Lord of the Rings* trilogy . . . the list goes on of epic stories whose themes invite the masculine heart to *more*. To adventure, to friendship, to journey, to the battle between good and evil.

And always, to love.

The best stories are, at their root, love stories. Oh, they may not appear to be at first, but take a closer look. Romance always works its way in. We resonate with these tales because they are telling us something about *our* story. They remind us that we too were made for something larger—for adventure, battle, and yes, romance. We were made to bear God's image, and if we long for and resonate with the good and noble themes such stories tell, then something of God must long for them too.

Have you noticed how love stories are always woven into these epic tales?

Neo meets Trinity and confronts the Matrix.

Maximus avenges the deaths of his wife, Selene, and his father figure, Marcus Aurelius.

Hawkeye tells Cora, "Stay alive. I will come for you. I will find you!"

Arwyn gives up her immortality to be with her true love, Aragorn.

And William Wallace, returning home to win the heart of the maiden Murron, takes her riding on his horse through the Scottish Highlands to a lofty overlook. There, sitting side by side with lake and valley spread below them and mountains stretching into the distance, they banter and flirt. William informs her that if he can ever work up the courage to ask her for their next time together, he'll give her more notice with a written message.

"Oh, it won't do you much good," Murron replies. "I can't read."

"Can you not?" Wallace says, gazing softly at her. "Well, that is something we shall have to remedy, isn't it?"

"You're gonna teach me to read, then?"

"Aye. And in what language?"

"You're showing off now."

"Are you impressed yet?"

"Why? Should I be?"

William (in French): *"Yes, because every single day I thought about you . . ."*

Shortly after, Murron, fascinated to hear William has been to Rome, asks, "What was it like?"

William (now in Latin): *"Not nearly as beautiful as you."*

"What does that mean?"

"Beautiful."

The Scottish peaks surround them. The misty twilight enfolds them. The scene fades.

Two hearts falling in love, with a dangerous destiny in front of them. Who can forget William's proposal? "I love you . . . always have. I want to marry you."

Does it not feel familiar? In chapter 13 of 1 Corinthians, Paul's famous essay on love, the apostle says that "without love I am nothing . . . and without love I gain nothing" (see vv. 2, 3). Sounds more like Shakespeare than Scripture. Of all the things that the Gospels are, among all the truths, themes, and messages contained in Scripture, the single great constant—powerful, and never to be over-looked or underestimated—is this: that the Larger Story is above all else a *love story*.

But don't think that because it is a love story, it is for that reason soft. Rather, that's what makes it all the more dangerous. The characters in love stories are always on a journey. They must learn to be courageous, must find their strength, and, eventually, must confront and overcome evil. All for love. The Larger Story is no soap opera; it is an epic tale for the ages, and we have each been written a part. In the words of author Brent Curtis, "Our lives are not a random series of events; they tell a Story that has meaning. . . . For above all else, the Christian life is a love affair of the heart. . . . Most Christians have lost the life of their heart and with it, their romance with God."[2]

So it is that the questions of earlier stages now make room for a new awakening of the heart. It is this:

If I was created for a sacred romance,
then my true destiny is this:
to love beauty,
to enter into mystery,
to know and be known.

It is in the sacred romance that our hearts will find both their path and their home.

Lover Stage

A love story requires lovers. The lover stage is foreshadowed in all the earlier stages of the masculine journey and, once entered, continues as a man becomes a king and, finally, a sage. But while the raw material is there early on, there is a distinct time when the lover in every man's heart awakens into the lover *stage* and his training begins. Woman is its centerpiece—the wonder and allure of her beauty, outward and inward. And yet, the lover stage is about much more, and goes far deeper, than just loving and romancing a woman.

The warrior stage lays the foundation and provides the proper perspective for the lover stage. That is why, ideally, the warrior comes first. Otherwise, feminine beauty will be approached by a man as a consumable item rather than a gift to be cherished, and he will attempt to get his strength *from* a woman rather than bring his strength to her. Sadly, this is exactly what happens with most men, and far too many women pay the price, deeply wounded by men who ought to be their protectors, not their consumers, let alone their predators.

In the lover stage, the formative years of boyhood and explorer make for either good or bad training. A man at this point either is settled through validation and initiation in the ways of the kingdom, or he is unfathered, unfinished, and disoriented under the influence of darkness.

* * *

Woman is beauty in human form. But a man must discover something richer and more eternal and transcendent than a woman. He must discover God.

He has thus far journeyed toward that discovery from the small world of a boy to the expanding, larger world of a man. It is a dangerous world, yet filled with beauty, wildness, and wonder, where the artistry of creation and, ultimately, of the Creator himself, is experienced. Now, here in the lover stage, a man discovers the nature of the heart.

Lover is the stage when *mystery* is embraced. A man moves from the academic to the transcendent. Learning the answer to "why something is" is not as important as simply *enjoying that it is* and appreciating its effect on the heart. Not everything can be explained by facts and flow charts; more parts of life must be *experienced* in order to actually "know" them. There is a *ginosko* that comes only as a man learns that God's heart toward him, and the resulting richness of his own heart, are the essence of life. It is out of his deeper, truer experiences of beauty and romance that he can learn to love a woman for who she is and what she was created for rather than for how she can be used and what she can provide.

In this stage, a man not only discovers romance but comes to see God as Lover, as the Great Romancer in his story. Settled in his own belovedness, the man is able to partner with God in validating and initiating other image bearers. In his relationships with women, he declares to them their worth and protects their heart because he sees them as God sees them. Thus, the lover stage is not about sex; it is about intimacy. Sex is a small part of that, but intimacy involves far more than physically making love. Intimacy is about knowing and being known.

And romance is what makes intimacy possible—pursuing and being pursued.

Initiating and Validating the Lover

I was fortunate, more so than many boys, to have a father who gave me his time and presence. During my first decade, I truly experienced what it means to be a beloved son.

The wheels started falling off during my explorer stage. That's when conditional love slithered in, and the lover part of my heart began to be seduced. Sports, grades, recitals, and even pornography started to plant deceptive seeds that would bear bad fruit in the stages to come. Competing for validation by teammates, classmates, and girls—winning and losing, proving or failing—became my new "theology." It overran anything and everything. And church didn't help with its weekly reminders that my performance was never enough—that I was the problem, but if I worked hard, try and try again, I could earn God's love and approval.

As I hit warrior, my personal theology was at full tilt. College scholarships and maintaining a position on the basketball team dominated my life. My worth was now fully connected to my performance. School was a place for which to stay eligible, and girls were a hobby as long as they didn't get in the way of my first love, hoops. Sadly, I managed that way for a long time.

But managing isn't the kingdom way. When I married Robin and we started having a family, the enemy was poised to rock my marriage and my kids with a husband and dad who was far more adept at trying to control than to love. It wasn't pretty, and my kingdom was in trouble.

Not until my late thirties did God penetrate the dark, unloved place in me. That's when renovation began. As my Father continued to reveal to me who I was to him, spoke affectionate words over my heart, and filled my mind with new images of acceptance, significance, and value, slowly the game changed, I changed, and life changed. God was romancing me with walks in the woods, songs, films, Scriptures, the care and wisdom of kings and elder-sages, and most importantly, validating words from his heart to mine. It is the love of God that transforms us.

* * *

Loving a son in all stages of his life is the greatest way to raise a lover. I don't mean hugging and kissing him all the time, or constantly complimenting and affirming him. Love isn't always soft; there are times when it flexes its muscles. Raising a child to know love also means telling him the truth. It means inviting him to hear instruction—not criticism, but caring, straightforward instruction. For a masculine heart to mature, it must cultivate attributes of respect, discipline, and responsibility, instilled at times through strong, loving correction. This is the protective and preventative side of a father's love, the side that comes across with passion and intensity—fierce sometimes; kind always. Always kind.

So much is riding on the instruction and modeling of what it looks like for a masculine heart to be loving. This is where we have been failed and why we have all but lost the war on masculinity. There's an unfetteredness to love, a goodness and a wildness we need to reclaim. Robert Bly wrote, "To be wild is not to be crazy or psychotic. True wildness is a love of nature, a delight in silence, a voice free to say spontaneous things, and an exuberant curiosity in the face of the unknown."[3]

* * *

As we open our heart to experiences of God's love that transform us into our true self, the warrior in us protects us. This is crucial, for the heart is the "fountain of life"[4] that is essential as we partner with God in the great battle for Life. Love is Life, and it is love that we offer to the world, because it is a love we have received from God.

Experiencing God's love is critical. His will is for our good (Romans 8:28); he assures us that he has "plans to prosper you and not to harm you, plans to give you a hope and a future" (Jeremiah 29:11). But his will is not always done. That is why Jesus instructed us to pray "on earth as it is in heaven." Sin is never God's will; therefore, both the warrior *and* the lover must fight for the kingdom to come—for it will take both to see love win the war.

The Wounded Lover

The lover stage is compromised early, long in advance of its actual arrival, when a boy is not shown and told he is the beloved son. When the foundation of the masculine heart is not properly poured and the materials are subgrade, then later in life, as the grown man moves into lover and then king stages, he will use his position and influence to make those he is supposed to love and lead provide the yes to his heart's core questions: *Do you see me? Do you love what you see?* No kingdom can survive a needy king; everyone will pay under an unsettled king's demands.

Similarly, if a boy's questions during his explorer stage—*Do I have strength? Can I come through—do I have what it takes?*—remain unanswered or disaffirmed, then that too becomes a wound. The lover part of his young heart can be crushed, for instance, when a father shames the explorer for his appreciation of art, creativity, and beauty. The false self that arises out of such a wound will play out in hurtful ways later on in the lover stage and beyond. The qualities of romance that a woman longs for, and that a man's children need, will be closed off to them because the man learned long ago not to offer those qualities.

Damage of another kind occurs when a man looks to a feminine heart as his primary source of validation. The lover is wounded when the woman is brought into the story prematurely and made to be its center. That's a forecast for ruin, both his and hers. A man must be in the warrior stage for a time and doing well there before pursuing a woman. Otherwise, failing to see both her heart and the true nature of the battle, he will try to conquer her rather than conquer the true enemy who opposes them both.

That is one of the grave dangers when love subtly gives way to lust. The drive for physical gratification is powerful and is the adversary's substitute for romance and affection. Lust becomes a huge enemy of the lover's heart, hindering its development. The desire to possess rather than protect, consume rather than provide, has taken many a young man down and kept him there for years and stages to come.

* * *

Imagine an engineer who marvels at a rainbow. An accountant who quotes William Yeats. A salesman who takes time to savor the colors and scents of a garden. There you have the makings of a king who knows a thing or two—because the lover in him nourishes and counsels his heart, soul, and mind.

Conversely, the lover stage never develops in young men who live their lives out of their heads. Men whose world consists of analysis and reason, facts and lists, competition and achievement. Rather than graduating to something deeper and weightier for their souls by embracing mystery, beauty, and romance, such men live in the shallows. They remain boys—boys who shave, drive, and acquire jobs, marriages, and families. They may be superb workers, producers, and providers, but their kingdoms will only go as deep as they are. Because while they may excel at thinking and doing, they're not so great at intimate relationships

A man who majors in his intellect but never taps into his heart becomes a man who will seek to fix his wife rather than love her. He will diagnose his children and friends, evaluate, lecture, and correct them. What he won't do is truly understand those close to him and offer not mere advice but empathy, compassion, and care from a strong and kind heart. That is what those in and around his kingdom need and want most—not an analyst, not a fixer, but a kind, engaged, and loving king.

Lost Boys

There was a reason Adam chose Eve over God in the garden. Darkness uses the feminine heart to lure the masculine heart into compromise; then darkness completes the loop by using wounded men to wound women.

We were made to experience kingdom beauty and noble romance. They are good things, and the lover stage is God's invitation for us to enjoy them both. But in this world . . . a curvy teacher, an older sister, maturing friends, images in magazines and movies: not bad things per se, but in a culture that has long adopted the idea that sex sells, how is a young man supposed to handle it all? He needs help navigating the sexual lures that surround him. Dad, or perhaps some other good king, needs to show up and help him see how and why the lover stage is about something more than women alone.

A boy is doomed to be lost when he gets his training from other lost boys. Peer pressure in every stage is a powerful thing, but nothing compares to the damage and confusion caused among grade school associates. Sharing images and videos on smart phones has made pornography more than available—it has made it handy. Recent statistics reveal that 35 percent of all internet downloads were pornographic. With roughly 42 million sites dedicated to pornography, the porn industry grossed an estimated 16.9 billion dollars in revenue. Compare that to the entire NFL, which in 2020 posted 12.2 billion in total revenue.[5]

Many men believe that once they get married, the pull toward pornography will go away. It won't. When the lost boy in a grown man remains lost, the allure actually gets worse. The tragedy with masturbation and orgasms, fantasizing intimacy with a woman on a screen, is that she is always ready for the man, always wants him, and never needs him to talk to her, care for her, and protect her. What real woman can compare with that or support such shallow and unrealistic expectations? Thus, even after he is married, the grown-up lost boy finds comfort in long showers or late nights in front of the computer.

While sex and sexuality aren't the only component of the lover stage, it's one the enemy prioritizes as their target. Darkness desperately wants an in with sex as early as they can get it so they can use it as long as possible. Why? Because they know any yahoo can have sex, but only a settled man can offer intimacy, enter into romance, and care for the heart of a woman. Anything less—false, shallow relationships with women based mainly on sex—will corrupt a man's internal system. That's the enemy's plan: to hijack the real and true objective of the lover stage so that instead of living intimately with God and others, men are trained to try to use God and others.

Sabotage on the Wedding Day

On a man's wedding day, his unhealed and unredeemed wounds go right down the aisle with him. They just acquire new symptoms—because wounds in earlier stages of the masculine journey, left undealt with, sabotage the lover in both husband and wife. A masculine heart wounded in the boyhood stage wants a mother, not a woman. The wounded explorer in a man sees the woman, not his walk with God, as the adventure. The wounded warrior sees the daughter of Eve as something to win or conquer rather than someone to love, cherish, and protect.

Meanwhile, in all fairness, the woman has wounded stages of her own, and she can use a masculine heart just as badly as she herself can be used. The result: two wounded hearts using each other. And who wants to be used?

Sadly, the manhood modeled for us as we grew up taught us that women were to be exploited, not cherished. The lessons began early, positioning the enemy to ruin the kind of relationship God intended for us: a man and a woman walking with him together. In choosing Eve over God, Adam granted the enemy one of his greatest and easiest war tactics, one he has used successfully against boys and men ever since.

So it is that a husband wonders why his marriage is a struggle and why he and his wife live miles from happily ever after. In both men and women, the wounded lover stage must be redeemed. Otherwise, one failed marriage becomes two, and two becomes three. Statistics show we don't get better with every attempt at marriage or relationships. Until the lover in us is healed, we get worse.

Healing and restoring the lover in us is the great priority of God, the kindest and fiercest pursuit of our Maker. Our part is to let the Great Romancer catch us—again and again.

CHAPTER 9
King
Ruling and Reigning for the Good of Others

"I will clothe his enemies with shame,
but his head will be adorned with a radiant crown."
—Psalm 132:18

Nearly all men can stand adversity,
but if you want to test a man's character, give him power.
—Abraham Lincoln

HOW DO I LOVE AND LEAD,
PROVIDE FOR AND PROTECT,
REIGN AND RULE WELL FOR THOSE GIVEN TO ME?

Greg's dad passed away from a sudden heart attack at the age of fifty. Greg was twenty-two. Not a day goes by that he doesn't feel the ache of losing his father.

Twenty-five years later, Greg stands in a circle with eleven other warriors and kings who have gathered to celebrate our friend SJ's fiftieth birthday. On this prestigious occasion, each of these men has brought a story of his friendship with SJ, a few words about SJ's qualities, and a token to validate him and remind him of this day. The rule is, the token isn't something you could run out and buy. You had to find it among what you already owned. It might be in a drawer or displayed on a shelf—something that reminds you of SJ.

Now it's Greg's turn to present his token. He stands in the circle and tells his tale of teaching SJ to fly-fish a few years earlier. We laugh at his description of SJ, six-foot-four and an XXL, being spooned by five-foot-eight Greg as he wraps his arms around SJ to teach him the rhythm of the fly rod. Like teaching a big ol' bear how to fly-fish. It was a great day and a great story.

As we catch our breaths from laughing and calm settles back over our circle, Greg turns his attention to his gift. It is an odd metal instrument, a tool from the 1960s.

Now, SJ is a gearhead. He knows more about cars than anyone I know. He and his dad used to work on the family cars, and while some boys might have read comic books, SJ read Chilton manuals and *Hot Rod* magazines.

"I knew right away what I was supposed to give SJ," says Greg. "God put it on my heart immediately. It required a little digging through a few old toolboxes of my dad's."

Everyone feels it when Greg says "dad's." This is going to be important. He holds up the tool so we can all get a good look. It is about eight inches long and three inches wide, and it has holes and hooks and handles.

"This was my dad's multitool. It makes me think of SJ and all the things he can do with tools and his knowledge of cars. But also with his knowledge of the kingdom."

Greg's eyes tear. He pauses; his voice catches. "As we celebrate his next steps in the king stage, I want to give SJ something to remind him that he is gifted and skilled in so many ways, but also that he is and will be a father to many, teaching younger men to walk in the kingdom. And as important as our weapons are, a good tool in the hand of a good king can get a lot done.

"Happy birthday, SJ. I love who you are, love our friendship, and am honored to call you my brother."

It is an XXL moment for us all. One good king validating another good king. Affirming him. Telling him, "I know who you are and how you are. You have impact. You have impacted me, and your reign will continue to expand further than you can imagine. You're a good king, and I'm so blessed that you're my ally and friend."

That's how validation in the kingdom works. It's part of how you grow a king. It clearly isn't easy, or we would see far more good kings. Recovering from the hard parts of your story comes with a price—goodness doesn't just roll out and into you—but the price is well worth paying.

Wounds of the Crown

I once heard that the injury rate in every season of the National Football League is 100 percent. All the players come into the league with a history of injuries from high school and college, and every NFL season, every player somehow and in some way gets hurt. Like rams squaring off again and again, NFL players line up against each other about 150 times a game for seventeen games a season, not to mention the practices and off-season training. No wonder the average career of an NFL player is three years. It's quite the accomplishment to get to that elite level, but they sure pay the price.

When I turned fifty, it was like a switch was thrown in my body. Kinda like when all the appliances at my house all came out of warranty at the same time; it was as if they had organized themselves and systematically took turns breaking down. Ditto my body. Years of wear and tear started giving way to pain.

It's not really the years as much as it's the mileage. When I was nine, I was knocked unconscious by a two-by-four that fell from a second story deck. When I was ten, I broke my leg snow skiing with my dad. When I was eleven, I almost sliced my finger off with a pocketknife. When I was twelve, I was stung nine times after stepping on a yellow jacket nest. Throw in a few more concussions, broken bones, and garden-variety bruises and pulled muscles over a few decades, and I'm glad to report I'm still here!

Life outside the garden takes a toll on all of us. Some injuries are done to us through the careless fault of others. Some are our own brilliant doing. All come at a cost. The physical injuries and their painful disruptions, those pretty much heal up. Pretty much. Not so much when the injuries are of the spiritual kind. In the spiritual realm, as in the NFL, all men "play hurt" and, unfortunately, have learned to live with the pain. Spiritual injuries will affect a man for years and years to come. Our hearts, souls, and minds, like our bodies, carry with us the marks from lost battles, the scars and souvenirs of life's injuries, spiritual and emotional pain that will eventually cause others pain.

Wounds to the heart work differently than wounds to the body. Arrows to the heart lodge there, and the infection is almost immediate and lasting, carrying guilt, shame, and fear from one stage of life to the next and the next when left untreated. How do we live with such pain?

We don't. Survive, maybe; live, no.

Everyone except the enemy loses when we wound one another. And in the king stage, where men attain the zenith of their influence, we have exceptional power to keep the wounding going. It is the stage of either great opportunity or great calamity, and every man enters it limping. If our pain were physical, our doctor would want to know two things: Where does it hurt, and what is its history? Those same questions apply here. But there's also a third question, and it's the most important one of all: Do we try to live with the pain, or will we go to the One, the only one, who can heal us?

The King Stage

We finally come to it: the king stage. The stage in which all the previous stages of the masculine journey play out for the good or the bad.

In the king stage, all the days of all the previous stages mix together to make for how a man will live, how he will see himself and the world, and how he will reign. This is the time of handling authority. The time of stepping into trials with the hearts of others on the line. Most importantly, it is the stage when how a man was loved over his lifetime will determine how he will love others at this time of his life.

The culmination of years—the collective work of trials and errors; the wounders and wounding moments over a lifetime; the agreements and vows a man makes; what he has come to believe about himself, others, and God; and the healing he has received, if he has received any—will all be on display in the king stage. The false self constructed in him the kingdom of darkness has over the first forty-some years of life—the man's coping strategies, the devices he believes will protect him, and the controlling methods he has learned in order to arrange life and manipulate relationships for himself—will no longer serve him.

In the king stage, a man begins to *feel* his life. His response may blossom into a midlife crisis (which, if he is a disoriented man, will drive him to seek futile remedies), or it can become the man's gateway to the path of healing and overcoming. Sixteenth-century philosopher and statesmen Francis Bacon wrote, "It is a sad fate for a man to die too well known to everybody else, and still unknown to himself."[1] Wise words. Thankfully, there is a better alternative.

* * *

If kings bear their unhealed wounds, good kings learn how healing brings great glory. Healed hearts heal hearts, sunshine is as real as rain, and it's the hope of being good kings that inspires us to cross the checkerboard of life. For the king stage is the time when a man wields power and authority—when his reign has expanded in ways that, for better or worse, have far-reaching impact. A bad king can do great damage. But a good king has the love, the resources, the connections, the reputation, and the wisdom and experience to tremendously benefit other hearts and lives.

A good king has learned how to handle wealth of every kind—money, relationships, influence. I like how author Bob Goff puts it: "God didn't give you influence so you could lead people better; He gave it to you so you could love people more."[2]

In the previous stages, a man has been learning how to hear God's voice and distinguish it from the many other voices that compete for his attention. He has learned how to walk with God and receive God's council both in day-to-day life and in weighing tough decisions. He has come to see his role as a partnership with God, one in which he is fathered by his heavenly Father even as he himself is like a father to many.

Now he has arrived at the hardest stage of the masculine journey. The king stage is the time when a man's wisdom, earned through all the trials and errors of many years, the healing of wounding moments, and the restoration from lost battles, can serve him well. Living and ruling from a wise and discerning heart is the objective of the king stage, and it's vital for a good king's role in the Larger Story and in the missions with which God entrusts him. Many depend on him; the part he now plays is big and affects untold lives.

But this is not only the time when a man is entrusted with more. He may also, in God's kindness, have things taken away. God will use anything, or partner with anyone, to see a beloved son healed, restored, and set free. Not every shipwreck we encounter is the enemy's doing; God has his ways of rerouting a man to help him discover his identity and destiny. Remember what Jesus said: We lose life (on our terms) in order to find life (on his) (Matthew 10:39).

Initiating and Validating the King

The COVID-19 pandemic was lifting a bit, and some folks were beginning to move about and reengage in events and gatherings. I had been invited to speak at a place called The Barn, and several of our Zoweh allies and friends—men who had bought one of my books, downloaded resources from our website, or been to one of the weekend conferences—got an invitation to attend.

It was a cool spring day in the Southeast. Winter hadn't quite given up, but a beautiful night was ahead. We had no idea how many men would show. (You know men—it's always hard to tell.) As they began to pull into the fields that served as a parking lot, it appeared this was going to be a bigger deal than we thought.

A good friend was manning one of the registration tables. We shook hands, gave each other the one-arm hug, and stepped into "How are you?" After a few minutes, one of the other men at the table, sitting at the computer, leaned back and, kindly interrupting, asked, "Have you registered?"

My eyebrows went up. "Well, that's a good question," I said. "I think I have."

"Last name?"

I liked where this was going. I took a step closer to where he hovered over his computer and said, "Thompson."

He scrolled down the Excel file. "Thompson, Thompson . . . hmmm, you're not here. Are you sure you're registered? How do you spell it?"

That was my cue. I picked up one of the books in a pile next to him and pointed to the name at the bottom of the book, Michael Thompson. And I waited for it.

He looked at the book, looked at me, looked at the book again, and then shot out of his chair in one of the best validating moments I've ever had. "Oh my gosh, oh my gosh, you're Michael Thompson! You don't know what your book has meant to me, what God has done in my life. Oh my gosh, oh my gosh, I am so sorry"—like a kid meeting one of his heroes. And I got to be the hero! God is fun sometimes.

We shook hands, and I thanked him for such a special moment, all of it. I was honored. I got to tell my new friend that he was an answer to my prayer, both years ago and that very afternoon: *Dear God, I pray that you would impact men's lives in these pages we wrote and bring them to deeper intimacy with you.*

Now we both were smiling, our hearts filled and warmed by how our Father arranged for a little moment that wasn't so little.

There are significant moments in every man's life. Graduating from school, getting married, having children, buying a house—all are major mile markers in a long journey. Making a team, being hired . . . thank goodness, not all of life is about wounds and wounding. There are moments when we are recognized. To be seen, to be invited, to be wanted, to belong—that's what love is, and we need it, need it badly, even as kings. We need to be strengthened by those we strengthen, validated by those whose lives we touch.

Because love is what fills our hearts, and the absence of love is what wounds them, we stay susceptible to wounding and in need of love in the king stage—as in every stage. For remember, the lover part of us exists in all stages, and every stage, once laid, remains a part of us. But given our heart's varied questions, love looks and feels different in each stage. Our enemy worked in every stage to wound us; therefore, in the king stage, the Father's good pleasure is to redeem love . . . in *every* stage. Discernment is what lets the good stuff in and the bad stuff go.

* * *

Because king is the greatest stage for healing, that makes it also the greatest time of validation and initiation. All men come into the king stage wounded, and most are oblivious to what it will take to get free. But in the kingdom, there is always the hope of resurrection. God is determined to see a man's wounds healed, see that man overcome his false self, and see him overcome the enemy who has hated him all his life. God is rolling away the stones, inviting initiation; it is our part to respond.

In every stage of your life, wounds happened—and still happen—in a moment, bringing messages of potential bondage and death. God will literally love you back to life through a great exchange. In it, he invites you to bring your naïve agreements with the false messages and vows of your past into a present moment in which you listen to what *he* has to say. A moment in which you trade the enemy's lies for the truth your Father wants to tell you. That's the great exchange. It's life-giving and life-changing.

God is committed to your comeback. To making good on all that wasn't good in your life. And in this stage of your life, that includes seeing that you receive love and its ongoing validations of your true identity as a man—how you are known in heaven.

A good king is validated when those under his care flourish. His kingdom isn't without trials, and he is initiated into new responsibilities again and again because the trials of those he loves are his trials as well. Thus, they are also opportunities for him to love well and rule well, inviting him to provide for and protect hurting hearts.

A good king knows how to counsel because God has counseled him. He has learned when to speak words of life and, more importantly, when to be quiet and allow a moment to unfold. One of the most powerful things he does is model for those in his kingdom what it looks like to walk with God.

Because his domain was given to him by God and operates in partnership with God, the king is generous with his time, treasure, and talent. He takes joy in seeing others flourish under his care. He looks for opportunities to pray with others (more later on how he prays), and he brings God's kingdom into the circumstances, declaring what is true and enforcing the truth against the enemy on behalf of others.

Such a king is often validated and initiated by the hearts, young and old, that he himself is validating and initiating. It's a two-way street. In God's kingdom, the giver gets.

Kindness

I've heard Graham Cooke say it dozens of times: "God doesn't see what is wrong with you; he sees what's missing." This is why the examined life and the healing path move in the same direction on the masculine journey. Exploring with God answers to the questions "What happened to me?" and "How did I get here?" are key to breaking free from the spell of quiet desperation.

No matter how much brokenness or how much goodness you bring into the king stage, God wants the job of fathering you. Every man needs that for his comeback: the Father to father him, Jesus to equip him, and the Holy Spirit to guide and counsel him in his masculine journey. Every man needs the Trinity to kindly walk him to freedom. And the Trinity needs a few good men in your life to partner with in, validating and initiating you with their words and presence. Your comeback and training require quite a team!

In all of it, one more thing is required: *kindness*—including your own attitude toward yourself. You will be called upon again and again to be kind to your own heart throughout the restoration journey.

It's never a weak thing to be kind or gentle. In fact, these are two of the most powerful fruits of the spirit. It's a gentle word that turns away wrath (Proverbs 15:1), and it's kindness that has the ability to allow for the flow of love. As the sun can melt ice, so kindness melts away the hard things of the heart. Therefore, we must learn to be kind, gentle, and compassionate toward our own heart if we are ever going to learn to be kind, gentle, and compassionate toward others. I have to remind myself from time to time:

I've never been here before.
I am an unfinished man.
Very few get it right the first time.
Father me, Father.

* * *

God's validation and initiation of a king looks like something. It is experiential, not mere theory. Love *feels* like something. Attention, affection, and kindness *look* like something. Care lands on our hearts as an experience that can overcome the evil of our past with good, sometimes in just a mere moment with God.

It's the love of God that transforms us, making all the difference. So look for it, listen for it, and you will see his loving work in your life. Look for it when it's just you and him, alone in conversation. Look for it from other kings and elder-sages. Look for it when God partners with your wife or your kids, even a stranger, to deliver a holy and grand package of his affection. If the enemy can use all these folks to wound you into being who you aren't, God can certainly partner with them to heal, validate, and initiate you into being who you are.

Remember: If it isn't kind, then it's not God.

Recap: Glancing Back to Move Ahead

We have crossed the checkerboard at last. Now is the time when we say, "King me!" and then journey back onto the board with new, greater influence and power. The king stage is the time of our widest impact, whether for good or evil, glory or shame. Our Father wants to do great things with us and through us on behalf of other hearts.

He also wants to do great things for us and in us. The time of king is the time of greatest potential for healing—the time when, if we seek it, God will expose our false self and introduce us to who we truly are. So let's take a quick look in the rearview mirror at the stages we've already traversed and the unresolved wounds we carry with us to this point.

Boyhood. A boy has two key questions: *Do you see me? Do you love what you see?* If poorly fathered, the boy grows up with "No" for the answer. (Mother wounds are also very real, but they happen on a father's watch—or absence.) *There is something wrong with me* is a brutal sentence to live under. And that wound of shame will spur the grown man in the king stage to avoid being seen or to continually use his power and authority to arrange to be loved.

Explorer. A boy transitioning to early adulthood asks a new set of questions: *Do I have strength? Can I come through—do I have what it takes?* A king who was not validated and initiated by his father in the explorer stage will attempt to reclaim this stage by arranging for adventure. In truth, relationships *are* the adventure, but a king wounded as an explorer will concern himself not with what he can bring *to* a relationship but, rather, with what he can get *from* it.

Warrior. Unvalidated and uninitiated by his father and other oriented men in the warrior stage, an unhealed warrior-king lacks vital answers and training for the questions *How do I discern between good and evil? And in a dangerous world, how do I offer my strength for good?* To compensate, he will pick fights and use his power to destroy others to prove his manhood. Or he may see his kingdom as a place to hide in order to protect himself. Either of those two options reflect a wounded, insecure warrior who views others as a threat. Fear has got him either way. And as a king, he will wound those around him through passivity, aggression, or both.

Lover. We'll linger on this one a little longer because it is foundational to everything a good king is about. From our earliest years, our heart is built with a component that longs for love, *requires* love—and that, as it grows, needs to give love. That lover part of our masculine heart is intended to mature during the lover stage of our journey, when mystery, romance, and beauty—significantly, the beauty of Woman—enter the picture. All of this is intended to woo us to God as the ultimate lover, who equips us in turn to love and be in love with a woman. In relation to both her and God, our concern in the lover stage is this: *To love beauty, enter into mystery, know and be known—this is what my lover's heart was created for and what I must know.*

But if a man has not been loved well though his lifetime, especially as a boy maturing physically and awakening to the magic between the sexes, then the wounds that play forward carry deep consequences. A wounded lover-king will take his core questions and needs for validation and initiation to a woman, attempting to get his strength from her rather than bringing his strength to her. He will consume her rather than provide for her. But a woman who is a man's source of life is also his harshest critic—a terrible arrangement, given that she bears her own unhealed wounds. And if pornography remains unhealed, then loving, honoring, and cherishing her will be impossible.

* * *

Those are the stages and their wounds in a nutshell. Now, are you ready for the good part? Flip those wounds around and you've got a thumbnail of what happens when a good king rises to his glory, walking in the footsteps of the King of kings. Each stage, as it heals through a man's personal encounters with God and through moments of validation and initiation by oriented men, locks in properly with the other stages to form a strong foundation for that man's kingdom rule.

Boyhood. A good king has experienced that he is the beloved son of his heavenly Father. His heart is settled in the assurance, *My Father sees me, and he loves what he sees.*

Explorer. A good king knows, *By God's love, I have strength. I have what it takes to come through for those who count on me.*

Warrior. Settled in his Father's love, a good king steps in, according to the circumstances and in whatever way he is called, to fight against darkness for the hearts and lives of others. He knows who and what his enemies are, and he can stand and declare to them, *Greater is he that is within me. You shall not pass.* The warrior learns the way of a wise and discerning heart, and he aims at all times to exercise his will for good.

Lover. With his heart opened to the mystery and romance of beauty in its many expressions, and drawing his life through an intimate love relationship with God, a good king brings his strength, his protection, his provision, his kindness—his love—to his wife and children . . . and beyond, to all in his domain. A good king with the lover part of him healed can say, *I know who I am, and I bring that to romance and beauty.*

That is the vision God has in store for you as you advance to the coronation square of the checkerboard. That is the healing, the promise, and the glory that lie ahead as you receive the crown and the beautiful words "Well done." That is what it means to be a good king—the King's good king.

You've Never Been Here Before

Don't mistake me as saying it'll be easy. Healing isn't easy, nor is exercising your reign, nor are some of the initiations you have yet to encounter as you seek healing and training to learn to rule well. You're going where you've never been before, and if the thought of that both excites you and intimidates you, good. You've got the right idea. Reclaiming your glory will come with a fight. The enemy will not give it back so easily, and it therefore may not seem at all glorious at the time.

We sat at a dining room table, two couples deep in the mire of a relationship going sideways. We four had been friends; now we were becoming something else. Healing and repair were eluding us. Forgiveness, though powerful, was a power we couldn't tap into. The toll on my heart and on Robin's was extensive.

I had to end it. And the worst blow, the brutally painful irony of it all, is that we are a ministry that specializes in redemption and restoration. Only not this time.

As I talked with Jesus and asked him to help me sort out the damage, he showed me:

Conversation like this? You've never been here before.

Confrontation like this? You've never been here before

Betrayal like this? You've never been here before.

And . . .

Initiation like this? You've never been here before.

Initiation? Yes. In every circumstance, every relationship, every drama, God invites us to walk with him and respond to his initiating us into something—for me, in this case, into the hard, uncharted territory of cutting off a cherished friendship truthfully, lovingly, and forgivingly. Accepting the invitation to navigate that territory well would make me a better man. If it is the ocean's storms that can make for good sailors, then it's life's trials that can make for good men.

We aren't initiated without going *through* something. That's why James tells us to "consider it pure joy . . . whenever you face trials of many kinds" (James 1:2).

Really? Joy?

Really. The Message translates the next verses, "You know that under pressure, your faith-life is forced into the open and shows its true colors. So don't try to get out of anything prematurely. Let it do its work so you become mature and well-developed, not deficient in any way" (vv. 3–4).

Every king will suffer. Hard circumstances, slaps in the face, losses, criticism, rebellion . . . pain doesn't stop just because you wield authority. The story I've shared involved a keenly felt personal betrayal. But that's nothing new. Jesus experienced betrayal, and so will we—the breaking of trust, a switch from walking-with to pushing-against that results in the end of a relationship. It's one of the many faces of loss. One day we're celebrating someone or something we feel is the answer to our prayers; then over time we come to wonder, "How did it come to this?" Jobs end. Friendships expire. Marriages go from "I do" to "I don't anymore."

Why, God? Why would you allow this to happen?

Never underestimate the unholy trinity: the kingdom of darkness, the false self, and life outside the garden. But take great comfort and reassurance in knowing that Jesus is with you. He will tell you what you need to know and what you need to do if you talk it over with him. Because it matters to your heart, it matters to his.

The reason a man's greatest healing doesn't usually occur until the king stage is, that's when his past finally catches up with him. All the old systems finally fail, and the false self is exposed. It is a great kindness, a time when God wants to take a man into deeper waters of personal restoration to become more and more whole-hearted. The restoration of the heart is so important to God that he will invite, disrupt, even provoke a man into healing. No one wants to see a king healed more than the King of kings. His love is our great hope—and only hope—of pushing back the darkness and walking in the freedom Jesus died to purchase for us (see Galatians 5:1). Being so loved is no guarantee we won't encounter the storms of life. But again, it's the storms that make for the best sailors—and it's the storms that give us the opportunity to walk on water.

There is nothing greater than to hear the voice of the King of kings calling you out to remake you into one of his kings.

Why?

So you can use your influence to open doors of opportunity for others.

So you can create possibilities that only a good king can see and provide.

So you can speak kind words of hope, encouragement, direction, and life born out of the long experience, the wisdom, the *ginosko* of a man on the journey to becoming a king.

So you can use your resources—your network of relationships, your finances, your position, your strength—to birth new kingdom initiatives, spark loving relationships, help restore relationships where love is dying, maybe even partner with God to empower life-saving care.

Success isn't the goal. Love is. And even with love, there is no guarantee things will turn out the way you hope. Sometimes they will, sometimes they won't. Because darkness still exists, and overcoming and becoming are your greatest offense and defense. Your job is this: being restored to your true self so you are free to love. But the results? Those are up to God.

All the healing and training are what King Jesus wants to do *in* you so you can do the things he wants to do *through* you. That's how you fulfill your role in the Larger Story—and in so doing, point others to him and help them find and fulfill *their* roles.

That's the glory of a good king. That's the reason to heed the call and step onto the kingly path of healing. Your story is maturing. Your power is at its peak.

And many hearts and destinies are counting on you.

CHAPTER 10

Elder-Sage
A Guide for the Hearts of Others

The teaching of the wise is a fountain of life,
turning a person from the snares of death.
—Proverbs 13:14

Often when you think you're at the end of something,
you're at the beginning of something else.
—Fred Rogers

HOW CAN I FINISH WELL?
WHO IS IN MY LIFE TO LISTEN TO AND,
IN LISTENING, LOVE?
HOW DO I BRING WHO I AM TO THOSE WHO NEED
MY LIFETIME OF WISDOM AND EXPERIENCE?

He moves about Middle-earth with a vast knowledge of its history. After all, he has been there for most of it, since the third age. He is confident in who he is yet humble with those he serves and guides. He is Gandalf the Grey, wise, cunning, kind, and good.

As the Dark Lord marshals his vast, evil hordes for war, it is Gandalf who strengthens the hearts of his friends with his presence and his words: "It is not our part to master all the tides of the world, but to do what is in us for the succour of those years wherein we are set, uprooting the evil in the fields that we know, so that those who live after may have clean earth to till. What weather they shall have is not ours to rule."[1]

You may say, "Gandalf isn't real." Oh, he is very real. Did he really live? That is a different question. Characters, whether fictional or historical, are real—real in their essence and in how they lived. The *quality* that is real about them, the thing they embody, is what we must see, what C. S. Lewis calls the "true myth."[2] Our desire for something *more* is just that: mythical until it finds us and becomes our reality. That is how proposition becomes truth. And truth is powerful.

I'm not suggesting truth is subjective. However, I believe deeply there are hard, fast truths that live outside our understanding. There is mystery. There is always more. And there is time, and journey yet ahead, for kings to discover that "more." We need those who have tasted the more and know it to be true to guide us crown bearers toward greater understanding through a right interpretation of our circumstances. We need the elder-sages.

J. R. R. Tolkien's mythical Gandalf the Grey passed through hidden, fierce fires and deep waters and emerged as Gandalf the White. What is it in the experiences of real-life elder-sages that has made them what they are? When and how did they transform from gray to white?

* * *

Merriam-Webster's defines an *elder* as "one having authority by virtue of age and experience"[3] and a *sage* as "one (such as a profound philosopher) distinguished for wisdom . . . [or] a mature or venerable person of sound judgment."[4] While the two words are similar in meaning, *elder* stresses age, someone whose influence comes from having seen and accurately interpreted many years of life, while *sage* puts the emphasis on wisdom. Connecting the two words into elder-sage gives a complete picture of this final stage in a man's journey. Not every older man is a wise man; not every sage is old (Jesus was only thirty when he began his ministry as a rabbi). But an elder-sage is both, uniting age and wisdom into someone both powerful and kind.

The best elder-sages know how to ask questions that help us discover the truth for ourselves, or they share truth that invites us to ask the next questions on our journey. I have had many such elder-sages in my life. Some, including Martin Luther, C. S. Lewis, A. W. Tozer, and Dallas Willard, are figures of both the long and the more recent past whose words have shaped my heart. Others, such as Aslan and Gandalf, are fictional yet real and impactful to me. Still others are very much alive and active today—men such as Graham Cooke, John Eldredge, Dan Allender, and my own father, Big Jim, who continue to speak into my life and whose journeys are of great comfort to me as I travel my own path.

Scripture is full of sagely counselors. The Epistles, for instance, are all written by older men. Peter, James, and John wrote thirty and forty years after their three-year expedition with Jesus. Peter was a changed man by the time he wrote his letters. His words "Clothe yourselves with humility" (1 Peter 5:5) don't at all reflect the brash Peter of the Gospels. That rooster did something to him (Mark 14:72). Wisdom hard-earned.

The ultimate elder-sage is God himself, who shows his heart toward us by his appellation *Father*. He wants to be known and trusted, and he wants to validate his sons and daughters for who they are and initiate them into who they can be. He does so both through direct, personal encounters by his Spirit and through his human agents, including elder-sages who see the glory in a person and call it out. These wise, loving souls see what stands in the way of that person's glory, his or her woundedness, and carry that man or woman to Jesus for healing.

Not every older person is an elder-sage, but you can learn something from every elderly person—what it is about him that you want to be like . . . or perhaps what you *don't* want to be like. Some elders bear such unhealed wounds that they have settled into a cynical, even profane character whose life experiences haven't translated well into wisdom. But if you are fortunate to have a true elder-sage in your life, a great question to ask is, "What do you know?" Chances are he (or she) will smile, take a deep breath, and then tell you the story of when they learned a lesson you yourself would be wise to heed.

The Elder-Sage Stage

The elder-sage stage characterizes men in their late sixties and beyond whose legacies started long ago. These are their years of final repairs and final blessings. Their presence, words, and actions will live on one way or another in the lives of those who follow. An elder-sage feels deeply the words of the Farmer's Insurance commercial:

"We know a thing or two because we've seen a thing or two."

Elder-sages need kings and warriors—and kings and warriors desperately need them. We would be remiss not to explore this stage of the masculine journey.

This is the season when a man is wanted for his wisdom, his experience, and his stories, particularly those that relate to the times and ways God has brought healing, validation, and initiation into his life. His kingdom is being passed on, handed over to a younger king or kings, bequeathed to the next generation. But his presence and his words must remain. An elder-sage's strength lies in gracious counsel, wise and gentle. He knows that kindness is stronger than anger and that love is the most powerful force of all. An elder-sage is a father to many, and the way he draws near to God is the most attractive thing about his life.

Proverbs 31, beloved in its depiction of the "noble woman," briefly says this about her husband: "[He] is respected at the city gate, where he takes his seat among the elders of the land" (v. 23). In biblical times, the city gate was a place of great significance where kings issued decrees, armies were commanded, and important governmental and societal business was conducted. The city gate was the town square of Jewish culture. People went there to be heard and to share wisdom and direction. The elder-sage occupied a prominent position in that very prominent of ancient places— and he still does, or should, in the lives of kings today.

* * *

Retirement, often forced upon a man at this time in his life, is something the elder-sage is apt to see more as a sentence than an offer—and he's not having it. Nothing wrong with retiring from a job or career, but he's not about to retire from life or his journey with God. He knows there is more life yet to be lived, and he believes his greatest contributions are in front of him.

"Encourage" is the motto of an elder-sage. More than an answer man, he is a listener, question asker, and storyteller. Indeed, he sees his chief job as listening and, in partnership with God, offering healing, training, validation, and initiation to the next generation. An engaged heart is his greatest invitation to others, and stories are his most powerful weapon. You know you are with an elder-sage when he can look not only at you but into you.

Entering the elder-sage stage is, as with any stage, a rite of passage into a new role with new assignments in life. With God, a man in this stage pursues any unfinished heart business of his own while also seeking to bring healing to any hearts he has been a part of wounding. As his life winds down, he feels the importance of finishing well.

The elder-sage is cunning, a spiritual warfare veteran dangerous for good. He has learned to watch, listen, and wait for God to open doors. He knows well the lowest seat at the table and prefers it, though he is seldom there for long. His stories are transparent, tales of both his regrets and his victories over a lifetime of learning how—and how not—to walk with God. His walk has in fact deepened to the point where he is a *friend* of God, and he lives with an orientation that invites and attracts other men to that same closeness with the Father.

All kings, warriors, and explorers need such a man in their life—an elder who sits at the city gate looking out for them. One who can listen, share, comfort, pray, and tell the encouraging stories of God's goodness in his life. Retire? Never. Not now, when all the years are paying off and wise counsel is the gift such a man has to offer. Not when friendship with God and friendship with others makes the elder-sage, like George Baily in *It's a Wonderful Life*, "the richest man in town."

Initiating and Validating the Elder-Sage

Hasn't a man who reaches the elder-sage stage been initiated and validated enough?

No. Living *through* something is not the same as being validated or initiated by someone *in* something.

To be recognized never gets old, and "well done" is always a powerful validating force. The settled elder-sage doesn't *need* such pats on the back, but he certainly appreciates them, and he is ready with a wink or a thank-you when one is offered. He's comfortable in his own skin and knows how to receive a compliment.

Many men don't. I've seen it often, and so have you. You say, "Thank you for your help. You are really good at that." And in reply you get, "Oh no, it's all God." Or "It's nothing. If you really knew me or what happened . . ." Or "God will use any old bush that will burn." It sounds so humble and spiritual, but it's really not. It's false humility with a spiritual veneer, and underneath it lies a wound. Such a response sends a kindly given package back to its sender unaccepted because its intended recipient's worth is held hostage. How godly and gracious is that?

An elder-sage doesn't create such awkwardness. He feels at ease simply saying thanks, and he wants to make sure those around him feel comfortable too.

Elder-sage is a time when a man's kingdom may be getting smaller, but his influence is getting larger. He is ready to bring the weight of his character and experience to younger men. Knowing when to speak, and how, is an art critical for the elder-sage. When he does speak, it is from a vast reservoir of *ginosko* and a settled heart, for he has nothing to hide, prove, or fear.

The advent of the elder-sage stage is a time of passing on the torch to younger men—for the older man himself is transitioning as he graciously allows, and even appoints, other men to be kings. Initiating others is an initiation of sorts for the elder-sage as well, and validation follows when he embraces what he has become: a fire-tested, broadly experienced source of wisdom, counsel, faith, spiritual strength, and powerful affirmation. Entrusting those following behind him with kingship, and blessing them in that role, is harder than one might think; yet it makes for some of the most powerful moments for the hearts of others and for the man himself. For the elder-sage is validated and free when he can freely validate others

Wounded Elder-Sage

Again, not every older person is an elder-sage. If there is a shortage of good kings, then it stands to reason there are even fewer elder-sages. And even the best of them aren't perfect. Wise and godly they may be, but they are still human. They may have experienced much healing, but they still bear their scars, and they remain susceptible to injuries, particularly those that are unfortunately common to this season of life.

Having built his kingdom, the elder-sage now is tasked with passing it on. And it's not easy for a man to entrust others with the future of something he has taken a lifetime to build. He is still keenly interested in his kingdom's welfare, and his insights are treasures he has to offer. He has something valuable to say about every stage in the masculine journey, and he needs to be sought for what he has seen and learned as a boy, an explorer, a warrior, and a king. Partnering with God, he is highly equipped to participate in healing and training the younger men in his life. It hurts when who he is and the wisdom he possesses is not valued and invited in the kingdom he once ruled. If he's not grounded in his friendship with God, he can easily agree with and subscribe to the enemy's lie, "You have nothing to offer."

The wound is compounded when a man's mileage catches up with him physically. His body is slowing down. Health concerns become more trying and real. Grieving the loss of his ability to do things he used to do is a challenging part of the elder-sage stage, and if the health of a man's bride of many years, or of his closest friend, is declining, that is another heartbreak. Funerals multiply, the losses add up, and the enemy attempts to play his last cards of fear, anxiety, loneliness, and especially, regret.

Our culture is quick to cast off its elders. Forgetful, slow, cranky, opinionated, irrelevant—that's the stereotype. When was the last time you saw a film or TV show with a positive masculine character over seventy who was critical to the story? Our elders are wounded simply by the way our society treats them. That is why a king can play an incredible, mutually redemptive role in an elder-sage's life by seeking him out for his priceless counsel. Without it, the kingdom suffers. But when a king invites an elder-sage to share his life, his story, and his wisdom, both men benefit, and the kingdom prospers.

Finding Peace through Forgiveness

Whatever a man has based his life on will be exposed in his latter years. Whether he invested more in people or in things will determine what surrounds him in his last season of life. That is not always a happy revelation. But as with Ebenezer Scrooge in Dickens's "Christmas Carol," the still-broken places of an elder-sage's heart that haunt him can also invite him to redemption. Regrets can be holy if we see them as invitations to intimacy with God.

Many older people are haunted by wounds they have inflicted on others, especially family or friends. The injuries they caused have become the ones they themselves bear. Among the elder-sages I have counseled, the burden of being unforgiven is common. Those men's regrets aren't holy; guilt and shame force them to live paroled rather than forgiven and free. Receiving forgiveness from those a man has wounded is a powerful antidote to guilt, shame, and regret. It is both an elder-sage's challenge and his opportunity. It is a courageous thing to pursue forgiveness, for it is a vulnerable space to enter. Maybe that is why so few do. The enemy has much to lose when forgiveness is pursued. Two hearts are involved, both of them have much to gain, and so does the kingdom at large. So there is opposition, with the potential for pain, and no guarantee the other person will forgive.

True, the Christ follower is already forgiven by God through the work of the cross and resurrection—but will he *receive* that forgiveness and allow God to weed the garden of his heart? Whose voice will he listen to? The enemy's: "You don't deserve this"? Or the Father's: "I forgive you. Stop trying to pay for something my Son has already paid for. Just receive it, and let me love you in the grief and regret.

Lay this down so I can hold you up."

Of love's great gifts, forgiveness—and the grace to *receive* forgiveness—is the greatest, and a very humbling one. The best elder-sages are the ones who have let forgiveness do its work in them, washing away the stains of guilt and shame and replacing them with powerful and empowering humility and grace.

We Need Them

Old men ought to be explorers
Here and there does not matter
We must be still and still moving
Into another intensity
For another union, a deeper communion.[5]

I am reliving a moment in my life—an occasion on which, like thousands of times before, my Pops is once again in the stands, here with me and for me. He's the same dad who made playing catch or shooting baskets together a normal part of my boyhood. He even coached my teams until the "official coaches" relieved him of that joy.

But it has been a few decades since the last time, and this is a different kind of setting.

The event is in Colorado at one of Zoweh's weekends for men. I'm excited for Dad and nervous for both of us. Speaking to hundreds of men sitting in their seats is challenging; I'd rather shoot a free throw to win in the last seconds or be up to bat in the bottom of the ninth. Yet it's my father's seat that still means the most to me. I'm fifty-four and he's seventy-seven, but when he is in the room, I feel as if I'm fourteen again.

Just Dad's presence is validating, but it's his words afterward that go even deeper, this time reinitiating me as a king. With tears and a quivering voice, he says what I never tire of hearing: "I'm proud of you." He can't say much more. His emotions are getting the best of him while at the same time inviting the best of me. I feel as if I am in a ceremony, a rite of passage, an acknowledgement from the man whose presence and words mean the most to me, my dad. He has stepped up and brought my heart with him.

One of the most precious things in all this is, I know his story. Dad is living on the emotional frontier, because my grandfather didn't deliver such good packages to my father's heart. So every time Pops ventures into this new territory, it's all the sweeter for me. How courageous of him. How beautiful. How important for the both of us.

The enemy isn't the only one who can get two for one. Love casts out fear, and a lot of love silences fear's voice altogether.

Nothing inspires a good king to do battle like the presence and loving words of a seasoned and oriented elder-sage. And nothing makes an elder-sage more proud, glad he is still alive and fighting, than watching a good king win a battle, or rescue a heart, or expand God's kingdom. He welcomes having a small part, simply being included and having the opportunity to offer love and encouragement from his heart as a seasoned Christ follower.

Good kings know how to call elders out of hiding (spelled "retirement") the way all good friendships start—with a question: "Would you tell me your story?" Elders welcome opportunities to share their lives and bring them into the present.* They need a good king to invite them to continue exploring the kingdom.

Paul's purpose for leaving Titus in Crete, he reminded the overseer of the Cretian churches, was that Titus "might put in order what was left unfinished and *appoint elders in every town*" (Titus 1:5, my emphasis). As kings, we too can appoint elder-sages, and those in our domain need to know who they are and seek their wisdom.

Temporary Confusion

Life is not stationary. Like the ocean, it is continually billowing, rolling, a vast expanse marked by both placid horizons and violent storms. The prevailing current will propel you to your next destination, yet you may not have learned what the previous stage was all about. And the storms are as capable of running you aground as they are of accelerating you on your way. But God is in both the current and the storms, and whether the waters at any moment are peaceful or roiled, his invitation stands: "Will you let me teach you how to live?"

The different stages, now that you've lived through them, remain in you to form the composite of who you've become, and life's current will carry you through them daily. You may have to buckle down on a Saturday morning to finish a project at work (explorer); then enjoy playing in the sprinkler with your kids in the afternoon (boy-

---

* If you are a king or a warrior, I strongly encourage you to do videos or audio-recorded interviews with your fathers and grandfathers. It is a tremendous way to honor a life and create a validating moment.

hood/king); then comfort your daughter through a breakup after dinner (lover/king); and at day's end, rescue your wife from the foul spirits of fear and anxiety before you go to bed (warrior/king). Just another full day in the kingdom.

Each stage of the masculine journey has its essential ingredients for making a man. We are always susceptible to wounding in any of those stages—until we learn how not to be. We all missed things; we all were missed; and the ingredients needed in every stage, and the transitions from one stage into the next, are challenging and fragile. In his book *The Masculine Journey*, Dr. Robert Hicks writes, "Understanding the stages as a journey also suggests that at every new place encountered there is a time of separation from the past, initiation to something new, transition from one place to the other, and temporary confusion. At every season of life these developmental tasks are required in order to keep moving on the journey without getting lost or stuck in the developmental mud."[6]

From boyhood to elder-sage, God has created all the stages. But he has subjected them to our own free will, and he also allows others to exercise their wills, for better or worse, to influence our masculine hearts. We are composites of power, pain, and promise; of wonderfulness, wounds, and wisdom. God has said, "I will work it all out for the good" (Romans 8:28), so if it isn't good yet, then God's not done yet.

In the last stage of the masculine journey, when white hairs and life experience commend a man as an elder, it's God's ongoing work in that man that makes him an elder-*sage*. The man has seen and learned much, but he has much yet to learn. He is wise yet still growing in wisdom. Healed yet still healing. And day by day he continues to prove his Father's promise:

"I will be your God throughout your lifetime—
     until your hair is white with age.
I made you, and I will care for you.
     I will carry you along and save you."
                    (Isaiah 46:4 NLT)

"I am as strong today as the day Moses sent me out," said eighty-five-year-old Caleb to Joshua. "Now give me this hill country that the Lord promised me. . . . The Lord helping me, I will drive [the Amalekites] out just as he said" (Joshua 14:11–12). It's never too late to reach for what God has promised you. Never too late to get in the fight for the heart, going back with God for the healing of your past in order to expand the life ahead of you into a life of *more*.

More of his love yet to experience. More of your true self to offer, with his help. More to be entrusted with.

Because more, always more, much more, is the kingdom way.

* * *

So concludes our exploration of the different stages of the masculine journey: their characteristics, their wounds, and their strengths. The foundational knowledge is in place. Now what do we do with what we've uncovered? With that question in mind, let's move ahead into the third part of this book.

PART THREE

The Glory of a King

Authenticity is the daily practice of letting go of who we think we're supposed to be and embracing who we are. . . . In order for connection to happen, we have to allow ourselves to be seen.
—Brené Brown

In part 2 we looked at the different stages of the masculine journey. But why is all that important? Why heal from our wounds and dismantle the false self that rooted in those wounds?

Because of the glory our Father is calling us to as his beloved sons and kings.

Part 3 is where things get real and things get good! God invites us to join him in tearing down the lies that have opposed his vision for our lives. We're about to explore how healing happens—and what it looks like for us to walk in our glory as kings in the Larger Story.

* * *

In the movie *The Lion, the Witch and the Wardrobe*, based on C. S. Lewis's classic children's book, winter has taken over Narnia. Jadis, the White Witch and self-proclaimed ruler, has the land under her spell.

The time for a reckoning is coming, but not without a fight. Aslan, the great lion and Christ character, has summoned the four Pevensie children, Peter, Susan, Edmond, and Lucy, to join him. As sons of Adam and daughters of Eve, they are key to overthrowing the White Witch's evil reign. But there is a problem: The children have no idea who they are in this story.

When the White Witch enters the camp of Aslan to lay claim to Edmund, the younger brother, for having betrayed the others, Peter instinctively takes out his sword and readies to fight her. The White Witch scorns the young prince: "Do you really think that mere force will deny me my right, *little king*?"

"Little king."

Truth spoken in mockery is still true.

God has a high view of mankind, of those who bear his image. As sons of the King of kings, we are royalty. Our enemy knows this about us. He knows who we really are. The question remains, do we?

How do you see yourself? What voices are you believing? Who and what is blocking you from walking in the nobility of your true identity?

You are the son of a good Father, the apprentice to a glorious King, and the companion of the wisest and wildest Guide who ever existed. You have a glory, and God wants to see it restored so he can turn you loose—because he knows that free men free others.

Your enemy wants you to remain ignorant of this. He doesn't want you to cross the board and receive your crown, because he knows that healing is for a purpose far greater than your small story. There is a weightiness and splendor to your life. It's what God had in mind when he made you uniquely in his image.

Let's go with God and get your glory back.

CHAPTER 11
The Healing Path: Trailhead

"This people's heart has grown dull,
and with their ears they can barely hear,
and their eyes they have closed,
lest they should see with their eyes
and hear with their ears
and understand with their heart
and turn, and I would heal them."
—Matthew 13:15

Healing in this life is not the resolution of our past; it is the use of our past to draw
us into deeper relationship with God and His purposes for our lives. We need a new
understanding of how to deal with past hurts, one that acknowledges the damage to the
human spirit while charting a path toward
the abundant life God promises
—Dan Allender, The Healing Path

X-rays show us a where a bone is fractured, but X-rays don't heal. Knowing what is broken is vital, but it's just a start; treatment and healing are another thing altogether. So it is with our heart: There is a big difference between understanding where our pain comes from and having God heal it.

Times when our false self takes over—when we hurt others or hide from them, when we seek to control, when we react out of our woundedness in ways that wound and alienate another person or reinforce our own pain—those times are invitations to come to God with questions: *Why do I believe that? Think that? Act like that?* Seeing is awareness, our part; but going to God is the key. He is the only one who can heal and restore a heart.

Over the years, I have heard the stories of many men. Some of them have spent countless hours and hundreds of dollars with counselors only to become more *aware* of their problems and pain but not *better*. Not healed, not transformed.

A man will describe to me a wounding moment in his life. "But I worked through all that," he'll assure me.

"So . . . what do you mean, you've 'worked through all that?' How? What does that mean?"

"Well, you know. I just worked through it."

"No, I don't know," I say, gently. "That's why I'm asking. What does 'I worked through it' look like?"

A few awkward seconds pass. "Do you think I haven't worked through it?"

"Would you say you have *experienced* healing? Heard God's voice? Felt relief? Seen a shift? Have you allowed God to show you what happened and why? And then let him give you something to replace the pain, heal the broken part of your heart? Has he helped you exchange the wounding message you've lived with so long for a loving, healing one?"

How would *you* answer those questions? Have you gone with God to examine the deep wounds, agreements, and vows of your past and experienced his healing? Have you heard him speak life-giving words to you that rooted out lies you lived with for years and replaced them with the truth of who you really are—of your beloved-ness, your enough-ness, your strength and valor as his man?

Healing is relational. It's an outgrowth of walking with and communicating with the Father, of talking with him and—very importantly—hearing him talk with you. What exactly will that look like for you? I can't say. What God has reserved for you is as unique as the way he designed you. It's as individual as you are. There are, however, some . . . what should I call them? Concepts. Tools at your disposal. Not so much steps to take but rather a direction you can go, practices you can cultivate, attitudes you can develop for going with God into the wounded places of your heart and discovering the reality of his voice and its healing, redemptive power.

Let me share with you just one of the many times this has played out in my own life.

* * *

Shame has a voice, and I was sick of hearing it. This time, when the accusation *There is something wrong with me* came up once again, I was just hanging out with some friends. Yet I felt out of place. *Why, God?* I asked him for eyes to see what might be operating within me that wasn't good. Then it came back to me—a scene I hadn't thought about for more than forty years. Sitting in its memory, replaying it, I started to feel anxious and sad. And my stomach knotted, just like it did that day so long ago . . .

The famous Sixth Grade Trip of my school had arrived. Four different homeroom classes—more than a hundred boys and girls—boarded the big yellow buses and headed to camp on the coast of Washington State. With us came our class projects—science competitions, group projects, geography and botany classes, team building, survival skills, and more.

In the middle of the campus, framed on all sides by the dormitories and other buildings, was a large courtyard. That's where my classmates and I played and had activities. And that's where the disaster occurred. How much trouble can a Frisbee cause? Plenty, trust me.

I was in a game of throw with several other classmates, and it was my turn to show my Frisbee skills, hum one hard for a distance record. I let 'er rip. The Frisbee sailed, caught some wind, banked hard, then—and here is where everything shifted into slow motion—headed toward the launch platform for the rocket module group. Boys who had spent the last few months building rockets in anticipation of this day were gathered around the pad, eager to launch their projects a mile into the air. I swear that bunch had to have been a hundred yards away. And what happened next, I couldn't have repeated in a million tries.

Like a guided missile, my Frisbee descended and smacked into the rocket on the launch pad, obliterating the rocket, trashing the pad, and scaring the crap out of the kid who built the rocket, the other boys, and worst of all, the sixth-grade teacher.

Scowling, the teacher surveyed the landscape and, out of the hundred kids out there on the courtyard, zeroed in on the one with his hands grasping the top of his head, his mouth wide open in shock, and his body frozen in horror. Like a lion coming after a gazelle, he crossed the field to me, grabbed me by the shoulders, and began to shake me in time with the words he hissed through his teeth:

"What–do–you–think–you're–doing?"

On he went with his shaking and venting. Ninety-nine other kids now also stood frozen with their hands on their heads, gaping at the spectacle. When he finally let me go, I ran, humiliated, straight back to my bunk in the dorm and cried—heavy, heaving crying. The punishment continued inside me, and I agreed with every accusation on the enemy's list:

You're an idiot. Yes, I'm an idiot.

You ruin things. I ruin things.

Look at you. You're all alone. No one cares. That's me, all right: all alone and no one cares.

"Surely I'm over that," I told God.

"No," I heard him say, "this one left a deep impression and led to a list of agreements that fear has used in your life for many years."

"Well, what can I do about it?"

"You know those messages you heard that day? The ones your false self and darkness have been beating you up with ever since? They're lies. Renounce them and unsubscribe from them. I have better things to tell you about who you really are and how much I love you."

We'll talk more about renouncing and unsubscribing in a bit (and also share this story's conclusion). Right now, it's enough to say that going back with God at age fifty to that wounding moment was one of the kindest things I've done for the explorer part of my heart—for young Michael, that boy who was shamed, who cried, but who never grieved or healed. The boy whose young heart needed the care of a calming presence and a consoling voice. That came much later. But thank God, it came.

How Healing Works

Fallen people in a fallen place can't help but fall on one another. So asking God when and how the harm happened and why it still hurts, and inviting him to tend to the wounded places, should be standard operating procedure for every believer's restoration. Your current false self is always a clue to your past.

Every man has stories of boyhood misfortunes, shaming mistakes, hurtful miscalculations, and the mishandling of his heart. And each man's wounds are unique. Your pain is yours, not to be compared with mine or anyone else's. Counselor and teacher Jane Travis wrote, "Comparisons come in 2 forms: They make you feel superior or they make you feel inferior. Neither serve any useful purpose."[1]

Your belief system has been shaped by a lifetime of experiences, especially during the formative years. Hurtful experiences are gateways for damaging lies. But none of us knew how to discern lies on our own when we were boys. Unless someone was there to teach us how to guard our hearts, false beliefs were free to slither in, embed in our hearts, and compromise our true selves, guaranteeing we'd lose our way and the life God created us to have.

Thank God, the glorious offer of the gospel is just that—*life*. Life we have lost. Life only God can restore. Because we are never more alive than when we are being loved—and God *is* love (1 John 4:8). That's why, in the conflict for your heart between the kingdoms of darkness and light, encounters that left lasting damage need to be replaced by new encounters with the God who is love—the God who loves you, whose image you bear.

That is how healing works, how it is accomplished. God reveals and loves aspects of you that weren't loved well or weren't loved at all. With God, you revisit a wounding moment in order to reclaim it for the kingdom of light. You do this by renouncing your agreement with shame, guilt, or fear and by replacing that agreement and whatever vow you made in response to it with a new agreement, a loving and kind agreement. This new one is an agreement with what Love (that is, God) says to you and about you. That's how you let Love have power in your life. Encounters with God are the key to healing.

There are things you can do to facilitate such encounters. That's the word, facilitate. You can't *make* those moments happen. After all, we're dealing with God. He determines the how, where, and when of things, and he's not bound to any formula. He's no insert-tab-A-into-slot-B, snap-in-place God, any more than your heart is a snap-in-place heart. But he does want very much to connect with you and love you into wholeness, and there are ways you can *position yourself* for that to happen. As you do, you'll discover that God has been waiting all along. You've just needed to get the ear muffs off and develop a greater sensitivity to how he communicates with you, and an expectation that he wants to and will.

Before we get into that in the next chapter, though, let's consider a few basics.

What to Do with Guilt, Shame, and Fear

The false self arises out of our attempts to deal with guilt, shame, and fear on our own, without help from oriented and engaged parents and apart from God and his ways. At its roots, the false self is the sum of all our bad beliefs about ourselves, God, and others, which leads to strategies to self-protect or self-promote.

It starts with guilt. Guilt in itself is neither good nor bad. It's just a fact: Something we've done or said was wrong or has hurt someone else. We can admit it or deny it, but either way, it is what it is, and in this life, it's simply going to happen. We all make mistakes. There's not a one of us who doesn't sin or just plain screw up.

The problem is, we don't like how guilt makes us feel . . . well, guilty. It's a painful feeling, especially when our actions might have consequences. So we cover up our guilt or excuse it. Few of us know how to handle the weight of guilt constructively. The rarity of sincere apologies and seeking forgiveness shows the power of guilt. It commonly becomes a doorway for something much worse: shame.

Shame persuades us to hide or, worse, pursue revenge. Brené Brown, a leading researcher on shame, writes:

> Based on my research and the research of other shame researchers, I believe that there is a profound difference between shame and guilt. I believe that guilt is adaptive and helpful—it's holding something we've done or failed to do up against our values and feeling psychological discomfort.
>
> I define shame as the intensely painful feeling or experience of believing that we are flawed and therefore unworthy of love and belonging—something we've experienced, done, or failed to do makes us unworthy of connection.
>
> I don't believe shame is helpful or productive. In fact, I think shame is much more likely to be the source of destructive, hurtful behavior than the solution or cure. I think the fear of disconnection can make us dangerous.[2]

Add fear to the mix, and the result is a powerful covert commentary:

Guilt pummels me for my behavior, commenting with disdain over something I did.

Shame punishes my very identity. It attacks who I am by whispering that something is wrong with me. Shame takes guilt the next step by insisting that the problem isn't merely what I did—the problem is *me*.

Fear glues it all together, compromising my future by reinforcing the lie that "I have nothing. I am nothing. I am on my own. Life is up to me."

* * *

Did you know that guilt, shame, and fear have a voice? They do—yours. Disguised as your own thoughts, they invite you to think something or do something, then give you a club to whack yourself with for thinking it or doing it. Almost always, they speak in the first person:

What was I thinking? What is wrong with me? Why did I . . . ?
I can't believe I . . .
How could I screw up so badly?
Why am I always such a loser!

Often guilt, shame, and fear are the internal echoes and amplifications of external voices we heard once upon a time, messages that came in through wounders' voices and lodged like poisoned darts in our heart:

"You idiot! Can't you do anything right!"

"Put that down! You'll break it. You know how clumsy you are."

"You are such a big disappointment."

"I wanted a girl. Instead, I got you."

"I wish you'd never been born."

Or they come from a *lack* of external voices and messages. No attaboys, no "I'm proud of you"s, no hugs, no kisses, no bedtime stories, no hand-held walks in the evening, no playing catch, no fishing on the lake, no initiations into new opportunities and responsibilities, no validations of our worth in all the ways, both verbal and nonverbal, that a good parent—particularly a good dad—conveys them.

The lack of good voices makes it open season for false suggestions on how to interpret one's circumstances, worth, and identity. The lying voices of guilt, shame, and fear are betting you won't ever detect them. Because if you do, you just might take them to God and exchange them for something far better: the truth.

We've discussed the collective impact of all these things in previous chapters. Now it's time to focus on the overarching, self-shackling ways we've responded—and how, with God's help, to get free.

Agreements, Vows, and Their Antidote

Countless are the guilting, shaming, and fear-producing messages the enemy aims at a man's heart. From early boyhood up to the moment when we finally learn to recognize and refuse those messages—which most men never do—we have too easily agreed with them. *Yes, I'm a loser. Yes, I'm a nobody. Yes, I'm unlovable.* These agreements attack our sense of who we are, and since we shape our lives according to that identity, the result is a self-reliance that is never good and often catastrophic.

Agreements can also target their lies against others. *Authority figures will hurt me. People are just out for themselves. Everyone wants to use me. No one is safe.* Lies that attack who others are, are just as damaging as the lies we believed about ourselves. Judgements play right into the hands of the kingdom principle of sowing and reaping. They're like boomerangs in the universe: Throw them at someone and, guaranteed, they'll come back at you.

Regardless of what form an agreement takes, the problem of agreeing with any lie is that in doing so, we also *subscribe* to it. "Sign me up for a daily delivery of *I'm Not Enough*," we tell the enemy—not out loud, of course; we're never aware of what we're really doing when we agree and subscribe, and the enemy prefers it that way. Once our name is on the dotted line, the subscription arrives more regularly than junk mail, along with all the other lies we've subscribed to through the years.

How does the false self cope with the pain of those agreements? By *vowing* never to put us in a position where more wounding can occur. A vow is our declaration of self-protection. We wall out the pain, or so we think, unaware that we're actually walling ourselves in with it. Vows take the form of "I will never" or "I will always":

> *I will never let anyone get close enough to hurt me.*
> *I will never trust an authority figure.*
> *I will always get the upper hand.*
> *I will never let a woman into my heart.*
> *I will always take advantage of others before they take advantage of me.*
> *I will never show tenderness (because it makes me look weak).*

Vows are our will's reactions to agreements. In response to the bad things that happen to us, we draw conclusions and make binding declarations—deeply personal, woefully naïve attempts to solve the pain our hearts have endured. We adopt them in a moment without weighing them with an oriented heart, and they secure a deep operational place in us. Stored in the belief system known as our subconscious, vows become part of the source and energy on which our heart runs. They're a powerful autopilot, reactions that will operate destructively—toward both ourselves and others—in the future.

The agreements and vows we subscribe to are like time-release poison pills, with one exception: pills disappear, but agreements and vows are self-replenishing, and they pave the way for more reinforcing agreements and vows. We may call all of this our personality: "It's just the way I am." No. It's your false self, and it is solely responsible for dragging you—the true you—into sin.

Fortunately, there's an antidote: As you pay attention and God calls them out, with his help, you can *renounce* your agreements and vows and *unsubscribe* from them. There's no trick to this. It goes like this:

Renounce—"Father, Son, and Holy Spirit, I recognize a lie I've been in agreement with, and I notify it, and my enemy who supports it, that I no longer agree."

Unsubscribe—"I cancel the lie's deliveries to my heart. I don't want it, and I'm no longer accepting it. Henceforth I refuse it, and if my enemy sends it to my door, I send it back with a note: 'Return to sender. Subscription cancelled in the power and authority of Christ.'"

Then Ask—"Father, what do you think of me? How do you see me? And what truth do you want to give me to replace the lie?"

This isn't just a mental process. It's best that you actually verbalize it out loud. Don't just think it—say it. God made you a physical being, integrating spirit with body, mind, and soul, and he gave you your voice for a reason. Using it this way taps into your will and invites the spiritual power and freedom of God's love and his kingdom to be declared in the physical realm.

What does that look like in actual practice? Let's return to the day when God made me aware of the impact on my heart of that humiliating accident with the Frisbee way back in sixth grade.

* * *

Some days in your life you can remember in color and with great detail. Those days, both good and bad, matter for their impact on your heart.

I was wrapping up a talk with some men, sharing my final thoughts, when God showed up bearing my memory of the Frisbee disaster in his hands. "One more quick story," I told the guys, and launched into my account of that day. But what's in the well comes up in the bucket, and up came my emotions along with my words. My voice began to quiver and my eyes swelled with tears as I relived that moment back in sixth grade. I saw it, felt it, and was given the opportunity to grieve what had happened to my young explorer's heart.

Afterward, I found a quiet space. I knew God was waiting, and we got right to it. "What was that?" I asked. Sitting still, listening, letting God have my heart, I could envision myself standing with Jesus beside the younger me. I really liked this kid, and I felt so badly for what he had suffered in his experience with the sixth-grade teacher. My heart grieved for him, for that young me who had been cruelly blindsided by the enemy's lies.

Jesus felt badly too. He didn't like what happened, and he was ready to make it right. "Here," I said, giving him the emotional files I had stored up from that day. "I don't want these anymore. I give them all to you, all the agreements and vows.

"All these years my agreements have told me I'm an idiot. But that's a lie. I'm *not* an idiot. And I *don't* ruin things. And I'm *not* alone, not at all. *You* care about me, Jesus. You are always with me.

"I'm tired of hearing those lying voices. I give them to you and ask you to take them away. I unsubscribe from believing what they told me, not only that day but so, so many days since. They don't apply to me, and I refuse to accept them anymore."

Next came the vows I made that day that had been fueling part of my false self:

I will never trust a teacher. Big one.

I will never retreat. This one had been a problem.

I will never let them see they hurt me. Great in a fight; not good for a marriage.

"Jesus, I break the vows I made and their power in my life," I said. "I give them to you for the renovation of my heart. They no longer serve me—I'm not sure they ever did. Father, I invite you to father both my sixth-grade explorer's heart and my fifty-year-old king's heart. Where I wasn't loved and handled well, I invite you to love and handle my heart for the life of *more*."

I was done. My heart felt quiet and receptive.

"Now at last you're agreeing with me, not the enemy, Michael," I heard Jesus say—not in an audible voice but in my heart, where the lies and agreements had lodged. "I'll gladly take those old files from you. They were never yours in the first place. I have much better things to tell you about you, and a better, freer way for you to live.

"Hear the truth, son: I've given you an excellent mind. I made that younger you an intelligent boy, and today you're an intelligent man. More than just smart: You are gifted with insight—no one knows better than I. And because that superb mind of yours is yoked with a good heart, you use it to help, to heal, to guide, and to restore. You are far from a ruiner—you are a blessing, a life giver, and a pathfinder in my kingdom. These things, not the others, are what is true about you. You were, and you are, always mine—my inquisitive and adventurous explorer. My good and able king. My prized and beloved son. I am so proud of you and so pleased with you."

The bell rang to reassemble. I wiped my eyes and caught my breath. Something young within me had just been touched, healed, and integrated, aligned with my true self.

We don't know when God schedules our appointments for healing until those moments arrive. For goodness' sake, I was the teacher that weekend—but God wanted me to be the student! I never anticipated that moment; I only knew it for what it was when it happened. But then I knew beyond doubt. That day is now one of those I remember in color and in great detail, the day when part one of that story in my life gave way to part two. Part one is often where tragedy invades. It takes a part two for redemptive love to have its more powerful way.

For while shame leaves a mark, so does love. Jesus wanted to take something hurtful from me and give me something better in its place. That is the great exchange, and it is that wild and that simple: love for shame.

Why We Need to Hear God

Ever since Adam and Eve hid from God in the garden, all human beings have responded to wounding the same: "I was naked, so I hid" (see Genesis 3:1–10). But there is another way. There is a healing path. And there is a Guide, an authority on your life who can walk you down that path, speak the truth, touch your wounds, counsel you, and melt away the lies. There is another Voice—one that calls to you in your wilderness and invites you to turn from all imposters.

> God is love. When we take up permanent residence in a life of love, we
> live in God and God lives in us. . . . There is no room in love for fear.

Well-formed love banishes fear. Since fear is crippling, a fearful life—fear of death, fear of judgment—is one not yet fully formed in love. We, though, are going to love—love and be loved. First we were loved, now we love. He loved us first. (1 John 4:16, 18–19 MSG)

It takes hearing the voice of Love speaking to us personally for healing to happen. Being loved is not meant to be something we just read about in Scriptures. It is supposed to be the normal experience of the normal Christian life—encountering God, enjoying him, and being enjoyed. Dallas Willard writes,

> God's visits to Adam and Even in the Garden, Enoch's walks with God and the face-to-face conversations between Moses and Jehovah are all commonly regarded as highly exceptional moments in the religious history of humankind. . . . However, they are not meant to be exceptional at all. Rather, they are examples of the normal human life God intended for us: God's indwelling his people through personal presence and fellowship. . . . We live—really live—only through God's regular speaking in our souls."[3]

Intense experiences of shame, guilt, and fear need to be replaced with deeper experiences of God's affection, his kindness, and our worth that lead our hearts to "faith, hope, and love"—among which, Paul assures us, "the greatest of these is love" (1 Corinthians 13:13).

So as you begin to explore the approaches in the next chapters, keep this in mind: God's words to you will be personal, loving, and hopeful. He'll speak with you truthfully but also deal with you graciously. He's out to build you up, never beat you down. So if a thought, or a voice, or an image, any message of any kind, leaves you feeling hopeless rather than encouraged, it's not the voice of your Father. He honors you when you come to him with a humble and hungry heart. "A broken and contrite heart you, God, will not despise" (Psalm 51:17).

Hearing from God, like everything else, takes practice. When you were little, there were many things you had to learn. That doesn't change as you get older. There is a way things work, and that includes communication between your heart and God's.

Do you believe every thought is your own? Are you critical of yourself and others? Do you hear a first-person commentary in your mind: *I am so . . . I always . . . I never . . . ?* Questions like these reveal how you think. And observing your thoughts is a great place to start the skill of listening to God. If a thought isn't good, if the inner commentary isn't loving or kind, then it isn't God, and it isn't the true you. The true you is always on the side of God, and together you and God create a force for life, love, and freedom.

* * *

When we talk about experiencing God's love, we are talking about communication. It's a simple idea, even though we're dealing with the One who made the universe. How encounters with God happen, and what those encounters look like, can be different for you than for me or the next man. There's no formula, just things to keep in mind and possibilities to explore.

The concepts we've examined in this chapter, and those I'll invite you to put in motion in the next, apply to all the stages. God wants to heal and redeem every part of you that's wounded and under a spell. He very much wants to validate and initiate you in every stage of your life. Step by step, intimately over time, the redeeming love of God works to free you to the point where there is more true man than false. This is how all the stages begin to work together rather than tear you and others apart. All so your glory as his king can be restored and you can be entrusted with more.

Got it? Good! Let's step at last into the action.

CHAPTER 12
Becoming You

"I will restore you to health and heal your wounds," declares the Lord.
—Jeremiah 30:17

The great discovery of the healing journey is that in getting a glimpse of God we see our past, future, and present from the perch of an eternal now. . . . The healing path takes us beyond self-discovery to God-discovery.
—Dan Allender, The Healing Path

Till now we've been talking about getting your heart back. *But how?* This chapter seeks to answer that question.

I'd love to give you some step-by-step method, a formula with some ABCs of healing that can guarantee, "If you do this, then God will do that." But God is far more glorious than that, unconventional and full of surprises.

Still, there is a way things work. The concepts here have proven themselves in my own life, and I've seen the difference they've made for countless men as well, some of whose stories you're about to read.

Each section in this chapter offers you an invitation and one way to go with God into the wounding moments of your story. Ultimately, that is what the healing journey is: intimate encounters between you and God for the restoration of you.

Here are some important postures to keep in mind as you embark.

Healing is an exploration with God that takes time. We all have endured many wounds, and multiple wounds call for multiple healing encounters. Each healing moment brings some kind of transformation, and the moments add up—one, then another, then another, causing us to become more and more our true selves. More and more like the One whose image we bear.

What we subscribed to in our youth, and the coping strategies we adopted, won't serve us as men. So we turn these things in to God to receive something far better, and a part of the false self gives way to the true. But just as the wounds happened over time, so healing happens over time. There's no deadline, only God's schedule as he deals with us about different things.

The wounding in later stages often happens because of our wounds in our formative years. This is because the components for each stage exist in us long before they mature into the actual stage. You've surely heard a child say something profound, but that doesn't make him a sage. Grade-school boys skirmish in playground battles, but that doesn't make them warriors. It just means the elements are present for something to come.

So if some vital element of a particular stage gets damaged early on, we'll feel the impact as we enter a later stage in life. Just as a physical injury when we were young can make us susceptible to reinjury or impede our ability altogether, so wounds to the heart can leave us compromised when it comes to receiving and offering love.

We are never immune. We can still get hit as grown men. A marital betrayal, the loss of a job, the death of a child or a wife or a best friend . . . wounding moments occur throughout the different stages of life, and what happens to us in any stage not only affects that stage but will bleed over into others. So it's important to understand how long-ago events and circumstances can affect us years and even decades down the road. In the stories that follow, you'll see examples of how damage that was incurred during a man's boyhood and explorer stages affected other stages of his masculine journey.

Remember the four charts in chapter 5 (pages 89-91)? Take a moment to review them, because in this chapter you'll see them play out in real-life stories.

The concepts are just helpful options, not a checklist you've got to complete. They point you to different directions you can take. Look at each one as a possible point of engagement suited to the moment. As you step into it, you'll probably find that others naturally enter in as well and work alongside each other.

While this chapter discusses each approach as if it were isolated, in actual practice, it's hard to separate one from the rest because they are interconnected and often flow with each other naturally. Healing encounters can begin one way and end up another, in a place you never anticipated! What matters, ultimately, is that you experience God intimately, in a way that makes a difference deep in your heart.

This has already been mentioned elsewhere in the book; I'm reiterating it because you'll see it displayed in the stories. I've chosen each story as a real-life illustration of a particular approach. You may think, "Yeah, but I also see *this* approach happening in the story, and *this* appoach, and . . ." Yes, I know—and great that you're alert. But for the sake of example, I'm spotlighting just one concept at a time.

By the time this chapter is completed, we'll have worked our way through all the stages of a man's life, from boyhood to elder-sage. Bear in mind, though—this is important—that *none of the concepts is limited to a particular stage. Each one works for all the stages.*

Healing comes to those who are humble, real, and thirsty. Most men have become so calloused to their boyhood stories that they don't realize how their false self

> uses humor to cushion the pain,
> wields sarcasm to deflect hurt,
> goes passive under criticism,
> gets loud in order to be heard,
> or tries to be funny when it's time to be serious.

It is how we learned to play the game, cope with the uncomfortable, and vow again that life is up to us.

After the fall, Adam and Eve hid from God behind fig leaves. We have fig leaves of our own: defensiveness, blame-shifting, minimization, resentment, self-justification . . . many are the ways we try to conceal our true condition, and the pain associated with it, from God, those around us, and ourselves. But of course God sees, and sooner or later, others do too. The one person we're fooling is ourselves.

Our one hope of transformation is to go to God as vulnerably as we know how. It is then that God can lovingly call out the wound, speak to us about it, show us why it happened, and reassure us that that he was, and is, in it with us. The result may feel like the removal of a thorn or cool on the burn. Or it may feel like the removal of a thousand pounds off our chest or the invasion of a peace that transcends understanding.

Healing, above all else, frees.

The utter relief of not having to live one more moment under the power, influence, and curse of a lie, with its emotional baggage and triggers, makes the courageous steps toward healing and freedom well worth taking. What have you to lose? Let's begin.

Start with Your Dad

Because fathers are the most influential person in the masculine journey, exploring the relationship between you and your dad—how he handled your heart—is the trailhead for healing and restoring your heart.

Raising us, blessing us, validating us, and initiating us into life in the kingdom—walking us into manhood and teaching us what it is to walk with God—these things were our fathers' job. Consequently, the ways we experienced him are where to look first for wounding. Whether Dad did the wounding directly isn't the point. He was responsible to help us navigate the masculine journey at every stage. Therefore, an honest inventory of what your own father did, and what he didn't do, is foundational to your healing.

* * *

The wound came early for my friend Scott. The healing came many years later, but come it has, in a way both sorrowful and glorious.

When he was a boy, Scott told me, he was a handful for his parents to manage. "There was no ADHD or diagnosis for kids who were 'wide open' . . . but that was me. The medication prescribed back then was spankings or worse. And I got a lot of 'worse.'" Scott continued:

> I was often more than Mom could handle, though she broke a few wooden spoons trying. So I got a lot of being wrangled to a chair in the corner of the kitchen, with the words "You sit there until your father comes home."
>
> One Saturday afternoon when I was about six, maybe seven, after the punishment, in my anger, pain, and tears, I shouted at my dad, "I hate you!

I don't want to live here anymore." Furiously, he grabbed me by the arm and pulled me upstairs to my room, left, and then came back in a flash with a small brown suitcase. He threw it on my bed, then yelled, "Here, pack it. PACK IT!"

My rage rose to meet his, and I grabbed two armfuls of clothes from the drawers of my dresser and dumped them in the suitcase. In one motion, my dad closed the suitcase and, with its handle in one hand and my arm in the other, jerked me back down the stairs, out the front door, and into the back seat of our car. I watched my mom grab my dad, pleading for him to stop, but he opened his door, and she jumped into the passenger seat while he started the car.

As we drove away from my house, it hit me: *This is really happening.* At that point, he won. My anger turned to fear. "Dad, I'm sorry," I said. "I'll never do it again. I'm sorry. I don't want to live somewhere else."

Still furious, Dad looked back over his shoulder and said, "You wanted it, you got it."

Like he was pulling into a pit stop at a race track, he hit the brakes, threw the car in park, pulled me and the brown suitcase out, and set us hard onto a street corner. Then he drove away, with my mom crying in the front seat.

I was alone and abandoned, frozen on a street corner with a brown suitcase full of underwear and socks. My body collapsed, Indian style, to the sidewalk, and the shock of it all gave way to sobbing. I felt helpless, powerless, and afraid.

I'm not sure how much time passed, but eventually I heard a car coming up the street from the same direction I had been dropped off. It was my dad. He pulled up to me, rolled down the window, and with a stern face asked, "You ready? You want to come home?"

My head nodded involuntarily *yes*.

"Then get in and apologize to me and to your mother."

I apologized, and Dad put the car in gear, and we went home.

The experience was over in real time, but the damage had only begun. For Scott had made an agreement with his father's wounding message: *You are weak, and you will be abandoned.*

"Yes," Scott tacitly conceded. "I am weak, and I will be abandoned." That message lived on in Scott through the years—as did his response to it. "It wasn't remorse that won the day," Scott told me. "It was a vow: 'I will never be powerless and helpless again. I will always protect myself.'"

Scott's vow got in the way of every relationship he has had. He said to me, "This wounding moment explains a lot—why I achieved so much at the expense of so many. My wounds left a lot of other wounded hearts in their wake."

But—and this is the good part—Scott's story doesn't end there. Since boyhood wounds occur in the earliest stage of life, they usually stay with us the longest. Healing finally came for Scott many years later as death drew near his father. By then, Scott understood something of his value in God's eyes. He knew he was the beloved son of a good and gracious heavenly Father. "I knew God was offering me a different way of seeing and believing. Instead of contempt for my young heart and a striving to please my dad, God offered me compassion, something that wasn't available to me for almost four decades."

Compassion—God's compassion. Compassion for a young boy's unloved heart, and compassion for a grown son's dying father. As a boy, Scott had felt helpless because of his father's maltreatment. Now it was Scott's dad who was helpless. Scott knew what that was like, and as an oriented man, he also knew God was in this final time with him and his father. Knowing that made all the difference.

In Scott's words, "Going to God with this boyhood pain and forgiving my father . . . this is going to change a lot of things."

The stories that could be told are countless. Stories of men who, like Scott, went to God with wounds from their earthly fathers and experienced the healing of their heavenly Father. There is healing for Tom, whose dad diminished him with constant scolding. Healing for Jim, whose father's absence told him he didn't matter. Healing for Greg, whose passive dad failed to protect him from his mother's physical abuse. No two men's stories are exactly alike, and many are vastly different, for all men are different, and so are their fathers, and so were the circumstances. One thing, however, is constant: the Father's love and its power to rewrite the story your own dad didn't know how to write for you, or didn't care to write, or wasn't there to write. The Father wants to go there with you, back to moments in time when you weren't loved, to provide the love you missed.

* * *

Boyhood was supposed to be about being the beloved son, but most of us got something else. This is not easy to acknowledge; it feels too much like we're betraying our father. Often men are unable to bear the idea that Dad didn't, wouldn't, or couldn't love us deeply and appropriately at each stage of our journey.

But how could he? He was, and might still be, a wounded man himself. Only when we can see our father's own brokenness as a man who, like us, is also in need of healing and fathering, can we extend empathy, compassion for his failures, and possibly even love for his story, and for who and what he is rather than judgment for who and what he is not.

This is not to minimize the damage. "My dad did the best he could"—I hear men say it all the time. It may be true, but you can't say it until you have earned the right. How? By exploring just what the heck that saying really means.

> What is your dad's story? What happened to him? How did his own father father him?

> What are the landmark moments, whether good or bad, in your life with him? What did he say? What *didn't* he say? What were the messages he delivered to your heart through either absence and passivity or frustration and aggression?

> What did your dad tell you about being a man, teach you about masculinity, show you about how to fight and how to love? Were these things modeled, taught, and caught? (The answer to this second question is always yes. The next question is, Was what you learned good?)

> Did the way he romanced your mom, cared for her, spoke to her, show you how to love a woman? Did he rise up to *protect* you from your mom (or siblings), in a manner appropriate to the occasion, when you might have needed protecting?

> Did your father ask you questions about your heart, or was it more about your grades, recitals, practices, and games?

> Most important of all, *what did he show and tell you about walking with God?*

A boy needs more than someone to help him with math and drop him off or pick him up from practice. He needs more than food, clothing, and shelter. He needs a father's presence and a father's words to help him become a man. That is why, sooner or later in your boyhood, the enemy will attempt to secure the lie that you are on your own. The one he is assaulting is you, and the one he is using and accusing is your dad.

At what stage—especially boyhood or explorer—did the lie "I am on my own" get delivered to you? Sooner or later it happens to every man. When and how did it happen to you?

What was your father's central message to your heart, and how did it impact what you believed about yourself, your dad, and ultimately God?

And . . . what is God's part in all of this today? How might your heavenly Father want to show up for you now to tell you a better story, a true story, and help you exchange the old message for a new, life-giving one?

Look for God in Your Circumstances

Your marriage, your career, your relationships . . . you live life in real time in a physical world. You have concerns, dreams, realities you face every day. Guess what? God knows all about all of it, down to the last detail.

Earlier in the book, we looked at how the spiritual and physical realms overlap and mix together. That's how God designed his creation to operate. He's not somewhere way out there. He's right here, right now, as close as your breath and every thought you think, deeply involved in your life.

So get this: God wants to speak to you in the midst of your circumstances. They're not small to him, not even the things you think are small. Every aspect of your life has the potential for his voice to break through with a healing message for your heart.

* * *

Through a series of remarkable "coincidences," my friend Jack had obtained a position at a leading Christian publishing house. It was a door of unprecedented opportunity, and he knew it was God who had opened it for him. Jack was excited, grateful . . . and terrified. In his midthirties, he had no prior corporate or professional experience. What he did have was a long history of menial employment perpetuated by crippling self-doubt. Now, suddenly, he found himself shouldered with responsibilities he had never envisioned for himself at a company whose mission dovetailed with his longing to make a difference in God's kingdom.

"It was my make-it-or-break-it moment in life, and I felt massively underqualified," Jack told me.

"In those days, I use to walk the railroad tracks regularly out in the countryside and pray. One morning before work at my new job, out there on the tracks, I told God, 'I'm so scared of blowing it. I have so much to learn. I need you to help me, Father. This position is way, *way* too big for me.'

"At that moment, I heard his voice strongly in my heart. 'You're right, son,' he told me. 'This position is too big for you.' I could almost see him smiling. 'It's exactly the right size.'"

Tears were in Jack's eyes as he remembered. "I felt like my Father was putting his arm around my shoulders. 'You can't do this without me, and that's how I like it. Because you *can* do it with me. I'm going to teach you, son. I'm giving you a profession that fits you. I'm going to father you in this area of your life.'"

That experience is imprinted deeply in my friend's memory. To the questions of Jack's battered explorer's heart—"Do I have strength? Can I come through? Do I have what it takes?"—God responded:

Yes, son. Yes. And yes. Trust me. You will see.

It was the beginning of a season of great growth for my friend. Thirty years later, he will tell you that he found far more than a profession during that great adventure. He discovered a deeper, experiential knowledge—*gnosko*—of his Father's heart toward him, and significant healing for his own heart.

* * *

What about you? What circumstance in your life might be one where God wants to meet with you, give you life-changing words, and exchange lies that have shaped your life for a new, courageous way forward?

In the months and years ahead, different stages of your journey will surface at different times for you and God to deal with. For Jack, a broken part of his explorer's heart needed initiation, validation, and healing. What stage, and what circumstance, might God be singling out for you right now and saying, "Let's go here"? This would be a good time—now, this very moment—to pause and ask him. And listen, and watch, for an answer.

Let Healing Come to You

The world tells us, "Make it happen." But while you can cultivate a mindset and practices that make you receptive to healing, you can't force it. Just let it come—and seize the moment when it does.

Healing takes time in the spiritual realm, just as in the physical realm. The lepers, blind, and lame of Jesus's day had stories full of pain and wounding right up until the moment Jesus touched them, and he didn't touch all of them at the same time. Those encounters were highly individual in timing and circumstance.

I've seen this in my own life. A wound in my explorer stage resulted in an agreement and a vow that profoundly affected me later in my warrior stage and continued to get triggered well into my king stage. That is when God finally brought healing.

* * *

I was at a carwash cleaning up the family Suburban. I reached for the "soaking brush" to give the exterior a good bath. But after a few seconds of leaning into the brush and going after the dirt, I could see the side of my vehicle wasn't getting cleaner—it was getting dirtier. *What the!*

The previous customer must have used the brush on some kind of oil and tar, and now that crud was slathered all across my driver-side door. Anger rose within me and quickly turned into rage. And though the gas station attendant wasn't responsible, he was the one I was going to make pay.

The result was awful—a full-scale false-self invasion that almost came to blows. Finally I returned to my vehicle and drove away, seething and making plans to sue. This injustice was headed to the supreme court!

But anger is almost always an invitation to go with God after healing, and in a few minutes he showed up right there with me in the car. My anger turned to sadness, deep sadness. It wasn't guilt; it was pain. I began to weep—hard. Huge sobs. Crying that hard while driving might be more dangerous than texting. Again, *what the?*

"God, what is this about?"

That's when the memory came.

I was hunched over my desk in seventh grade science class, doing a homework assignment along with twenty other classmates. Brains hummed, but the room was quiet. Strict silence was the teacher's mandate.

"Pssst! Michael." It was my buddy Jeff behind me. *"I need your help."*

"Shhh! We're not supposed to talk."

"Mr. Thompson and Mr. King!" the teacher barked. Great—just like that, busted. "Did I not say very clearly that there was to be no talking?"

"But—"

"Both of you come up here *now*."

Whoa, he sounded mad! To the front of the room we marched, and it was clear that no explanation would suffice. This teacher cared about one thing, and that was to make an example of us to the rest of the class. My protestations of innocence fell on deaf ears.

Corporal punishment was still acceptable back then. Steve and I went in turn, the guilty and the guiltless alike. Standing with hands on knees, we each got one sharp smack on the butt in front of our wide-eyed classmates. It hurt, and it was humiliating, but far more painful than the spanking itself was the injustice of it.

"I had no voice," I told God. "I was powerless."

"I know, Michael. Your teacher didn't listen and didn't care, and you had no adult to speak up for you. But today I want you to know that I'm your advocate. I know you were innocent. You were treated unfairly and punished unjustly. Your teacher was wrong. What he did was wrong, and it hurt. I understand so well. My son Jesus got treated the same way."

In that tender moment, God allowed my heart to grieve. No longer was I dwelling on what had happened moments ago at the carwash; now I was feeling what had been done to me many years back in grade school. I could feel my heart leaning into my Father's and hear his comforting words: "I got you."

I renounced and unsubscribed from the lie I had believed that "I am powerless," and from the vow I made as a result: "I will never let myself be treated unfairly again." I had harbored that vow proudly for many, many years. Classmates, roommates, and teammates, referees and umpires, servers and cashiers . . . too many of them saw it. My wife and girls, especially when they were young, felt it. That false-self part of me wounded a lot of people. Off it came, like a weight. And my hair-trigger reaction to any potential injustice or unfairness hit a turning point toward a slower, more patient way. A good way. A God way.

* * *

You can't manufacture moments like the one I've just described. They come when and where they come (I mean, a car wash of all places!). What you *can* do, though, is be alert to what God might want to do when one of those moments arrives. You've got two options: Proceed as always, false-self business as usual, not seeing beyond the surface, and miss the opportunity. Or develop a sensitivity and consider your emotions in the light of what God is reaching for inside you. Live aware of his restorative involvement in your life. Be ready to ask him, "Why do I feel this way? What are you up to with me right now?" And then listen for his answer.

Make Time to Ask God Questions

Have you ever noticed how kids love to ask questions? They have to. It's in their nature.

"Dad, what's that?"

"Dad, where are we going?"

"Dad, how long till we get there?"

Asking questions implies, "I don't know. I need help." It can also mean, "I'd like to know what you think," which implies, "I trust you enough to want your feelings or opinion on the matter."

Jesus said, "Unless you repent . . . and become like children [trusting, humble, and forgiving], you will never enter the kingdom of heaven" (Matthew 18:3 AMP). Asking questions is an arrangement for trust, connection, and intimacy, and it's the best way for us to stay childlike.

God promised through the prophet Jeremiah, "You will seek me and find me when you seek me with all your heart. I will be found by you" (Jeremiah 29:13–14). Or, as Jesus put it, ask, seek, and knock (Luke 11:9–10).

* * *

Greg's teachers about girls were the world and other boys. Like the rest of us, he was taught to be a consumer, not a protector—not surprising, since Greg himself had never been protected. His dad died when Greg was twenty-two, leaving him and his brother with a mother whose care from his earliest years felt like Dr. Jekyll and Mrs. Hyde.

"I never knew what I was going to get—fits of rage or open arms," Greg told me. "When my dad was alive, I never understood why he didn't intervene. A lot of the time, he was right there. I think that, like me, he was afraid of her."

The father wound of passivity and the mother wound of dominance during Greg's early stages damaged the lover components in his heart. The result, as his body matured and the lover stage arrived in full force, was a sexual addiction that would haunt Greg for years. "Who I was and what I did in the dark, I really don't want to talk about it. I asked God for years to take it away. But it was much bigger and deeper than I knew, and it was going to need a massive dose of love in order to heal."

That day finally arrived for Greg. Taking a pen and a notebook, he got away with God. "I had heard about asking God questions, so I tried it: 'God what do you think of me? Who am I to you?'

"The next thought I had, I couldn't believe: 'You are my beloved son in whom I'm well pleased.'

"There's no way!" my heart reacted. So I asked again, and God said it again: 'You are my beloved son in whom I'm well pleased.' Tears.

"And again. 'You are my beloved son in whom I'm well pleased.' More tears.

"My pen moved as if on autopilot. Again and again I wrote it down. Like desert soil drinking in the rain, the hard and crusty cracks in my heart began to be filled with God's love.

"It was amazing! In that moment, God showed me how, out of a wounded heart, I had turned to women for worth and validation, willing to settle for a cheap imitation of what I really longed for. God showed me how I was determined to make women love me, and how I controlled and used women to fill my aching void. Wildest of all, God wasn't mad. To my amazement, it was more like he understood. And what had plagued me for three decades, kept me away from God, and almost cost me my marriage and family, was healed.

"It wasn't about stopping doing something; it was about receiving something I had no idea was available . . . until I knew it was.

"I was romanced by God and given back a lover's heart."

* * *

Greg's story involves the healing of his lover stage. God takes this stage very, very seriously because it is the part of our heart that is most connected to his. Since this stage is so far-reaching, with its components spanning virtually our entire life, let's soak in it for a minute. God is, after all, the lover of our heart.

As a reminder, though, the practice of asking God questions, like all the principles in this chapter, applies to every stage, not just one stage in particular, and it can touch several stages at the same time.

Getting still and quiet is often key. Romance doesn't happen in a drive-through; it happens by candlelight. So make a reservation. Set aside time to step into a place of beauty and stillness—the woods, a lakeshore, a hiking trail, a porch, or just a quiet place in your home. Like Greg, you may want to take a pen and notebook with you.

Take a few deep breaths and say out loud, "Here I am, God." Ask the Father to show you and tell you who you are and what you mean to him. Invite him to love you. And then . . . pay attention.

Walk with God back into your story. Listen for how you were trained to see particular aspects of it. For example, how were you trained to see love? What agreements and vows did you make about love?

Search your heart for answers to, and illustrations of, what you have come to believe about your value and significance. Are you worth loving? Were you worth Christ's dying for? If the answer is anything other than *yes* and *yes,* then something isn't right. What is blocking your ability to receive God's love? Whatever it is, guaranteed, it is also blocking your ability to send love out.

All of these are good questions. Others will occur to you—questions that come to you from your heart and life experiences. What counts is this: Ask God.

Ask him.

Then listen and watch for his response.

This isn't supposed to be novel but, rather, normal.

At any given time, God may want to walk with you into circumstances or things that happened to you during different stages of your masculine journey. If, as for Greg, it's the lover stage, keep this in mind: For the lover to be healed and restored, you must give your heart back to beauty and romance. Back to the expressions of God's beauty and goodness in a mountain range, a poem, music, the scent of pines, the dance of shadow and light on a footpath, the captivation of a campfire. Psalm 104:24 says, "What a wildly wonderful world, God! You made it all, with Wisdom at your side, made earth overflow with your wonderful creations" (MSG). Your Father is in these things, calling to your heart, telling you that he is good, and loving, and trustworthy. Listen for what he wants to tell you about himself—and about you.

Romance *is* the progression of knowing and being known. And friend, God wants you to know him—for he knows you, with deep affection.

Seek the Guidance of Oriented Men

One of the ways God restores the damaged and missing pieces of our heart is through the counsel of oriented men. (Note that word *oriented*. We'll come back to it later in this section.) Wise guidance is one of the ways we hear from God. To this point, we've looked at the power of encountering God one-on-one. But the loving insights God offers through good kings and seasoned elder-sages are a close second. Experienced brothers can ask questions, help us dig deep into our story to uncover the wounds, identify the lies and vows, and even tear off the roof tiles[1] to lower us to Jesus in order to exchange the bad for something very good.

In the stories in this chapter, I've been drawing examples stage by stage to show how the approaches we're looking at apply to every stage, across the board. Since this next story illustrates healing for the warrior stage, let me emphasize a point I made earlier in the book: Healing doesn't come without a fight. And that's good. Because healing the warrior *is* learning to fight. The counsel of oriented men can show us how—for many of us were never taught.

* * *

"Carl, what is wrong with you?"

It was his father speaking—his ever-capable dad. "Why can't you _____ (fill in the blank; there was no end of blanks)? If you would just *apply* yourself! You know what you need to do? You need to toughen up. Get mad and be more aggressive."

When I met Carl, my immediate impression was that he was shy and a little insecure, lacking confidence. He had come to me for counsel, and as we began to unpack his story, he told me about his bigger-than-life dad, his highly accomplished brother, and their ongoing commentary on Carl's own failure to measure up.

Standing in the shadows of others teaches you to hide in the shadows when you're older. I asked Carl, "Hearing such stuff growing up, what did you believe about yourself?"

"That kind of constant criticism? You don't hear an invitation to do better. You learn that whatever you do, it will never be enough. I learned to just take it and how to fly under the radar.

"I couldn't wait to get out of the house. So I decided to join the army."

You're kidding me, I thought. *Why in the world would you do that?* Before I could ask, Carl continued. "I thought, *I'll show them.*"

There it was—the lie: *Something is wrong with you.* The agreement: *I can't do anything right.*

And the vow: *I'll prove that I'm capable.*

I asked, "Did it work?"

He smiled at me as tears welled and, wordlessly, shook his head a couple times as if to say, "Naaa, it didn't work."

Carl told me stories of how he actually excelled in the army . . . right up until he ran into his dad and brother there. Not literally, but through a superior who embodied their qualities. Advancing to a new company and taking on new challenges and responsibilities, Carl acquired a new commanding officer. The man was sarcastic, moody, and sought to motivate with negativity, just like Carl's dad and brother. The boyhood wounding caught up and found Carl. Depression came calling, as did anxiety. The army wasn't a good fit anymore.

The more Carl shared with me, the more the theme of shame unveiled itself: *Something's wrong with me.* The voices from his world growing up had become the voices in his adult head and heart, and resignation was his constant companion. Like all of us, Carl wanted to matter. He wanted to be strong. But also, like so many men, he hadn't been trained to be. Just the opposite.

I was hopeful. Over the next several weeks, God began to move and work. I asked Carl to bring me the play-by-play from his previous days: what he heard and felt going on inside his heart and head. One by one we ran his thoughts through to their end and took them captive (2 Corinthians 10:5).

We began to address accusations that brought fear, such as "You don't know what you're doing."

"Is that true?" I asked Carl.

"Well, yes, kind of . . . I've never had a project this big at work." (At the time, Carl had just taken on a large assignment.)

We prayed and invited Jesus to give Carl his take on these circumstances. Carl heard Jesus ask, "I wonder why they chose you for such a big project. Why do you think they chose you?"

Carl tried resignation. "I don't know."

Jesus pressed in. "Yes you do."

Carl, his eyes closed, started to smile. My eyes weren't closed, and I asked him,

"What's the smile about?"

Tears welled up, as during our first meeting, but this time Jesus was with him. "Jesus is putting his arm around me and smiling. I didn't know I was smiling too." Still with a smile, "I guess I couldn't help it."

We went on to renounce the lies Carl had agreed with, and he invited Jesus to continue to speak. "Jesus, how do you see me?"

Carl told me later that he about fell out of his chair when he heard the reply: "Strong and capable."

Strong and capable. Wow. Jesus's view of a man who thought he was anything but. "Do you know how long I've waited to hear those words?" Carl said.

Tears and smiles often accompany healing times with Jesus. Over time, Jesus healed Carl's warrior heart. One day he came in for our time together and said some of my favorite words: "You're not going to believe what happened."

"Try me," I replied with a grin.

"My wife and I were talking about my son and what he 'needed' to do. She wanted to give him a pep talk. Usually I would have let her step in and give her lecture. Not this time. Something rose up in me to step in myself. I told her, 'I don't think that's going to be helpful. Let me talk to him.'

"She looked at me with surprise on her face and a little put out. Then she said, 'I don't know if I'm mad with you for disagreeing or excited you want to do the talking.'"

There was another smile on Carl's face. I had learned to look for them.

"Can you believe I did that!" he said.

He told me how he asked his son some questions and began to see and hear the old, familiar voices sneaking into his son's heart and mind. Carl's own heart responded in strength: "Not on my watch! I won't let it happen to him."

Several silent, holy seconds passed, during which Carl's words hung there. Then I said what came naturally. "I'm proud of you, Carl. Well done! Looks like things are changing."

He smiled because he knew it was true. Like Gideon stepping out of hiding to become a warrior for Israel (Judges 6:11–14), Carl was stepping into the fight for his own heart and for the heart his son.

* * *

When we were young, not knowing how to fight or not having someone to fight for us in the spiritual realm takes a toll. That is why learning how to fight is so healing, and it's why later in your journey you will be invited to go back into your story and fight a battle your timeline says is *waaay* back there. In eternity, it was just a moment ago. Eternity knows no time, and you are an eternal being.

This is where the counsel of God through oriented men can be invaluable—to help you uncover the different wounds, the lies and vows, and show you how bring them to the Father to dismantle them with the truth that heals and restores. Men to stand with you and show you how to fight today what you didn't or couldn't fight back then.

The trick is to find a man or men whose wisdom you can trust. In the church, you can find plenty of people who are free with their advice, often accompanied by a Scripture or two. But to find an *oriented* man—a man who

- knows who he is, where he is, and the good God is up to;*
- knows how to listen to your story and ask you questions that help you really hear it yourself;
- will help you bring your story to the Lord for his insights, healing, grace, and direction; and
- has been around the block enough not to offer glib, prefab advice

—for that, you'll need to be selective. Few men are truly wise, and just because a person quotes the Bible doesn't mean his counsel is biblical.

My encouragement: Chase after God first. Let him catch you again and again. And let God bring you a teacher. Ask him to . . . and then seek, and watch for, the right person. Meet God's provision on the road while actively walking toward it.

And be ready for when he decides it's time to bring *you* a student. For that's what becoming an oriented man and a good king is all about: learning how to walk intimately with God and live loved, so you can walk in redemptive relationships with others.

Moving On

We've looked at several different ways you can enter into healing encounters with God, ways you can partner with him for the restoration of your heart at every stage of the masculine journey. We'll get to a few more in the pages ahead.

---

* See the footnote on page 19.

They're not formulas, and they're certainly not magic. God isn't manipulable. He is, however, responsive, present, communicative, and beyond eager to help you dismantle your false self, with its agreements and vows, so you can live in a way that's true to who you really are:

A beloved son, settled in who he is because his Father has told him.

A brave and adventurous explorer, discovering the wildness of God.

A strong and courageous warrior, trained in love to be dangerous for good.

A kind and patient lover who has learned both to pursue and to protect beauty.

A noble-hearted king, good for all those entrusted to his care.

And ultimately, an elder-sage, wielding wisdom for the hearts of others.

In this chapter, we've used examples from the four earlier stages to show how the approaches we've discussed have played out uniquely in men's lives. In chapter 13, you'll read of a couple more principles that helped a king and a sage find restoration for their hearts. We'll then have covered all the stages—but not all the powerful insights the next chapter contains.

CHAPTER 13
Healing Encounters

Praise the LORD, my soul, and forget not all his benefits . . . who redeems your life from the pit and crowns you with love and compassion, who satisfies your desires with good things so that your youth is renewed like the eagle's.
—Psalm 103:2–5

If broken lives and souls are to be healed, it must begin with teaching the practice of the presence. . . . To abide in the presence of the Lord is to begin to hear Him. To follow through on that hearing is to find healing, self-acceptance, and growth into psychological and spiritual balance and maturity.
—Leanne Payne: The Healing Presence

In this chapter, we'll conclude the *how* of healing moments with God. The stories in the first two sections deal with the crux of this book, the king stage, and with the elder-sage stage. Healing is as important in these latter two stages of a man's journey as it is in the first four. We'll also explore a vital question: What does it mean to "hear God's voice?" Some men are familiar with the idea; others, not so much; still others, skeptical if not outright leery. Since the healing of our heart involves encounters with God, it would be good to get some clarity on the matter.

Shifting gears, let's look ahead just long enough to put the healing journey in its proper context—the glory of being a king in the Larger Story. That's what draws us onward: something higher and more compelling than healing alone.

There's a glory that awaits us—that of kings free and empowered to have king-dom-of-God impact on the lives around us. That's the goal and payoff of healing: the strength, authority, influence, and love the King of kings wants to invest in us and through us on behalf of others. We'll unpack that vision and how to bring it into reality starting in the next chapter.

With that in mind, let's look at the remaining practices for the healing of the heart.

Let God Lead

"If something doesn't feel right, it likely isn't right." Heard that before? Observing and taking responsibility for the emotions and thoughts that stir in our heart is critical to healing. Often, this is where God's invitations to healing begin, and learning to let God lead will enable a man to walk with him intimately.

Where God will lead is often not where we think we're going. This is the beautiful thing about walking with him: He knows the ways to the roads less traveled—through the beautiful gates to the narrow roads that lead to Life.

* * *

I was thirty-eight when God awakened me from the religious coma I was in. By then, my false self had done a lot of damage—my wife and children can attest to that. Ironically, I was a Christian counselor, working to "help" others through my full-time ministry. Nothing like a hypocrite to not only wound people but justify his actions with a Bible verse.

By my early fifties and in the king stage of my life, I had done considerable work with God on renovating my heart. Yet there came a particular season when I felt "off," restless, out of sorts. More times than not, I've learned, that feeling is from God, not the enemy. So when the nagging sense that "something is wrong" persisted, I called a counseling friend.

"Bill, I need some time. God is after something in me, and I think I know what it is, but I would very much like your help." We made an appointment.

A few days later, I sat in the familiar chair at his practice, and we consecrated our time, locked out the enemy, and invited God to come. "So, what's God stirring up?" Bill asked.

"I think it's about some mother wounds." I had been home with family for the holidays a few months earlier and felt some old, familiar frustrations, pressures, and accusations.

"OK, let's go," Bill said. "Close your eyes, settle in, and let's invite Jesus to come and help you sort it out."

We did, and the King of kings came. "He's taking me back to a memory with my younger brother. We're playing Monopoly. He's winning, and I'm not good with that. I lose and tell him, 'You won, so you need to pick up the board.'

"'That's not how you did it last time, when *you* won,' my brother said. 'You made me pick up the board then too.'

"'Well, at least I didn't cheat.'" Hurtful words, and painful to recall. My younger brother started to cry and called for Mom.

Here we go. This is what I came in for, I thought.

Frustrated with me, my mom made me pick up the game and then sent me to my room to think about my conduct.

"Where are you and Jesus now?" Bill asked.

"In my room. Jesus is showing me the agreement I signed: *Losing makes me a loser. I have to win; losing isn't an option*. And the vow from my feelings of humiliation: *I'll do whatever it takes to win. And if I lose, I'll win by making them pay*."

OK, this was *not* what I came in for. This was not about my mom at all.

"What's Jesus doing now?"

"He's got his arms around my shoulder, and we're looking at something. Kind of a small hill, a bump really, but it's got an iron cover on the top of it."

"OK, anything more?"

"Jesus is giving me a tool. He wants me to take the bolts off the cover."

I did, and what happened next was like something out of one of C. S. Lewis's Narnia stories. The iron top exploded off the little hill from the pressure behind it, and then, like lava oozing from a volcano, slime oozed from the opening. Borne along in the goo were game pieces, boards, cards, cleats, balls, bats, uniforms . . . anything and everything that had to do with competition, and there was a lot of it.

I knew what Jesus was after: the agreement that *I have to win; losing isn't an option*. It was a huge piece of me that hadn't been, nor would ever be, good for my kingdom. Winning may get you some trophies or awards, maybe a big house and lots of stuff, but it won't grow people or your kingdom. When you see everyone as a competitor, every conversation as a challenge, and every day as an opportunity to win and not lose, you will lose more often than you know.

I turned to Jesus, deeply saddened by what I saw. "I'm so sorry, so sorry I did that. I don't want to live with that still in me."

He said, "It isn't anymore."

Then he gave me a white cloth. Somehow I knew it was for tending to the opening where the iron lid had once resided. I could see that now for what it was. It wasn't a hill; it was part of my heart. As I started to gently wipe around the opening, Jesus put his hand over mine, and the hole began to dwindle. The black rim where the iron cap had been fastened turned a beautiful pinkish red and closed in until the hole was gone. Jesus and I were standing together by a part of my heart that now was healed.

Healing is how God grants us the freedom to move in a new way. I noticed right away that the pressure to win a discussion, have my opinion validated, or defend my turf was lifted—and it has remained that way. My family and friends took a little longer to see the change as I quietly went about wearing my new way. Healing the heart doesn't require an announcement: "See? I'm new and improved!" It does, however, invite us to a brand-new walk, a different way to offer, share, and especially, love. Healing will always bring about a change in our ability both to receive and to offer love.

* * *

The enemy isn't the only one who provokes or disrupts. God has his ways of wooing, inviting, and disrupting our lives so we might bring him our wounded places for healing. Whether through an unfortunate moment when our false self is on display, or whether the Spirit prompts us *before* we step into a pile of something, God will provoke us to engage in our own healing.

The Father has asked me many times, "You want me to help you with that?" What about you? What might God be provoking in *you*? What kind of pain might he be allowing to surface so you'll bring the hurt to him? When you do, you may find him leading you toward something you've already suspected—or, as with me, in an utterly unexpected direction.

The point is, when you sense God wanting to lead you in a particular direction, whether it's one you expected or one that surprises you, let him. Follow where he wants to take you.

If you're in the King stage, as I was then and am today, know that the healing of a king's heart is going to take a few years. The false self that the enemy took decades to construct and reinforce won't deconstruct overnight. Be patient, persistent, and hopeful. With your engagement, God's help, and God's love, he will chip away every-thing that does not resemble "the Lion of the tribe of Judah." Everything that isn't you.

Share Your Story

If intimacy is knowing and being known in a way that enhances acceptance and trust, then sharing our stories of pain and loss will always be a path for healing. That's pro-vided the person listening knows how to listen and values our story for what it is. Not everyone recognizes it's an entrustment, not a project for Mr. Fix-It.

In a safe, loving environment, sharing your story is one of the most power-ful things you can do. Cracking the lid on a sealed or unvisited compartment of your life so others can see into it lets light and fresh air into a dark, musty interior. It's an invitation for God to show up—and he does, because you give him something to work with.

But it gets even better. Being real about your struggles, sins, and pain frees up others to be real about theirs. Openness encourages openness. Honesty begets hon-esty. And revealing what the enemy and your false self have kept hidden breaks the grip of shame, not only from yourself but from others as well when they realize they're not alone. Your story is both Big Medicine and a potent weapon in the war for hearts.

* * *

My dad's dad came home from WWII and did what all those veterans tried to do after the war: reenter their home fronts. I can't imagine how hard it must have been after seeing what they saw and doing what they did. It would be sixty years before a few of those men talked, and the country heard the stories of what they lived though.

In the meantime, countless sons of those men—boys like my father—were left to wonder, *Do you see me? Do you love what you see?* When silence is the answer, the next generation is wounded. So it was with my own dad, though I never suspected—until . . .

Dad was in town for a visit, and we were having lunch after playing a round of golf, something we enjoyed doing over the years. "Did you ever play golf with Grandpa?" I asked. That's all it took, that simple question. In the unforgettable, sad but healing conversation that followed, Dad told me:

Growing up with him [his father], I just felt like something was wrong with me. He never came to a game. We never played catch. He was just shut down—unless you "disobeyed an order." Then there was hell to pay.

I would come home from school or baseball practice and ask where he was. My mom would tell me, "Oh, he went hunting," or fishing, or golfing. Not once did he invite me. What are you supposed to do with that?

I vowed, "I'll never be like that." And so I set out to prove that I was going to be a better man, a better husband, a better father.

It didn't work. Because the one vote of approval I desperately wanted was his, and he never gave it.

Never, "I love you."

Never, "I'm proud of you."

Never, "Come with me."

What are you supposed to do with that?

What indeed?

As a young family, we would travel several hundred miles back to my parents' hometown for holidays. When we finally arrived after the two-day cross-country excursion, we three boys would jump out of the station wagon and run into our grandparents' house. Grandpa was always positioned in his recliner, waiting for us, and that was where we pounced. With his big Popeye forearms, Grandpa would curl us up and down, or pin us to his lap or to the side of the chair, and we would laugh, and so would he.

Trailing behind until he stood in the doorway, my dad would watch. I don't remember my grandfather ever getting up or even greeting us at the door. Never did I see him move toward my dad or hug him. My dad told me, "I would just watch on as a familiar question played in my head: *Why wouldn't you engage with* me *like that?*"

Through all the years, my two younger brothers and I never knew our dad was suffering from a wounded heart and an agreement that something was wrong with him. Not wrong with Grandpa, which was the truth, but with him. As I sat with my dad and his tears, hearing him recount from the earlier stages of his masculine journey, I loved him more and felt more love from him than I had ever known. Was God in the midst of it? How could he not be? Wherever love is, God is.

That day my dad got a part of his heart back, and I was there to see it happen as I partnered with God in listening. What an honor to hear Dad share! And in the sharing, there was healing for each of us, a holy "two-fer." It brought my dad a new sense of being heard and understood at the heart level, and validated, and cherished. And it salved my own father wounds with new understanding of the man who was my dad, and gave me compassion for the wounded boy inside him.

That's the power of a hard story told well. Shackles fall off a man's heart, and what was old, painful, and ugly gets traded for something new, free, and beautiful. Today, my dad and I enjoy a deeper connection. A stronger bond between father and son, yes, but also an important friendship as man to man. All because we were willing to go together into matters of the heart.

* * *

The stories that most need to be told are often the ones that go untold. And so the wounds fester for years, even decades. It takes courage to open up. Doing so involves two concerns: *who* and *what*.

Whom can you open up to? Who is trustworthy? My dad trusted me; whom do *you* trust? It could be one person—maybe a close friend, a good counselor, or a skilled kingdom therapist. It could be a small group, such as a band of like-hearted warriors, kings, and elder-sages—oriented brothers who know how to listen with open hearts.*

Then there's *what*. What is your untold story? Chances are you know the answer: It's the one that's too painful or shameful or scary to share. The one that, if people knew it, you're certain they'd never understand. The one that haunts you. That story.

Or maybe not. Maybe your story involves something you've minimized and lived with most of your life. It's just one of those things, the kind you stick in the "Shiz Happens" bin and pretend to forget about. It might not be so inconsequential. What if bringing it into the open could help heal a wound you never knew you were bearing and turn your life in a new direction?

Pray about your *who* and *what*. Think on it with God. That's part of the *how* of this section.

The rest is . . . be willing. Some stories are easy to tell; others are costly. Some emerge naturally in the moment; others take forethought. But every story begins with the choice to tell it. Remember, your story has the potential to free others as well as yourself. Dad's opening up the files of his heart to me brought healing to my own heart. It offered me the opportunity to forgive him for some of the father wounds he had unknowingly inflicted on me, and to see him like never before:

---

* For further insights, see the section "Seek the Guidance of Oriented Men" in chapter 12.

as another man whose broken story mattered and whose healing comeback was glorious.

Not until he was an elder-sage did Dad share that part of his life with me. The elder-sage often lives with pain, both from the long past and from injuries unique to a man's elder years. No matter how old you are, it takes courage to heal. So bear in mind: If you are an elder-sage, although your kingdom may be getting smaller, your opportunity to offer your presence, your words, and your life-tested wisdom will grow larger if you pursue healing.

Hearing God's Voice

God is *the* master of languages and communication. In Genesis he speaks creation into existence. The apostle John writes, "In the beginning was the Word." In the second chapter of Acts, on the day of Pentecost, God spoke through the disciples with clarity and grace in many languages, and the multinational crowd listening to those disciples understood their message.

Is it any surprise, then, that God can speak in more ways than we can imagine? An inner impression . . . the quiet flame of a sunrise . . . a dream imbued with significance . . . the wide-eyed gaze of an infant . . . a display at a museum . . . a Scripture verse that leaps into the heart . . . the kind words or wise counsel of a wife, a friend, or a stranger spoken at just the right time . . . the silvery rush of a waterfall . . . even a bumper sticker (as we shall see) . . . the ways God speaks are limitless.

So it's important that we understand how God speaks. After all, it's a huge part of having an intimate relationship with him. And every healing encounter with God is an intimate encounter. What, then, should we look for? How can we know it's really God, not just our imagination?

No way can I cover in one section a topic on which entire books have been written. Sam Williamson's richly insightful *Hearing God in Conversation*, Ken Gire's eloquent *Windows of the Soul*, and the masterful classic *Hearing God* by Dallas Williard are all wonderful, and there are many others. I recommend that you read at least one. My goal here is to give you a solid overview of what hearing God means and what it doesn't mean, and to offer you some reassurances for any reservations you may have.

* * *

Between the cessationist insistence that God speaks only through the Bible today, and the questionable stuff some believers attribute to "God told me," there lies a balance. It's not always easy to pin down, but that doesn't mean we shouldn't try. For one thing, the Bible never points to itself as the end-all of God's communication with us. Quite the opposite: It depicts God speaking through various means that will only cease when we see him face to face and know him as fully as he knows us (1 Corinthians 13:12). We're not there yet.

Meanwhile, Jesus said his sheep know his voice, and that means there's a voice to be heard. As a beloved son, you are equipped with spiritual ears to hear it. Here are a few thoughts to guide you, beginning with the one that's obvious and foundational.

God speaks through the Scriptures. Kind of a no-brainer. The Bible is God's essential, authoritative means of connecting with us through the written word, and it's the plumb line for discerning his other modes of communication. Spending time in the Scriptures sensitizes us to God's voice in all its forms, from the biblical text to the "still, small voice" of inner impressions and more—because the goal of reading the Scriptures, ultimately, is so we can know God better. Then when he wants our attention, we're more apt to recognize him. We're also better able to filter out what's *not* him, because he'll never say anything that contradicts his written word.

The Bible is largely a collection of stories, just like your story, just like my story. Stories of real people—not exceptional people but ordinary folk and their relationship with God. A multitude of *examples*, not exceptions, of what it looks like to walk with God. It is in reading these stories that we are invited to see our own story, and to respond as the Holy Spirit woos us to the life of more.

One thing the Bible is *not* is a huge library of isolated verses, from which we cherry-pick certain ones. The verses need to be put in context. Try reading the Scriptures out loud and even listening to the Lord about what you read. Ask questions. Imagine what it would have felt like back then. What might you have thought had you been the main character in a story? Or one of the many engaged bystanders watching on? You may find that your times with the holy text often evolve from simply "learning your Bible," which is a good thing, to having conversations with God, which is even better.

God speaks through an inner voice. One of God's main ways of communicating is through inner impressions. When someone says, "The Lord told me . . ." or "The Lord showed me . . . ," that's usually what they mean.

But how do you know it's not just that person's imagination? Chances are you don't. Here's another question, though: What if our imagination is supposed to be involved? Imagination is the ability to see and perceive something from within. Hearing God will at some point recapture the good for which your imagination was intended. Time will often tell. We're all learning how and how not to hear from God.

What matters is your own relationship with the Holy Spirit. We're all invited to ask, seek, and knock; that's our part. His part is to answer, be found, and open doors.

Sometimes an impression is so strong that it's a conviction. You simply *know* it's God. But not every impression is a God impression. So what's the answer? Go slow. Develop those discernment muscles you have. God's inner voice often works with your imagination, which God gave you for a reason: because it can usher you into life-changing encounters with him. So don't be afraid to let him inhabit it. Commit it to him in prayer: "God, I give you my imagination. I consecrate it for our communication and conversation; it belongs to you just as I belong to you."

Your imagination lies in the tension zone between two realities, between the flesh and the spirit. Be assured that the false self and the enemy aren't the only ones wanting to use your imagination. God does too. And you are equipped with spiritual ears to hear your Father's voice. Like Solomon, we are after a *wise and discerning* heart. Credit your ability to hear a loving Father who wants very much to speak to your heart.

God speaks through the world around you. Here's where it gets really good!

God is the Voice who spoke all creation into existence, and his speech now permeates that creation. He can use any means he chooses—anything at all: circumstances, timing, places, coincidences, dreams, nature, objects, people, trials, and unexpected blessings—to get through to you. No one knows the language of your heart like God does. Your Father knows how something that has no significance to anyone else can have a profound and powerful meaning to you.

No need to elaborate. Instead, let me illustrate with a couple brief stories from my friend Jack, whom you heard from in the last chapter.

* * *

"For many years, I used to take long walks on the railroad tracks out in the country-side in the evening," Jack told me. "They were my 'prayer closet'—a place where I could go and be alone with God. Nothing but fields, farmland, and forest all around, with only an occasional train to interrupt—and I love trains."

He continued:

A time came when I was feeling discouraged. All those years out there walking the tracks, praying and reading the Bible . . . what was I accomplishing? Was I just fooling myself to think I was making any kind of a difference? To look at my life, I sure couldn't tell.

So I took the matter to God. I asked him about it. And then one night shortly after, I had a dream. I was walking along the tracks in the evening, out there in the middle of nowhere, when I ran into a guy walking toward me. Like the sower in Jesus's parable, he was scattering handfuls of seed on either side of the tracks, and behind him, spreading off to the left and right far into the distance, the fields were full of wheat from the seeds he had cast. It was amazing!

"What's your secret?" I wanted to know.

His reply was kind of gruff. "You just have to do it," he said. "Just do it." And that was that. End of dream.

A short while later, I think even the same week, I was slowing down for a red light at a busy intersection. As I pulled past the guy to my left in the left-turn lane, a bumper sticker on the truck ahead of him came into my view. On it was a picture of a railroad crossing blinker and the words "Keep On Trackin'."

That just blew me away! I mean, what were the odds? I never saw a bumper sticker like that before, and I've never seen one since.

God really was listening to me. He really did see. I can't tell you that my circumstances changed in a big way, at least not right away. But just knowing God was with me like that—that his eye was on me and he cared about me like that . . . wow! That made all the difference.

A dream, a bumper sticker, and the uncanny "coincidence" of their timing—those were God's voice for Jack at the time. But he had yet another story for me. This time he was shopping for a couch at a used furniture store. As he walked through the doors, he saw a local radio crew on hand. The store was hosting a drawing for a TV set to generate publicity, and a crowd had been gathering for the last hour or two.

"I went about my business," Jack said. "By and by, the announcement came: Last chance to enter the drawing. 'What the heck,' I thought. 'What have I got to lose?' So I filled out my name on a card and stuck it in the box. I had no great expectations. Lots of people were in the store for the drawing, and they'd been there a lot longer than me."

Still, he got to thinking. He had never owned a TV set. It would be kind of nice to have one. "Lord," he said, "it sure would be great to have that TV."

Immediately, in his mind, too strong and clear to ignore, came the words, "Why don't you ask me for it?"

"Okay, Lord," Jack said, surprised, as the host picked up the boxful of entries and shook it up. "Can I have that TV?"

A few seconds later, he heard his name being called. He had just won the drawing!

Now, Jack had envisioned a small, inexpensive portable television. But what got carted to him on a two-wheeler was a large, pricey set—so big he had a hard time getting it into his car.

Jack told me, "Winning the TV—that was great. But what mattered to me by far was, my Father gave it to me, and I *knew* it was him. It was his way of saying, 'I see you, son, and I love you.'"

The Road Ahead

As we draw to a close on the chapters on healing encounters, it's worth stressing one more time that each approach we've covered applies to *all* stages of the masculine journey. From boyhood to elder-sage, the stories you've read have portrayed how men received healing at every stage.

Most of your healing will involve looking back, observing your life history and journeying with God through the memories of your masculine stages in order to exchange lies, unholy vows, and binding agreements for the freeing, life-giving truths of how the Father sees you.

Maybe you could expand on what we've covered. I don't claim it's exhaustive. But it's enough to take you down the healing path into ever-increasing freedom. Everything we've covered can be summed up in three words: intimacy with God. The pursuit of healing and the pursuit of God are one and the same.

Knowledge is good, and behavioral changes may produce some positive results, but only God can heal deep wounds in a profound and lasting way. Sometimes that can happen in seconds, in a flash of revelation, but usually God takes the jigsaw-puzzle approach to restoring your heart: A piece here, a piece there, and over time the big picture comes together. One step at a time you claim holy ground; bit by bit the false self gives way to the true. God wants to do it all with you.

But liberating as it is, the healing journey is just part of a greater adventure. Healing is like clearing the deadfalls that block your progress and removing the overgrown brush that obscures your way a toward a goal of surpassing grandeur.

What if there is an amazing secret about you that God wants to reveal? What if your life is meant to show and tell other people what it looks like to be free? And what if who you are is intended to be lived on behalf of others, loving them wholeheartedly as Jesus commanded us to do (John 13:34–35)?

In Christ, that's exactly how you are equipped to live. You have a glory to your life. You've always had it. It's a beautiful, remarkable, and unique part of you, like your smile, or the color of your eyes, or the shape of your toes. Your glory is the one-of-a-kind way you bear the image of God. The world needs it, and many are waiting for it. The more healing you receive, the more your glory will emerge. It's what the enemy would rather you not know. It's what God longs to show you.

And now at last it's time. Time to look deeply into what your glory is and what it is for.

CHAPTER 14

The Glory of a King

We all, who with unveiled faces contemplate the Lord's glory, are being transformed into his image with ever-increasing glory, which comes from the Lord, who is the Spirit.
—2 Corinthians 3:17–18

We have heard a lot about original sin
but not enough about original glory.
—John Eldredge

In 2002, Pastor Rick Warren published his runaway bestseller, *The Purpose-Driven Life*. Warren begins his book this way:

"It's not about you.

"The purpose of your life is far greater than your own personal fulfillment, your peace of mind, or even your happiness. It's far greater than your family, your career, or even your wildest dreams and ambitions. If you want to know why you were placed on this planet, you must begin with God. You were born *by* his purpose and *for* his purpose."[1]

Warren's book has sold more than 50 million copies, so you probably should take my next comment with a grain of either salt or sugar. I believe his opening sentence is half right. On the one side of the coin, it isn't about you. Yet on the other, God makes it clear . . . it's all about you.

The Father sent his Son, Jesus, to die on the cross for you. And when Jesus rose from the dead, he miraculously brought you with him as a new and holy creation inhabited by his Spirit. With your heart having become his home and your spirit now aligned with his, God makes it his aim to guide, teach, and counsel you on your journey to becoming *more*. More whole, more free, more loving, more oriented. More the you he created you to be. Your purpose was and still is intimacy, intimacy with God. God desires you.

"I know the plans I have for you, says the Lord. They are plans for good and not for evil, to give you a future and a hope" (Jeremiah 29:11 TLB). God has plans, big plans, and they include you. Before you could do anything for him, God arranged for you to be with him.

Jesus said we would do even greater works than him (John 14:12). Oh my. That's hard to fathom, but those are his words. It is what entrusting looks like, and it is why, as his apprentices, we must recover our glory and learn to live as the freemen we are in Christ. Then we can partner with God to provide for and protect the hearts of others, model what it is to walk with God, and tell the stories of his goodness in our journey. This is how we get to play our part in the kingdom of God, sharing in the mission of seeing hearts become free. That is what a disciple, an agent of the kingdom, a good king, is and does. What an honor! What Jesus has, he shares with us, his co-heirs. It's very much about you!

I Have a Glory?

Your life has a glory, and it is time that you walk with God to discover just how wonderful it is . . . how wonderful *you* are.

But what does that mean, "Your life has a glory"?

To experience the glory of anything—a rose, a horse, the Grand Tetons, the Atlantic or Pacific Ocean—is to take it in and allow it to touch you, influence you, affect how you feel in its presence. Your glory is the effect of your life on the world around you, especially on the lives of others.

In the Scriptures, the Hebrew root for *glory* has to do with weight. Your life has a weightiness to it, a massiveness, an ability to move, stir, impress, influence. Your character has substance. Your words and ways and who you are have impact. But that's not all. There's a splendor to your life, a radiance that emanates from the way you are. A goodness about you that people notice—because the Spirit who lives in you is shining through you.

This is what glory means and what glory does. The prophet Isaiah said it this way: "You will be a crown of splendor in the Lord's hand, a royal diadem in the hand of your God" (Isaiah 62:3).

God's glory is surpassing and tangible. It affects our hearts because it is something we can experience. The goodness of his love, the weightiness of his care, the kindness of his voice, his relentless pursuit of the sacred romance with our heart . . . all this and more so we might encounter him, be affected by God. That is what having an encounter with our Father's glory looks, feels, and, in the psalmist's words, even tastes like.*

And because you are his image bearer, there is a glory to your own life that is meant to reflect the glory of God. When we offer the glory of our hearts, we are bearing the image of God in the most tangible way we possibly can, and others lives are affected for the better. For glory is a relational term: one gives, another receives, and both are enriched.

The glory of your life is a precious, exclusive, one-of-a-kind thing, unique in the universe, like a snowflake or a fingerprint. You are an original. Your glory is what you are to offer the world. It is part of your Trinity DNA, yours and yours alone. It is *why* you are here. Through wounding, darkness works to mute the glory of your true self by substituting a false self. But through healing, God works to restore you and your glory.

In the following chapters, we'll explore ways your glory can—and must—display itself tangibly in your kingdom, particularly in your marriage and family. But first let's explore more fully what this matter of having glory means.

* * *

You cannot go to the world to find out who you are; you must go to God and then bring who you are to the world. For there are no small parts or insignificant roles in the Larger Story. God made everyone, everything, and every day epic. That's a hard lesson to learn. One of our greatest challenges as image bearers is to resist and overcome the gravitational pull to live small.

---

* "Oh, taste and see that the Lord is good! Blessed is the man who takes refuge in him!" (Psalm 34:8 ESV). It's a metaphorical invitation to draw close to God and experience his goodness. It's also a reminder that the God who created our senses can engage us through any of them. Something to think about next time you hear a bird, watch a sunset, or eat a grape!

It was C. S. Lewis who wrote, in *The Weight of Glory*,

There are no *ordinary* people. You have never talked to a mere mortal. Nations, cultures, arts, civilizations—these are mortal, and their life is to ours as the life of a gnat. But it is immortals whom we joke with, work with, marry, snub, and exploit—immortal horrors or everlasting splendors. . . . Next to the Blessed Sacrament itself, your neighbor is the holiest object presented to your senses. If he is your Christian neighbor, he is holy in almost the same way, for in him also Christ *vere latitat*—the glorifier and the glorified, Glory Himself is truly hidden.[2]

Paul writes to the Corinthians,

We all, who with unveiled faces contemplate the Lord's glory, are being transformed into his image with ever-increasing glory, which comes from the Lord, who is the Spirit. (2 Corinthians 3:17–18)

Hm . . . "ever-increasing glory." That sounds pretty good. Yes, all glory and honor is due God—he has, and he gets, the capital-*G* Glory. But he radiates it through us. We are "born of God" (1 John 5:1), and his spiritual DNA is in us. We bear the family resemblance to our Father. We may fall, but we don't fall far from the tree, "for in him we live and move and have our being" (Acts 17:28).

The life God has afforded us is far more than just "being saved" and hanging on until Jesus parts the eastern sky. It is far more than just trying not to sin. The Father, Son, and Spirit intend to carry out their original plan for creation, sharing their glory and kingdom with the sons and daughters of God. Jesus said, "I pray also for those who will believe in me through [the disciples'] message. . . . I have given them the glory you gave me" (John 17:20, 22).

If God is giving us glory, he must want us to discover it, protect it, enjoy it, and offer it.

The Impact of One Man's Glory

I met Gary in 1990. Well, actually, I knew of him. We worked in a large global ministry at the same time. He was a director in Colorado, and I was on staff in Ohio. Shortly after I joined the team, Gary left.

Fast forward to 2002 at a Young Life camp in Colorado. I was sitting with a few friends and 250 other hurting and hopeful men to hear author John Eldredge take us deeper into the principles of his book *Wild at Heart.* Can the heart of a man be changed in a weekend? Mine was, and my life along with it. I've never been the same.

During one of his talks, Eldredge invited one of his friends to come to the stage and share a few stories from his life. As he began to speak, a déjà vu feeling came over me, and a few seconds later I worked it out: *That's Gary Barkalow.*

During the next break, I hunted Gary down to remind him that we knew each other. Since then, Gary has become one of my closest friends and greatest allies. Nobody has taught me more about the glory *of* my life, God's calling *on* my life, and his purpose *for* my life than my friend Gary. His book *It's Your Call* was, for me, one of those rare, profound game changers in my walk with God.[3] Gary is a very good king.

The glory of who Gary is—his wisdom, his experience, his perspectives, and above all, his love and presence—ripples not only through my own life but also through the lives of thousands of other men.

It was Gary who helped dispel a couple misconceptions of Christianity that preachers preach and teachers teach as if they were verses in the Bible. They're not. Contrary to popular belief, God doesn't want you to "get out of the way and let God." That makes a snappy bumper sticker, but it's bad theology. God also doesn't want to *use* you. Jesus didn't use his disciples—he *entrusted* them with the mission and ministry of loving one another.

If St. Augustine is right that "the glory of God is man fully alive," then the holy alliance between our heart and God's is a partnership. We are more than mere vessels, though we carry the Spirit of God within us. We are more than instruments, though we play a part. We are more than just servants, though we are to love one another and there is work to do. Our glory is *how* we carry, how we play our part, how we love and serve. God wants to *partner* with you, do life with you and through you—his glory and yours integrated, impacting the world; life in the Larger Story for good.

At the right time, when he and they were ready, Jesus announced to his disciples, "I no longer call you servants, because a servant does not know his master's business. Instead, I have called you friends, for everything that I learned from my Father I have made known to you" (John 15:15). Validation! What an amazing initiation! A new role from which to operate, a new position in which to live.

Your glory has been with you all along, in every stage of your masculine journey. Even when you were young, it was part of you, expressing itself in how you organized your room, how you played, and what you loved to do. To rediscover your glory—the unique way you carry the Trinity DNA—you need to explore and reclaim three things: the Larger Story, your story, and your desires. Like the three satellites needed to triangulate a GPS signal, God will use these three coordinates to show you the glory of your life, invite you to live from it, and equip you to protect it.

The Larger Story

In the 1998 film *Les Misérables*, the recently paroled convict Jean Valjean is lying on a park bench to sleep for the night when an old woman approaches the bench. "You can't sleep here," she says.

"Get away from me," Valjean replies, gruffly.

"Why can't you go to an inn? . . . Did you knock on doors, ask people?"

"I asked everywhere. Leave me alone!"

"You didn't ask there. Knock on that door."[4]

She is only in his story a few moments, but her seemingly small and disruptive contribution will change Valjean's life forever.

Our hearts recognize and resonate with epic stories because they invite us to remember we are important after all and the story of our life matters. Yet sadly, most of us still see ourselves as less-than, and therefore we live lives of "quiet desperation" (Thoreau). The belief that there is nothing special about us, nothing epic about our days, is a lie, and falling to it is one of the greatest tragedies of all.

In *It's Your Call*, Barkalow writes, "The story you believe you are living determines how you interpret and react to life."[5] There is always the pull either to shrink into the shadows or to believe your story is all there is. Either way produces a small life, and that isn't the part you were created to play. Love is after you. He is pursuing you, wanting you to be found.

We've lost our sense of amazement and wonder. But brother, God lives in that place of amazement and wonder all day, every day, and he invites you to live there with him. You have a significant part to play, and he wants you to rise to the occasion. How can you do so? Only by living mindful that your story unfolds within another Story fantastically larger than yours alone.

Your Story

Epic stories move us with such elements as love, hope, and the promise of good triumphing over evil—with the idea of "happily ever after," for we know, deep down, that we were made for happily ever after.

Your story—your masculine journey, especially its wounding moments—provides coordinates for discovering who you are and the ways that the kingdom of darkness has attacked your capital-*L* Life. Their goal is to hijack your God-given glory. But, as with the old woman interrupting Valjean's repose on the park bench, God partners with many of his image bearers to provoke, disrupt, and even woo us in order to steer us in the right direction.

"We need to be aware of defining moments throughout our lives," Barkalow writes: "the people that entered our story and their deposits or withdrawals; the moments when we were most alive and the times we felt wholly lost; the things we have dreamed about and the things most feared; the stories and the toys we loved as children. All of these various aspects and themes are part of our unfolding story and are meant to bring revelation to who we are."[6]

You are a story, and you live in a story. Journey is how you move within that Larger Story and see your own story written. A good king and sage of mine, Craig McConnell, once told me, "If you want men to be sailors, don't tell them how to build ships. Tell them stories of the sea." Unlike many people who want to fit our lives into their own agendas, Craig didn't tell me how to feel, or what to think, or what to do. What he did do was invite me to move ahead on my journey by telling me stories of what happened to him on his. Craig taught me that having "God stories" is the key to seeing your journey with God and inviting others to see theirs.

Craig is a good teacher. Not all teachers are. God brings some people into our lives to show us what *not* to do, who not to become, and how not to live. They too have their role to play.

Eventually, we too will become teachers. The question is, what kind? When you are ready, God will point your students to you. Because who you are and who you are becoming in the kingdom equips you to encourage others that wounded hearts can be healed and live free. Your story provides perspective; journey gives direction; and both reveal *desire*, the longing and hope for more.

Magnificent Desire

Discontent isn't innately bad. It can carry us away from God, but it can also bring us to him. The same is true of its twin brother, desire. It can tempt us to compromise, to sin, and to live a life of less. But desire can also woo us to goodness and glory—a life of more.

Your glory is not new, though the idea of it may be new to you, and it is connected to your desires. Paul wrote it this way: "It is God who is producing in you both the *desire* and the ability [i.e., your glory] to do what pleases him" (Philippians 2:13 ISV, emphasis mine).

What is it you most long to do?

What do you do when you aren't even trying?

What do you do that brings Life to you and to others?

Pondering these questions will open amazing doors to more intimacy with God and more clarity as to why you are here.

What is it you want? Long for? Hope for? How you answer points toward the glory God has etched in you. You don't manufacture it. And you can't copy it from anyone else—because your glory is a part of you. It's woven like gold threads into the fabric of your life, and if you pay attention, you'll see it shining in the deep longings of your heart and the things that most make you come alive.

That's why desire, rightly guided, is indispensable. That's why it is a gift of God. It's supposed to work like this: God will entrust you with a desire and then, in turn, invite you to trust him to bring it into reality. We don't "make it happen." However, we may need to do our part—which sometimes means just being still and waiting patiently in order to see God meet our desire. While we wait, we watch and trust that God is at work.

* * *

Here's the problem: Desires *have* gotten us into a lot of trouble. Not waiting on God, taking matters into our own hands . . . that's how we get Abraham with Hagar, Moses with the rock, Judas and the silver. What we like to call honest mistakes can disrupt a lot of lives. Judas might well have believed he was forcing Jesus to lead a political revolution as opposed to nailing his friend to a cross.

It's not our desires per se but, rather, where we have taken them—to whom and to what—that often gets us into trouble. Ours is a journey of learning right from wrong, good from bad, and the way things work. And while our desires can move us to selfish and even evil deeds along the way, they can also move us to profound and glorious acts of love. The latter is the right focus for desire, and it is why we need to reclaim it, not cast it aside.

God invites you to live as your truest self. Whatever it is he's calling you to, he will first—if he hasn't done so already—give you the desire to do it (Philippians 2:13). And then he will provide the things you need to see it through. That's how it will be for everything he invites you to—for there will be more than just one thing. He has a big life for you to live, with many a surprise and opportunity awaiting you, guided by the desires he implants within you.

Your longing to matter, to contribute, to come through, to offer something good . . . your desire to be seen, wanted, invited, and belong . . . these are standard equipment for you as an image bearer. They're a part of your Trinity DNA. They're in you to move you toward God. In becoming yourself, you don't become a less needy man. You become a *more* needy and wanting man, a more hopeful man, a man whose appetite deepens for the best things—for more Life, more love, more freedom.

There is only One who can handle the weight of such want and hope. And that is how our desires can actually serve us, not enslave us. The more we take our heart with all its wants and needs to God, the more we discover that *he* is what we want and need.

Wildly, the more you and I make it about him, the more he makes it about us.

The Right Things in the Right Order

Theologian and civil rights leader Howard Thurman once said, "Don't ask what the world needs. Ask what makes you come alive, and go do it. Because what the world needs is people who have come alive." Thurman knew what God knows: You, fully alive, are a masterpiece, a priceless work of God, one he felt was worth dying for in order to see you recovered, restored, and turned loose. The Father bought you because he is crazy about you. *You* are your greatest gift to him, and he wants to be the greatest gift to you. Your glory is his gift to you, and living in your glory is your gift to him.

Your glory is how you express both your identity and your purpose. The question of identity—*Who am I?*—comes first; then comes the question of purpose—*Why am I here?* Identity, then purpose. Get that backwards and, guaranteed, you become a broken "human doing." And we don't need any more of those running around. A man who gets worth *from* what he does rather than bringing his worth *to* what he does will be a harmful and dangerous king.

That's the pitfall of "service." Rightly motivated, as an outflow of our identity, serving is a loving and powerful thing. But ask any five-year-old, "What do you want to be when you grow up?" and he won't say "a servant." Maybe there is more to what Jesus said in Matthew 18:3: To enter the kingdom, we must become like little children. Children don't dream of serving. They want to be loved. They want to matter. They dream of being like their heroes. Service before love gives you Saul, not Paul; Martha, not Mary; religion, not freedom. This is why our identity as beloved sons comes first, *then* purpose.

From his first disciples up to today, all of Jesus's friends become *more* when they let Jesus love them. His love—*for* us, grounding our identity, and then *through* us, overflowing into action—has always been the only solid basis for how he invites his friends to the mission: "As I have loved you, so you must love one another" (John 13:34).

Peter, James, John, and Paul were all very different men, each with his own particular glory, with a unique way of seeing, sharing, writing, and interacting with Jesus and the world. So it is with you and me. God calls us to unique assignments, gives us missions, specific roles to play, and so on . . . but in all of it, always, always, always his foundational invitation is for us to walk in intimacy with him. Do that and you won't have to find or create your mission in his kingdom. He will make sure your mission finds you.

Over the course of your masculine journey, through trials and errors, wounding moments and validating ones, God is revealing your glory. Let's look more specifically at what it is, what it isn't, and how glory works.

Glory, Roles, and Assignments

Our glory is deeply knit into who we are. Always has been. Yours was in you from the day you were born. It is what God has uniquely entrusted to you and you alone. Over a lifetime, it must discovered, uncovered, cultivated, and protected. Maybe this is why so few know and live with their glory. In our everyday conversations, we don't give the matter much thought. When someone asks us what we do in life, we say, "I'm an accountant."

"I am a husband."

"I am a father of four" . . . and so on.

But we are so much more—so very much more.

Such things do say something about who we are. But that's not our glory; those are the *roles* we play, and they are different from our glory. We bring our glory to our roles.

My friend Bob plays a mean saxophone. That's just one of the things he does. Sax player is a role for which Bob has practiced very hard and become talented at. Bob plays because he loves music (jazz, to be specific). He loves being part of a team, making a contribution, working out complex notes and devising smooth harmonies. But if you think he does that only when he plays the sax, then you don't know Bob. Bob *is* a great teammate; he comes alongside other hearts to bolster their voice. That's what harmony looks like in the kingdom. Bob cares deeply about how the notes of another person's life are played, and he wants others to find their part in the symphony of the Larger Story and a life with God. That's Bob's glory.

* * *

Now let's talk about *assignments*. And let's start by remembering this fundamental truth:

You are the beloved son of your heavenly Father.

Everything you are, everything you do, and everything you become, flows out of this core identity.

Apart from belovedness, your glory has a faulty foundation. But with that foundation in place, you can explore how your glory plays out in life.

I'll offer myself as an illustration. I am a husband. I am married; therefore, I have a role as husband. And my assignment? My wife, Robin. My glory is something I'm to cultivate and offer her, as a man after God's own heart. Not a perfect man, but a good man on a good journey, learning how to love and lead well. In my role as husband, God partners with me. And he invites me, through my role *and* my assignment, to learn how to love a woman and be entrusted with her heart, and to explore what it looks like for a specific woman, Robin, and a specific man, me, to walk with God together.

I am also a dad. That's another of my big roles. I have children; therefore, I am a dad. That's not a "calling," just a reality: A man either is or isn't a dad. The *glory* in my life is to be the kind of dad I have it in me to be. My *assignment* is three Thompson girls: Ashley, Hannah, and Abbey. The question is, will they experience a dad living from his good heart, becoming his true self, offering them his glory as he is discovering it himself along the way?

To that end, my three children have been my teachers. God has used the role of fatherhood to bring me closer to him and show me who I am. And he has certainly used fatherhood to show me where my false self was and how *not* to love and lead my kids.

Discovering what your glory is takes time. You had it once; then the wounding came. When you get your glory back, you'll know. It gives you the freedom to say no to roles and assignments that don't fit. Sure, you might help out for a time, but the longer you remain in a role or assignment that doesn't fit your glory, the more a slow death sets in: yours.

You've witnessed this in others. Someone you can think of has stayed in a role longer than he ever should have. Perhaps he was assigned to a department or a school, and he hung on for safety, tenure, or money. In any case, he's been at it too long. And men in that situation are often like fish in a fridge: they begin to affect other lives.

When a man is in one title (role) at one place (assignment) for more than a decade . . . something is fishy. Men weren't built to play it safe, be domesticated, shackled to a cubicle or caged in a corner office year after year after year. Sooner or later, a man needs to step out in faith.

Maybe even break out in faith.

Escape with God and see what God has for him out there.

Bust the chains of monotony and discover what he's really made of. We call it risk and reward.

Men, over time, should outgrow their roles and assignments. Either that or step into a new frontier in their present role and assignment, because their glory has grown the things and people around them to a higher level. New challenges, more people to love, harder battles to fight, greater problems to solve—all these come to a man who is growing things with his glory. The going doesn't get easier, but it does get better and better.

For each of us, certain words can describe key pieces of our glory. Here are some that God has revealed to me about the glory of my own life: *encourage, guide, counsel, teach,* and *love.* These words describe me and touch on the things that make me come alive. Showing the fingerprint of God's handiwork in my being, they are essential to who Michael Thompson is. How they get expressed will change over time, but these qualities themselves will always remain, hardwired into me, the essence of whom God made me to be and whom the enemy would rather I not become.

Other men may possess these same characteristics, but no one else will display them the same way I do. And that is true of you as well. So, what words describe *your* glory?

Glory Is in You and Entrusted to You

During the course of our lives, we take on many roles: son, brother, friend, teammate, student, husband, father, employee, employer. Roles change or evolve. A role and assignment that one day was an answer to your prayers will likely give way to a new role and assignment. The transition may be a happy one, but more often it is challenging. A layoff or firing, a death or a betrayal, the end of a project or a life season . . . a man finds himself thrust into change, and the pain can be awful. But when the dust settles, the man discovers that God was in it with him, redeeming, restoring, healing, and training him, arranging for his freedom and a life of more.

The Bible story of Joseph comes to mind. David too. Moses as well. Follow a story long enough and you'll see all that goes into the making of a man as well as what comes against him. What is entrusted is taken away, then reentrusted, then taken away again so something else can be entrusted . . . and so it goes. Because God is after your glory. So is your enemy. But what was lost will be found. God promises.

It works like this: You bring your glory *to* what you do, not get it *from* what you do. Take the uniform off, take the instrument away, remove the job, title, or responsibilities, and your glory remains. It's just no longer on display in that role or on that assignment. If your glory was your role, or if came from an assignment or something you did and even excelled at, then your glory could be taken away. But the great news is, that's not possible. Your glory can be muted or covered up. People may dislike it and wound you because of it. But it is still in you.

Jobs change. Careers change. Activities change. Even relationships change. Old doors close and new ones open. What doesn't change is the glory of who you are. The calling on your life is to bring that glory to all your roles and assignments in your kingdom journey and all it touches.

So here's what's paramount to understand:

A role and assignment can show you more of who you are and what you are meant to offer—but *they are showing you something that is already in you.*

The glory of your life is far larger than some letterhead or business card, larger even than your family. It can be assaulted, misunderstood, mishandled, even go dormant or be put in the dark. But taken away? Removed from you? Nope, no way. Your glory is the most powerful way you bring the kingdom of God and the life of Christ to the world around you. It is violently opposed—because it is how you, as a son of God, uniquely bear his image.

God Has a Name . . . for *You*

My friends and I have an ongoing game we play with names. It came from a war film a few years ago called *Fury*, a story about a WWII American tank of the same name and its crew. Each member of the team had a "war name," a nickname bestowed on him by his peers—Wardaddy, Bible, Gordo, and Machine. Such important and affectionate names identify us and solidify our place within a brotherhood. They are names that affirm, encourage, and at times, with quirky affection, speak to a part of someone's glory.

As men on mission together, from time to time my friends and I bestow such names on one another, try them on to see if they fit. My friend Christopher is "Upgrade," Tom is "Dr. Love," and Jim is "Coach."

What's in a name? Identity. And much, much more.

A good name [earned by honorable behavior, godly wisdom, moral courage, and personal integrity] is more desirable than great riches; and favor is better than silver and gold. (Proverbs 22:1 AMP)

During a man's life, he will be called many things. Not all of them will be good, and the old adage, "Sticks and stones may break my bones, but names will never hurt me," rarely applies. Being diminished, insulted, even cursed, hurts. It leaves a mark.

This includes self-talk. It's one thing for us to say or be told we did a bad or stupid thing. It's quite another to be called stupid or bad. It's even worse when we allow our false self to adopt that label and speak it over us daily. That's when we know we're harboring an agreement with a lie. The enemy is quite happy to name us, hand us the agreement to sign, and then give us a stick so we can beat ourselves up.

But God has better names for you and me. They are bestowed in two ways. One is when someone experiences the weight and goodness of who we are in the kingdom, and God prompts them to deliver a package to our heart in the form of a compliment. Our job is simply to receive it and thank the messenger. The other way is when God skips the middleman altogether; in a moment of personal encounter, he comes straight out and tells us, "You are my _____."

God has given me many names, new identities, some validating, others initiating, all affectionate: *You are my Barnabas. You are my Aragorn. You are my Abolitionist, my Medic, my Braveheart, my . . .* Ask, seek, and knock for God to give *you* affectionate names—for he has them for you, as surely as Jesus did for his disciples. James and John he named the Sons of Thunder; Peter he named the Rock. Jesus himself is known by many names, and you bear his image. God will name you too, and more than once. When he does, however it happens, receive the name he gives you. Take it in and let it wash over you. And remember: The blessing of a new name is powerful because of the One who gives it to you. May you know such intimate naming moments with your Father!

Revelation 2:17 tells of a white stone "with a new name written on it, known only to the one who receives it," which Jesus will give those who overcome in the kingdoms-clash between good and evil. In that moment of ultimate validation, your new name will feel familiar, even fitting. Maybe it will be something you didn't even know you wanted until the moment it was presented. But in that great ceremony, I believe each of us will somehow recognize our true name on the white stone. And our longing to be seen, and our desire to be known, will be fulfilled.

Your Glory Is for Others

Your glory is what intimately connects you to the Father, and him to you. You are to offer it to others without strings attached simply because you can. Thus you fulfill the main purpose of a good king: to love and lead, protect and provide; to help others come to Jesus for their healing and training; and, in partnership with God, to offer the glory of your life in order to validate and initiate others in the glory of theirs.

Live free in your glory as a king and you won't have to convince anyone to pray a "sinner's prayer" or explain why your theological argument is superior to theirs.

Simply living the way you do, as a free man loved by God, is convincing enough. It's where Life truly is. "Prepare an answer for the hope that lies within you" (1 Peter 3:15)—be ready to tell stories of the good God has been up to in your life—and you will point other hearts to the Lord of your own heart.

Whatever your unique glory looks like, it will affect people around you. Not always positively, mind you—even Jesus didn't win them all. But for those who are listening, helping them discover for themselves the Larger Story and their place in it with their own story and desires is always a better way than telling them what to think or how to feel. As Vicktor Frankl wrote, "The meaning of life is to help others find the meaning of theirs."[7]

God makes it all about you and then invites you to make it all about him. Your glory is for you and then for others. How you live as a king in this war-torn world— this is what a kingdom Life is all about, brother. It's a life of deep impact on the lives of others, and it will take courage to live it. But God will give you that courage. Courage to fight for your home front, your kingdom, and the world around you.

What does that look like? That's what the next and last section, part 4, is all about.

King Me

PART FOUR
The Reign of a King

We must let go of the life we have planned,
so as to accept the one that is waiting for us.
—*Joseph Campbell*

It's a long way from "Once upon a time" to "And they lived happily ever after." The timeline is fraught with dangers and pitfalls, with continual opportunities to overcome and become. The journey requires learning how things work—most often the hard way. That is the invitation of the masculine journey. God is up to something, something good in the hearts of his children, growing them up into whom he designed them to be. Sounds a bit ominous. And it should, for without him we can't do it. But with him . . . you bet we can.

In parts 1, 2, and 3 we explored what a king is, the journey of his heart, and what he can become. In part 4, we focus on what a king does, starting with those closest to him and moving outward.

* * *

There is only one reason to start a conversation with "Don't be afraid": There is something to be afraid of. I imagine Jesus's tone was very loving and compassionate as he spoke those words in John 14:1. I imagine it was his way, kindly yet firmly sharing his heart.

Jesus was hanging out with his closest friends. They had just had dinner—their last dinner together. They had journeyed together for three years. That's quite the camping trip. It was a mission inside a mission. Jesus knew his path and what he had to do personally. The Father and he had worked that out way, way back in time. The rule and reign of Jesus required going through a cross in order to reclaim what had been lost—us.

His other mission was to prepare his followers for what was to come. "I have told you these things, so that in Me you may have [perfect] peace. In the world you have tribulation and distress and suffering, but be courageous [be confident, be undaunted, be filled with joy]; I have overcome the world. [My conquest is accomplished, My victory abiding]" (John 16:33 AMP).

John was there. Likely seated right next to Jesus. John heard every word, and the seeds of what Jesus was teaching and describing went deep. It's how encounters with Jesus are supposed to impact us—deeply. We get an amazing opportunity to see what those seeds grew into, what fruit of wisdom they bore. John wrote to the early believers what he knew about the journey of overcoming and becoming.

> I am writing to you, fathers [those believers who are spiritually mature], because you know Him who has existed from the beginning. I am writing to you, young men [those believers who are growing in spiritual maturity], because you have been victorious and have overcome the evil one. (1 John 2:13 AMP)

Your masculine journey is about you—and far, far more. The mission within the mission is *for the hearts of others*. Experiencing from God who you are, hearing his voice, being validated and initiated in order to reclaim lost ground in your heart . . . these are powerful ways of healing you from your past. And all of it is also training for how to love others, starting with the vital inner circle of your family and reaching from there to other relationships. Your influence is great, greater than you know. From one King to another, Jesus wants to powerfully train and equip you to reign and rule like he does—with love, in love, and for love.

A Note to Single Men

The following chapters are from the perspective of a marriage between a man and a woman, and of fatherhood. However, this is much more than a "marriage and family" book, and I want to acknowledge that many men are not in that space. The Scriptures speak to being single with both honor and encouragement. The apostle Paul and Jesus himself were both single, and by no means were they second-class kings.

Whether never married, divorced, or widowed; whether by circumstances of life, someone else's choice, or your own doing; if singleness is the current path you find yourself on as a man and possibly a single parent, I encourage you to read on. Singleness is a big topic. However, I believe and hope you'll find the pages on "The Queen," "Heirs to the Throne," and most certainly "Kings at War" to be powerfully relevant in your life as a single king.

If you're divorced, one of the bravest things I've ever seen is a king choosing kindness toward his ex-wife—especially the mother of his children by how he talks about her to them. I'm sure that is more easily written than done. And if you've never married, I am hopeful that these chapters will better equip you to see women as Jesus did, love the women and young people God has placed in your life, and prepare your heart for a day when, if appropriate, *the* woman will yet enter your story and kingdom. May the pages that follow guide, inform, inspire, and strengthen you with hope in your walk with God going forward.

King Me

CHAPTER 15
The Queen

Jesus said to them, "Why are you bothering this woman?
She has done a beautiful thing for me."
—Matthew 26:10

A woman's heart is a deep ocean of secrets.
—Rose, Titanic

She stands in the middle of an intersection, surrounded by the intimidating structures of a concrete jungle. Hands on hips, chin up, and her ponytail bent by the wind, she stands her ground, staring down the danger in front of her—a raging bull, poised to charge. It is a moment frozen in time, the four-foot-two bronze statue Fearless Girl by sculptor Kristen Visbal defying another statue, the Charging Bull of Wall Street, at the intersection of Broadway and Whitehall Street in New York. Visbal said, "I made sure to keep her features soft; she's not defiant or belligerent, she's brave, proud, and strong."[1]

Yes she is.

My wife and daughter quietly stand beside her, taking it all in. Robin says, "I want my girl to know that this is how I see her, what I believe about her, more than she does." Then my wife's thoughts turn to herself, to all the times she wished she had stood her ground, stared down an enemy, and guarded her heart. Tears come as she thinks of the journey of every feminine heart. Of what has happened to each of them . . . and of whom they might still become.

Their world is not safe. Specifically, men are not safe. So much pain has been caused women by fathers, stepfathers, uncles, brothers, stepbrothers . . . in general, by all the uninitiated and disoriented boys who masquerade as men. Most of those unfinished males are consumers at best, and at worst, predators. It's amazing that any feminine heart is still standing.

The male gender has been at the forefront of wounding women. Regrettably, I have been part of that assault. It has been passed down through the generations. But we can learn a lot about how to see and care for the feminine heart by looking to our king, Jesus.

Jesus with Women

One reason Jesus got into so much trouble in his day was his scandalous way of respecting and befriending women. Hanging out with women? Including them in his posse? And caring for them in public? That definitely added to his maverick reputation. Stasi Eldredge wrote in her book *Becoming Myself*:

> When Jesus came onto the scene, he turned misogyny on its head. A rabbi at that time wouldn't speak to a woman in public, not even his own wife (this is still true for orthodox rabbis). . . . Jesus didn't abide by those rules. During his ministry Jesus engaged with women many times. He spoke to them. He touched them. He taught them. He esteemed them. He had women minister to him physically, touching him, washing his feet, anointing him with oil and with their tears. He had women disciples traveling with him, supporting him, learning from him, and "sitting at his feet."[2]

The world's message to women is that they are less-than, they can be used, and they need to know their place. Sadly, bolstered by a theology of feminine diminishment, the church's attitude is often worse than the world's. And it's compounded by the sexual scandals that regularly occur with pastors and leaders who know the Scriptures but who, as broken and wounded kings, wield their power and authority to use women. Their behavior makes men look really bad, Christianity look worse, and Christ seem irrelevant.

It's time we men joined Jesus in honoring, loving, protecting, and promoting women. God created *two* image bearers—male and female—and Image Bearer 2.0, taken from the side of 1.0, was not created inferior. She was entrusted to our care not because she is less, for she is not, but because she is precious.

A Very Good Year

In 1967 Elvis married Priscilla, the Beatles released *Sgt. Pepper's Lonely Hearts Club Band*, and Disney premiered *The Jungle Book*. There were some incredible firsts that year: the first heart transplant, first ATM, and first issue of *Rolling Stone* magazine. In 1967 the average cost of a new house was $14,250. The average per-capita income in America was $7,300, and minimum wage was $1.40.

But most important, in 1967, at just the right moment—3:37 a.m. on March 16—Lieutenant John Willett and his bride, Linda, became the proud parents of a little girl. Two days later they paid the Navy Hospital in San Diego their bill of $7.50 and went out the door with their treasured newborn. That was a Thursday. Little did I know then that my own world had changed, and my life was set on a collision course. I was only two and a half; the Willetts' priceless daughter, Robin, and I would not intersect until July 3, 1989.

At another "just the right moment" millennia ago, the first woman was created. Conceived of the Trinity and born from Adam's side, she was the final stroke of a masterpiece. God might well have been saving the best for last. Eve was the answer to a dilemma. "It is not good for the man to be *alone*," God said (Genesis 2:18). So he did something wild. In order to create another original, rather than going back to the dirt to fashion a woman, God went after Adam. By pulling Eve from him, God fashioned a suitable partner for the man: a feminine heart, created to share in the great adventure of life with God. Henceforth, it would be life with God *together*.

Wait a minute. Man wasn't alone—he had God, right?

Apparently we men can't do this without woman. She's here to be more than merely our "helper." She's here to be our partner, our equal.

* * *

In the world's first marriage, Adam and Eve were united and a new trinity of man, woman, and God was forged. With the institution of marriage came both privileges and responsibilities. Genesis 1:28 in the Amplified Bible says it this way:

> God blessed them [granting them certain authority] and said to them, "Be
> fruitful, multiply, and fill the earth, and subjugate it [putting it under your

power]; and rule over (dominate) the fish of the sea, the birds of the air, and every living thing that moves upon the earth."

Summing up that first union, Genesis 2:24 says, "For this reason a man shall leave his father and his mother, and shall be joined to his wife; and they shall become one flesh" (AMP).

Unfortunately, not long after the words "I do" came the words "This woman you gave me . . ." (see Genesis 3:11–12). Adam blamed Eve for his own sin, and a brutal, ancient cycle began. The truth was, the two of them ate the fruit of the wrong tree *together*. Some say Adam chose Eve over God; after all, Adam was standing right there, but instead of stepping in, he went passive. In any case, the couple's naiveté was used against them, and they went down together. And so it continues today, affecting the hearts not only of men but also, very deeply, the hearts of women.

The Four Core Desires of a Woman's Heart

As the feminine image bearers of God, women carry his likeness uniquely. They are deeply relational, made to love well and fiercely, to nurture and comfort. They care deeply and are amazingly empathetic. (When children scrape their knees, whom do they call for?) Women offer their strength in their kindness, care, and mercy. They are life giving not only in having babies but also with kind and loving words, gentle touches, and the beautiful environments they so often create.

God made women a certain way for a certain purpose, and their design is revealed in their desires. It would be silly for me to assume I can present a comprehensive list of those desires, for every woman's heart is deep water. Still, we men need some essential coordinates for launching our exploration of Eve. Every feminine heart shares four core desires:

1. She wants to be loved—to be seen, known, and wanted. Like you and me, she wants to be the *beloved*.

2. She is designed and desires to offer *beauty*.

3. She longs for *romance*—to be pursued for who she is.

4. She desires to play an *essential role* in a Larger Story.

In each of the next four sections in this chapter, we'll do three things. First, we'll explore one of the core desires.

Then we'll look at how the enemy assaults it.

Finally, we'll close each section by considering how you can explore your queen's story, encourage her, and possibly partner with God for her healing. This is so important. Her story is every bit as unique and impactful as yours, containing clues both to the wounds of her heart and to her unique glory—for the two are intertwined. Her wounds need to be healed and her glory validated and invited.

Don't expect this to happen quickly. That's not how it works. A story that has taken a lifetime to write will take time to tell, page by page, and the sharing of it will itself become a part of her story . . . and yours. You're learning the journey of her heart, and you must listen with your own.

The point isn't to solve her problems or "fix" her; it's to know and understand her more intimately and validate her in ways she finds meaningful. It takes a special man, an oriented man, to patiently plumb the depths of her heart and uncover the pain and disappointment, as well as the beauty and strength, that reside in this remarkable woman who is beloved by her Father . . . and entrusted to you to learn how to love.

Core Desire 1: To Be a Beloved Daughter

When God created people, he made them male and female (Genesis 1:27; 5:2). He made them with gender. We were made relational *for* one another and *for* God. It is the best part of being an image bearer. We desire to be loved because we are designed for love.

When your wife was young, her questions were the same as yours: *Do you see me? Do you love what you see?* As she grew, those questions became more nuanced: *Am I lovely? Do you think I'm beautiful? Do you want to be with me? Am I worth your time?*

Fathers and mothers, grandparents, and others have the opportunity to answer these questions *yes, yes, yes* and *yes.* The foundation of belovedness needs to be established in a girl before the world starts to insinuate its opinions and the enemy uses others to provide answers that are untrue. Otherwise, she will take her questions to the world, just like we men do.

Women never age out of the deep desire to be the beloved. They are no different from men in that respect. Their desires and ours are intended to align. When that happens, we—men and women together—offer more of the image of God to each other and therefore a greater measure of God and his kingdom to the world.

Belovedness Assaulted

Because women are born with a deep longing to be loved, they also have a great capacity to trust—and hence the painful potential of being betrayed. Men, in turn, have a deep and complementary longing to be trusted. Yet by taking our own core questions to women, trying to get strength and identity from them rather than bringing our strength and identity to them, we have established a track record of taking awful advantage of women.

Casual sex, "friendship with benefits," and extramarital affairs compound the wounding. All too often she gives, we take, and the elements of brokenness are masked by the intensity of intercourse. In a woman's heart, this pattern of intimate interaction and then breakup and rejection, regardless of age, continues a recycling of painful agreements: *I'm not enough* (or, *I'm too much). Something is wrong with me. Nobody wants me. I am on my own.*

Men and women taking their core questions to one another in bed will never be the answer. Although men are often credited with spinning this painful orbit, women too can live falsely as consumers rather than providers. And when wounded women take their questions to uninitiated and unfinished men, the broken cycle is reinforced. Like two cars siphoning gas from one another in order to run, sooner or later both end up on the side of the road with their love gauges on E.

Exploring Her Story, Validating Her Glory

As with you, the first man in your queen's story is her father. It's vital that you discover how he handled her heart as a little girl and on into her teen years.

Did her dad cherish her? Delight in her? Make her feel safe? In other words, did she grow up knowing what it means to be the beloved daughter?

Maybe she was Daddy's little princess as a young girl. But then, distracted by work, or overwhelmed by life, or uncomfortable with his daughter's physical or social changes as she got older, or otherwise ill equipped to handle her increasingly dangerous world, Dad got lost in his journey instead of protecting hers. What happened then? Did her father distance himself out of awkwardness? Did the cuddles and closeness and words of endearment stop when she needed them—needed *him*—the most? What message did her father deliver to her heart?

How did her dad shape the way she thinks, what she believes, and how she has related to men in the different stages of her feminine journey, including you today? Much of this you inherited, and some of it you may be reinforcing.

Start with her dad, but don't stop there. There's so much more to explore. How did her mom handle her heart? Was she critical or kind? Understanding or demanding? Did she lovingly engage, or did she belittle, nitpick, and nag? How did she treat her husband, and what messages did she convey about men and women overall?

Even if your wife was loved well at home during girlhood, inevitably she met girls who weren't—wounded hearts who attempted to wound hers. Also, what were her early experiences with boys? What lies did she receive from them and agree with about what she is for and where her worth comes from?

The sheer act of actively listening as she explores such questions is in itself a huge way of telling her, "I see you. I want to be with you. I love you."

Core Desire 2: To Offer Beauty

Veiled, the bride walks down the aisle, her father at her side as a symbol of his protection. Together, they head toward the ceremony that will change both their lives. The moment comes when the father presents her to the groom. Gazing into her eyes through the sheer covering, he tells her without words, "I see you, and I love what I see." Then, lifting her veil, the father reveals what every daughter is to have in her father's eyes—beauty. More than just the outward beauty others see; he knows better. He is unveiling the beauty within her—how he sees her and the love he holds for her in his heart.

It is a holy unveiling, an act of the father's love and affection—and permission. Permission for another man to take priority in his daughter's life. We call it "giving her away." While the groom and guests smile, a part of the father dies. What was entrusted to him, he must now commit to someone else. In that moment, the groom can't possibly know what the father knows: the deep inner beauty of his daughter.

"Beauty," writes counselor Jan Meyers Proett, "cannot be captured—it can only be responded to. Beauty is a grand collision between the glory of God within you and the particularity of the beauty set within your heart."[3] I love how she puts it. First and foremost, beauty is set within, an internal quality that belongs to every woman. Inner beauty must be discovered and *unveiled,* and then responded to, in order to truly be experienced by others.

"One thing I ask from the Lord," wrote the psalmist. "This only do I seek: that I may dwell in the house of the Lord all the days of my life, to gaze on the beauty of the Lord and to seek him in his temple" (Psalm 27:4).

As Jesus captures more of a woman's heart, she is transformed into his image, strong and beautiful. Yes, *beautiful*. That is the Lord's intention for her and the Spirit's work in her (2 Corinthians 3:18). Life is meant to be beautiful. Love is meant to be beautiful. Jesus is both. And with beauty comes strength.

True beauty brings increase. It opens our eyes to God's creation, the artistry of our surroundings, and the glory of each of his image bearers. And of the myriad ways the Father invites us, his sons, to experience beauty, none comes close to the wonder, the mystery, and the flesh-of-our-flesh intimacy he wishes to unveil to us in the hearts of his beloved daughters.

But because they have a beauty to unveil, that same beauty can be assaulted and marred.

Beauty Assaulted

Three hundred thousand dollars—that's how much the average American woman will spend in a lifetime *on face products alone*. From rouge to eye creams, lipstick to mascara, and from the morning ritual to the evening one, the average woman uses sixteen products a day. And facial products are just part of the approximately $70 billion annual US beauty market. Seventy *billion* dollars. Pause and let that number sink in. It's roughly the same as the 2022 gross national incomes of Puerto Rico, Bulgaria, and Myanmar.[4] Yet it's just 13 percent of the $569 billion women spent across the world in 2020. That figure only continues to grow, and rapidly.[5]

The beauty industry fuels the enemy's ability to distort what beauty really is. TV and video commercials, internet ads, and airbrushed magazine images at the grocery checkout taunt women. Those who allow these voices authority in their lives typically respond by either trying harder ("I will make this happen") or falling into resignation ("What's the point?"). And men who fall for the world's standards of beauty add to the weight and pressure of comparison women feel every day. The beauty industry's very existence hinges on the message "You need enhancements." In other words, "You're not enough."

Too many women believe they don't possess any real beauty of their own. No surprise—for the fallen archangel Lucifer, once the most beautiful of all God's created beings, has lied to women from the start. "You were the seal of perfection, full of wisdom and perfect in beauty," the prophet Ezekiel wrote of him.[6] *Were.* Past tense. Eve took Lucifer's place in creation, and he would not bow to her crown. Transformed into Satan, he rages with jealousy toward women. And in as many ways as he can, he distorts women's understanding of beauty (and men's) to their ruin.

Women often wound other women through their insecurity about feminine beauty. The teen years can be particularly unkind. Some girls "got it," some don't, and comparison begets envy. As girls grow into womanhood, some hide while others learn to use their physical appearance to get attention from men. Either way, underneath lie the same core questions: *Do you see me? Do you love what you see?*

Beauty is God's idea, for God *is* beauty. Women and men alike must therefore come to him to accurately grasp its nature and satisfy their longing for it. Women need someone other than men to answer the deep questions of their heart. And men need a source other than women to fulfill their desire for beauty—for women display beauty, women long to offer beauty, but women are not the wellspring of beauty. God is.

Exploring Her Story, Validating Her Glory

Helping your queen reclaim her beauty starts by reclaiming your personal experience with beauty—that is, your understanding of its true nature and purpose. Getting your heart and mind right about beauty will invite her to reclaim the beauty that is innately hers.

Every man has been infected with the enemy's lies regarding beauty. Some men are deceived worse than others. If beauty is outward to you, then that is how beauty will operate in your kingdom. You'll relate to women's beauty as a consumer rather than a protector, and thus be a means for the enemy to wound your wife. When God brings healing to this part of your masculine heart and gives you back your strength to protect beauty, then he can entrust her inner beauty to you.

So, what lies have you believed about beauty? Those are the place to start. Break the agreements. Turn them in. Renounce the vows and give God those moments in which you made them.

Then ask your Father, *Where is beauty within my queen?*

Listen. Look.

Is she an artist with the ability to create beautiful works with color and craftsmanship?

Does she offer beauty in hospitality? In how she sets a table or organizes a gathering?

Is her beauty in how she loves and leads others at work, or mothers your children, or cares for her parents . . . and perhaps yours?

Is she gifted with the ability to grow beautiful things—gardens, animals, classrooms, or friendships?

How do you feel when you're around her? Are you captured by her smile? Excited for the next conversation? Inspired to write her a note or even poetry? Most importantly, does she make you want to be a better man?

When you look for beauty, you will find it. Often it exists in hidden, unsuspected, or overlooked places. When you see it in your wife, point it out to her. Validate her for it. Express your love and appreciation for the beauty of who she is and the things she does. In private is a good place to start, but also look for those moments when you can compliment her in front of family and friends. The point is, tell her. As her king, your words and gaze have more power in her life than you can possibly imagine.

Core Desire 3: To Experience Romance

The North Carolina peaks and valleys were aflame with the scarlet, orange, and gold of October. It was a spectacular setting for a Zoweh Rendezvous Weekend. There in the heart of the Blue Ridge Mountains, Robin and I were exploring marriage with a few dozen other couples who were taking time away with God and each other.

Joe and Maureen, married fifty years, had decided, "Why not?" So there they were in our circle that Thursday night among the couples introducing themselves and sharing why they were there. Now it was Joe's turn. He said, "Honestly, after fifty years, I don't think there is much more to learn. We're just here to enjoy a getaway. Maureen thought it would be good for us."

Watching Maureen force a smile, I thought, "I can't wait to hear what Joe has to say on Sunday morning." He had lost that loving feeling. He had lost *romance*. It's easy to do. One thing that is death to romance, whether with God or between two persons, is routine.

Fast forward to Sunday morning. With all the couples circled back up, I asked, "What did God do this weekend? Why were you here?" This time Joe didn't look up and speak to the room when his turn came. Instead, he turned to Maureen, reached for her hands, and looked into her eyes. "This weekend," he said, "I fell back in love with my wife."

Ah, there it was—romance! Joe continued, "I learned more about my wife's heart and her story, her wounding and her glory. I was wrong. There is *always* more." Maureen beamed, Joe smiled, and we fortunate souls watching on . . . well, we all reached for the Kleenex.

How could there ever be love without romance? God loves romance! He made pursuing one another foundational to being *in* love. There is a lover stage in both the masculine and feminine journeys because God is the ultimate lover. Routine? Never! He is the ageless romancer, the one whose image we bear. The Trinity made us for a sacred romance—a love affair of the heart, inviting us to a mutual pursuit between the new trinity God created between man, woman, and himself.

Romance between a man and woman involves the emotions and acts of intimacy, of knowing and being known. It is as old as Genesis and the garden, when "Adam knew Eve" (Genesis 4:1 KJV). Interesting that in the first reference to sexual relations in the Bible, the Hebrew word *yada* ("to know") is used to reflect that deeply intimate connection between husband and wife. Sex is, or should be, an intense and loving expression of intimacy. But intimacy is bigger than sex alone. I would define it as one person experiencing another person's truest beauty, strength, and goodness while offering one's own and having it received in return. Intimacy has been described as "Into me, see." Intimacy is absolutely essential to romance.

The *Cambridge Dictionary* offers several related definitions of romance, like facets of a diamond. Romance, it says, is "a close relationship between two people who are in love with each other . . . the feeling of comfort and pleasure you experience in a relationship with someone you love . . . a quality of excitement or mystery connected with an experience or place . . . a story of love between two people, often containing exciting events or magic."[7]

The Bible describes our relationship with Jesus as bride and bridegroom: lovers created for one another and happiest when they are intimately pursuing one another. Earthly marriage is, at its best, a reflection of that heavenly union.[8] The heart of woman is made for the heart of man, and man's heart needs woman's. The benefits of romance were created to be mutual.

Romance, embedded deep in the heart of a woman, is God's wild gift to man. It cannot and should not be tamed, but it can and should be treasured, protected, and deeply respected.

> I will get up now and go about the city,
>   through its streets and squares;
> I will search for the one my heart loves. . . .
>   The watchmen found me
>   as they made their rounds in the city.
>   "Have you seen the one my heart loves?"
> Scarcely had I passed them
>   when I found the one my heart loves.
> I held him and would not let him go.
>   —Song of Songs 3:2–4

Romance Assaulted

Did you know that romance fiction regularly outsells all other genres in publishing? Romance novels outsell inspirational books two to one—and 90 percent of the buyers are women. Romance authors and publishers tap into the feminine heart. They know that women desire to be caught up into a larger story, long for adventure, want to be fought for and pursued. They long for the love story because, deep within, they know they were made for the love story. Instead of mocking this, we men should be stepping into it.

When our relationships become routine, complacency slithers in, and boredom replaces romance. Instead of pursuing and being pursued, both hearts feel gypped, trapped, and sooner or later the sense of isolation gives way to pursuing elsewhere in the hope of once again being pursued. Lies are agreed to, and vows are made in response.

Exploring Her Story, Validating Her Glory

"Why should I pursue her? She's not pursuing me." Sound familiar? It's an agreement and the enemy's invitation to passivity. Don't sign it and don't say it. When a critical spirit comes knocking on the door of your heart, remember, you're in a battle.

Remember, and break the spell, first yours and then hers.

Queen

Remember why you fell in love in the first place. Remember how you once pursued her and what it was that drew you to her heart.

And what drew her to yours.

You see, romance between a man and woman involves two stories intertwining, and her perspective on how that happened and why it happened might be a little different from yours. How would she tell that story? Not just the facts of your history as a couple but

what she thought and how she felt when your two stories merged.

what things you did that made her feel special—that made her fall in love with you.

what things you do today that still have that same effect . . . or that you no longer do that she misses.

what she finds romantic. Do you know?

Another strategic place to go with God is into her history before the two of you met. How did her parents' relationship shape her view of romance? Did her mother and father model mutual affection, laughter, and togetherness for her in her formative years?

Forging ahead in pursuit of her heart starts by learning to ask caring questions—and not just about her past. "How was your day?" is a good place to start. But lean in. Look for ways to invite more clarity: "Really, you talked to your mom for an hour? How was that? How is she?" The more you learn to ask questions and genuinely care, the more romantic you will be in your queen's eyes, and the likelier she'll be to open her heart to you again.

Core Desire 4: To Play an Essential Role

What would movies be without women in pivotal roles? Just a bunch of men fighting. God made woman essential to the Larger Story. In the stories that matter, she isn't there to take her clothes off; she is there to bring something very important.

Women desire to play an essential role, an irreplaceable part, in an epic story . . . because God created them to do so. It's in their name, their ancient and original name. When God created the first woman, he chose a name for her that bound her to himself in a very special way: *ezer* (Genesis 2:18). It is a word that speaks to a woman's intended identity, her high calling, and her coequal partnership with man in the Larger Story.

Ezer is typically translated as "help" or "helper," but that doesn't fully convey the word's richness and dignity in reference to woman—for *ezer* is in fact a name God also embraces for himself throughout the Old Testament. For instance:

> Who is like you [Israel],
>> a people saved by the Lord?
> He is your shield and helper [*ezer*]
>> and your glorious sword.
>> —Deuteronomy 33:29

> But as for me, I am poor and needy;
>> come quickly to me, O God.
> You are my help [*ezer*] and my deliverer;
>> Lord, do not delay.
>> —Psalm 70:5

Notice the military sense of the word. God is a warrior, and woman taps into that part of his nature no less than man does. There's a reason for the term "mama bear"! A wife can be a formidable battle companion in the fight against darkness. And she's so much more besides. In the many ways her "ezership" plays out in her husband's life—or can if it's invited and received—she is a reflection of God himself and a powerful vehicle of his grace.[9]

No wonder the devil hates her. No wonder he does everything he can to oppose her role in the Larger Story. And no wonder she longs so deeply to play such a role. It flows from her very being. How a woman plays it—both in a man's life and in the world at large—is unique to her as an individual. But the desire to play it is embedded in every feminine heart and is a key part of her journey.

It takes two image bearers, a man *and* a woman, to most fully bear the image of God. She needs us, but we also need her—not just her body for our pleasure, but *all* of her for our Life. We need her intellect, her heart, her vision, her faith, her wisdom, her kindness, her courage, her fierceness, her loyalty, her encouragement, the strength of her character, the completeness of who she is as a person. Until we understand this, we will be lesser men.

Ezer Assaulted

If you know your wife's core desires, then you know the areas in which the enemy has sought, and seeks, to plunder and destroy her. Most of the enemy's work was done long before the wedding day. Understanding her wounds, agreements, and vows gives you insights on what darkness will use against your relationship as her false self and yours conflict.

She may keep the attempts on her Life (and thus yours too) well hid, blunting the pain with denial and minimization, but they're heartbreakingly common to what women face in this world.

For instance:

• Roughly two-thirds of women have been sexually harassed in public, and one in five has suffered an attempted or completed rape.

• The workplace and the glass ceiling continue to deliver the message that women are less valuable than men.

• Women who grew up in dysfunctional families—an alcoholic dad, a narcissistic mom, a sexually abusive uncle, or a home shattered by divorce—typically bear the wounds of long-term emotional trauma.

Your queen may have experienced none of the above; she may have experienced all of it and more; but one thing you can count on—her heart has been wounded in ways that hinder the role she longs to play in the Larger Story.

Exploring Her Story, Validating Her Glory

As you journey with your wife (or daughter, mom, sister, or friend) to explore different parts of her life, you'll probably discover that any one wounding experience can have affected more than one of her four core desires. Here are a few helpful tips:

• Take time to listen patiently without trying to advise, fix, or correct.

• Don't tell her how, or how not, to think or feel. This is the death of intimacy and the ruining of trust.

• Ask thoughtful questions that encourage her to unveil her heart more deeply.

• Affirm her emotions and treat her with a gentleness, compassion, and respect that can help remove thorns from her heart.

• Show her a protectiveness that reassures her she is safe and secure with you. This can be as simple as opening a car door, having her walk on the inside of the sidewalk, or carrying a blanket or extra jacket in your car in case she gets cold.

• Be prepared to revisit the same story more than once over time, for it likely has many facets, each with its own impact on her life.

When you are a student of her heart, you will become a champion for her glory. Learning her story can expose her agreements with lies like "You have nothing of value to offer," "You are not beautiful," or "You're weak, and you are alone." Listen for such lies. The enemy is not bashful. Rise up and fight the lies on your queen's behalf. As she is willing, ask her questions, and accompany her in bringing the wounding moments, the lie, and her agreements and vows to the Father. Don't just tell her a lie isn't true; ask her first why she thinks that way. Where did the lie come from? When has she felt that way before?

Validate her strengths and her wisdom, and humbly and gratefully receive them when she offers them to you. Request them, for you need them, and she needs you to seek them—for in doing so, you pursue her.

Also, think of ways you can support her in her personal pursuits and dreams. Affirm their worth. Celebrate her achievements, and let her know what a remarkable person she is. When was the last time you told her how much you value her partnership and appreciate the ways she enriches your life?

Her Heart, Her Glory: Your Mission

What is it your wife (or your daughter, your sister, or your mom) uniquely brings to the world? Does she set a table of hospitality? Is she a gifted and empathic listener? Perhaps she's a natural at sports and physical activities, or a fierce advocate for the oppressed. What are the things she loves to do and the things that flow from who she is?

Like you, she possesses a glory and a particular way she bears the image of God. She too has had, and will have, unique roles and assignments along her feminine journey. And the enemy fears what she might become, for darkness knows she has a glory of her own.

Could it be that Satan came after Eve rather than Adam not because she was the "lesser or weaker one" but because she was *critical*? Take out the *ezer* with a lie and get the man too. Regardless, the serpent's goal was a two-for-one, and it has been that way ever since. So, against man and woman's common enemy, our greatest weapon as warrior-kings is blessing our queen by speaking words of life over her. Affirming her glory. And patiently partnering with God for her heart while pursuing God for our own.

* * *

I hate it when my enemy uses me, taking advantage of my false self to make a scene in my marriage. A belittling comment, a sarcastic jab, a facial expression that bruises . . . arrows, arrows to my wife's heart, reinforcing what the enemy has done to her over the years. A husband may win the argument, but he'll be losing the war. And every woman has her moments too, when her false self comes swinging.

False self summons false self. But the good news is, your true self can summon her true self. It's your choice. Being married doesn't make you a better man; being married invites you to see what kind of man you can be.

Your wife's wounds and her glory are your mission. And mission invites you to bring your masculine strength. You can't undo the past, but it isn't too late to bring valor to the years ahead. So, in the words of the *Mission Impossible* film series, "Your mission, should you accept it, is . . ."

Start with your own heart, walking with God to replace the lies you have believed with the truth. And as his love increasingly heals, transforms, and frees you, partner with him for your wife's heart . . . and the hearts of the next generation.

Taking the frontline position in that fight will require everything you've got—not because your wife is that needy but because the enemy will not give her up that easily. She's not a damsel in distress; she's another POW, and it takes a free man to free a woman. Just remember, your weaponry is counterintuitive to what men have been taught. Gentleness is more powerful than force. Kindness is more compelling than control. And honor, protection, and patience are holy requirements in a man for inviting a woman to walk in her glory.

* * *

Passivity may be the greatest enemy of masculinity. But aggression is not the solution; engagement is. True, sometimes the best course of action is to do or say nothing—but even inaction needs to be intentional and led by the Spirit. You must walk with God. That is what a good king does—not just on behalf of your wife but also your children. They are next in importance after her.

Fortunately, you have what it takes to fight on both fronts. And the more healing and freedom your *ezer*'s heart gains along with yours, the more effectively the two of you can lock arms in protecting, nurturing, and strengthening your heirs to the throne.

CHAPTER 16
Heirs to the Throne

Your sons will take the place of your fathers;
you will make them princes throughout the land.
—Psalm 45:16

Since it is so likely that children will meet cruel enemies, let them at least have heard of
brave knights and heroic courage.
—C. S. Lewis

My friend Jay tells the story of taking his then five-year-old daughter to breakfast at McDonald's for a daddy-daughter date. As they sat down with their trays at an intimate table for two, Jay's cell phone went off. He tried to listen to his little girl as she shared her thoughts on which Disney princesses were her favorites and the reasons she prefers sandals over flip-flops, but you know how distracting that little device can be. After he had broken eye contact one too many times and given his daughter the pretending-to-listen "uh-huh," she slid off her seat. He didn't even see her until she was right there, standing directly in front of him.

Reaching up with both little hands, she cupped his face. *Now* she had his attention. Tilting her head, she said, "Daddy, listen to me, look at me . . . ask me anything."

* * *

What do our children want from us? Same thing we wanted from our dads: engagement. *Listen to me, look at me, ask me anything.*

Loving engagement is the most powerful way to impact the heart of a son or daughter. It's *how* to fight for their hearts—not just in moments of crisis but in the simple day-to-day connections. "Mundane" interactions may not seem like battles, but they're the front lines where our children's hearts are won or lost.

Whether your child is five or fifty-five, never stop listening. Never stop giving them your time and attention. Never stop lovingly engaging. Whether across a McDonald's table for two, riding in the car to the store, or walking a trail, invite them into your world while at the same time doing your best to step into theirs. This is how we fight. What you talk about in those moments, and how you listen, is the difference between merely being with them versus connecting with their hearts.

Looking back, I see many of my messes. It's one of the few things hindsight is good for: seeing what you missed. That "missing them" is what gives the enemy opportunity to speak. My busyness, distraction, misplaced intensity, unhelpful anger, inappropriate facial expressions . . . what is a young person to feel, think, and eventually come to believe from moments when their heart is handled so poorly by their dad? I'm banking on the verse "Love [which includes engagement] covers over a multitude of sins" (1 Peter 4:8).

This chapter is not an indictment of us fathers. Rather, it is an invitation for us to love the heirs to our thrones with an engaging love befitting good kings. No matter how old our children are, engaging them and bestowing on them words of blessing—*I love you, I'm proud of you, I'm thinking of you, I want to be with you*—are powerful ways we partner with God to provide for and protect their hearts.

Father-Shaped

My grandfathers, Lawrence and Charles, are the two men who impacted my life by fathering my mom and dad. How they handled my parents' hearts, how they loved and how they wounded them, has profoundly shaped me. God designed it that way. One of his great intentions for fathers is to pass down Life through blessing. Wounding exists only because our enemy has hijacked the importance and beauty of blessing. How we engage our kids with our words brings either life or death. If—and more likely, when—we look back and see we brought death, the good news is, there is resurrection.

The word *father* means different things to different people. To some it speaks of passivity, absence, betrayal, demandingness, control, even abuse. To others it is a term of endearment, a reminder there was, or still is, someone out there looking after us, someone who makes sure we are alright no matter what the cost or inconvenience is to him.

How your kids see and experience you is vitally connected to how they see and experience God, because "Father" is the primary way God chooses to be known. No wonder the role of father is under such assault—God created fatherhood to mirror his own identity. The enemy uses father wounds to give both dads and God a bad rap.

* * *

Here's the problem: Wounds in one relationship are guaranteed to hinder other relationships. We can't help it; we project our past experiences onto our current realities. Only our heavenly Father has the ability to take the father wounds so many of us have borne for decades and, in their place, give us new names, new messages, new seeds of Love and Life to be sown for generations to come.

God is inviting every father to a heart-shaping assignment that is his alone as he fathers his children. Yet even as I write these words, I feel the weightiness of my own failures.

It's the enemy's way—accusation and doubt, the doorways to guilt and shame: "Who are you to write about fatherhood?" As Billy Graham purportedly said, "A good father is one of the most unsung, unpraised, unnoticed, and yet one of the most valuable assets in our society."[1] If that's true—and I'm certain it is—then we see why the enemy's whispers and accusations slither frequently into our thoughts.

Here's the truth that gives me, and you, hope: The legacy we leave behind isn't determined by how we started (though that may very well need to be cleaned up) but, rather, by how we move forward from here. That's what will make the difference in how you and I will be known to our grandchildren and even our great grandchildren. To move consistently in the right direction, we need Fathering as we father.

Falling from Our Pedestal

The last thing any of us dads want to do is wound our kids. But sooner or later we say or do something that hurts our child's heart. When it happens, we need to own our culpability. If your dog bites someone, you are responsible, and ditto for your false self. Your kids don't care for explanations about the false self. What they do deeply care about is how you respond afterward. Even though your false self got loose, your true self can still show up and answer their core questions. Even your mistake can become an opportunity to show them you love them.

Most dads have no idea how badly they have wounded their children and therefore are still wounding them. But the good thing is, when God shows you how you've hurt your child, that moment of hard revelation becomes an invitation. God believes you are ready to see what you did so you can own it and attempt to make amends, so your son or daughter can hopefully entrust you with their heart once again.

Their memory of how a wound happened may be very different from yours. What matters is the record in their heart: how they perceived the wounding and how it made them feel. Conversations about wounding moments are no time for excuses or discounting your child's memory of what *really* happened. Rather, they are a time to step into the invitation to listen, pursue understanding, hear how they feel, and offer care. In doing so, you bring the first wave of healing to your loved one's heart and point your relationship in a good direction.

Every father falls from his pedestal. My own fall, which happened long before I was even aware of it, allowed God to help me up. When the painful realization finally hit, it was a great mercy. God was inviting me to be Fathered in the midst of my fatherhood. Despite my past failures, God continues to help me move forward. He's training me to love my kids better by tuning in to their hearts more, and to wound them less by tuning in to my own heart with God.

Fighting for the Hearts of Your Kids

When my daughters were growing up, there were times when I had to step in—not *at* them but *for* them. When Ashley was in fifth grade, she got called to the vice principal's office for something she didn't do. Living close by, I dropped in, engaged, and confronted the authority who was wrongfully confronting her.

In middle school, Hannah was pursued by a boy whose text messages required a firm response. I confronted the boy at a school function with his mother standing by. It seemed like the right time and place to bring the matter to light. I was kind but made it very clear I was not happy.

When the coach for my youngest daughter's travel soccer team shamed her one too many times with his "motivational" tactics, I requested a meeting. The coach thought I wanted his evaluation of Abbey's performance. I made sure he understood I was evaluating *his*.

These are a few of my wins, moments when I recognized the opportunity to fight for my daughters' hearts. Unfortunately, there have been losses too. I was a very disoriented man when my kids were growing up. A Christian, yes, but disoriented. And I'll bet you can say the same. We dads have a learning curve all our own, and our training as dads walks hand in hand with our healing as a man.

So what do your kids need from you in the fight for their hearts? Above all, they need *you*. The real you. The authentic you.

By now you know: That all starts by getting back your own heart. As you do, you'll become increasingly equipped to hear and validate your kids in the questions they're asking. They're the same ones you were asking when you were a boy:

Do you see me?
Do you love what you see?
Do you want to be with me?

Whether your son or daughter is still a child or a grown man or woman, I guarantee that, one way or another, they too are asking these core questions. Are the answers settled in *your* heart as *yes*, *yes*, and *yes*? If not, then it's extremely likely they are not settled that way in your child's heart either.

Becoming a beloved son *as* you father is the way to learn how to father beloved sons and daughters. Being loved is the way to learn how to love. Being healed is the way to learn how to partner with God for your children's healing when you or someone else wounds them. Being fathered by God is the greatest way to learn how to father the hearts he has entrusted to you.

On the timeline of your children's life experiences, your love comes before God's. You are their first authority figure. How you handle their hearts shapes their ability to love and trust others. Either your love will help them make an intimate connection with God or your wounding will encumber it.

How do you wish your father had loved you? The key to loving your own kids better may well be contained in your answer to that question.

Building Strong Children

I'd imagine you're familiar with the verse "Train up a child in the way he should go: and when he is old, he will not depart from it" (Proverbs 22:6 KJV). Sadly, it's often misapplied to justify a heavy-handed parenting style of discipline, control, and conformity. There can be a huge difference between "the way he [or she] should go" and the way *you think* your child should go. That controlling way can crush their soul. Just ask all the preachers' kids who could not wait to depart from the path their dad pushed them on. I've heard too many of their stories.

The Amplified Bible sheds a clearer light: "Train up a child in the way he should go [*teaching him to seek God's wisdom and will for his abilities and talents*]" (my emphasis).* In other words, help the child grow in the way God designed him or her. Rightly understood, the proverb invites parents to go after their children's hearts, not just their behavior. This has been the most lifesaving and life-giving parenting principle in all my fathering days. God had to change my heart before I could implement that concept; then I could go after the hearts of my daughters. By then, they were well into the explorer stage, and much damage had already been done. But now I had a new plan in sight to guide me: Find each daughter's glory and train it up.

Fatherhood is an exploration of the heart whose discoveries, over time, build trust, wonder, and blessing. But with exploration there is always danger. The things we build are fragile, and accidents or sabotage can occur in seconds. A harsh word, a missed opportunity to engage, and precious ground is lost. Raising children in the Larger Story is not for the naïve and the walking wounded. You gotta know your way around if you're going to show your kids around the Larger Story and how it works. As the legendary seminary professor Howard Hendricks used to say, "It is impossible to impart what you do not own."

Adding to the challenge, so much happens outside of a father's knowing. How can a dad fight what he's not even aware of? You can't slay the dragons you don't know exist.

So . . . how do we reclaim the ground we lost with our children? How do we fight for their hearts? There's no one all-encompassing answer; rather, there are a number of approaches that work together. We'll explore some of them in the next few sections.

---

* In the Classic edition of the AMP, the bracketed content reads, "[and in keeping with his individual gift or bent]."

Ask Questions and Know Their Story

You would think, living with your kids, that it would be easy to know their stories. But consider: How much of *your* story did your parents really know? Living under the same roof isn't the same as knowing what's going on in your children's world.

Do you know where each child is in their masculine or feminine journey?

Are you aware of what the enemy is up to in his or her life? And what God is up to?

Can you discern what your son's or daughter's heart needs in training, validation, and initiation?

Why is your child doubting? What are they afraid of? Who is hurting them? Why did they say or do what they said or did? This is what you want to see, where you want to explore, *before* addressing their heart. How? Lovingly engage them with good questions. "How was your day?" isn't a bad question. But if you know what the day held for them—an algebra test, tryouts, choir practice, a doctor's appointment—then you can be specific.

You earn the right to ask your children intimate questions by starting with simpler ones and by listening, not lecturing. For too long I used to ask my kids questions so I could talk. I was more concerned about giving advice and "being right" than listening for their hearts. That's a bad way to train up your son or daughter in the way they should go. Asking questions for the sake of listening and understanding is far better. That's how you find out where your child is in their story and how God wants to partner with you to love them in the moment. If you take that approach, then just because a moment doesn't go well—your kid raises their voice or storms off—that doesn't mean you didn't handle it well. You're not in charge of their response; you're in charge of yours.

Listening is the one of the most loving things you can do. Listen not only with your ears but also with your eyes, your body language, your time, and very, very few words on your part. Give your child your undivided attention; it is impossible to listen well and be busy with other things at the same time.

Our most powerful weapon as dads in the battle for our children's hearts, no matter how old they are, is our presence. A close second is our words. Good questions, listening, and kind words are what we ourselves needed from our dads growing up. And they're what we still need from our heavenly Father in order to recover and grow as men.

We Shall See

When Abbey, my youngest, was applying to colleges, she had high aspirations: Stanford, Duke, Vanderbilt, Emory, University of North Carolina, and Richmond. She had worked hard and she had the grades.

As she was applying, though, I felt the sticker shock. And darkness, as it loves to do, brought God into question: Could I trust his heart, his will, and his way for my daughter? The enemy shot arrows of doubt at me: *You don't know what you're doing. You can't provide. She's going to be disappointed with you.*

Too many times I had fallen for those lies. Not this time. This time I counterpunched with "We Shall See."

"We shall see" is a great declaration. It's a strategy that relieves pressure and invites time for God to work in us and for us. How did I know which schools Abbey would get in? Or what kind of financial aid she might get or merit scholarships she might receive? My daughter's dreams deserved my support. And my support depended on God to take my little girl in the direction he has planned for her. *We Shall See.*

It was weeks before we heard back from the schools. What I didn't say during the wait was, "Honey, we can't afford these schools." Instead, I let it play out. We stayed the course together, father and daughter, hitting each mile marker as it came to us. And together, sure enough, we saw which doors opened for her and which ones closed.

During Abbey's second semester of her freshman year at UNC, I asked her, "Looking back, Abbs, are you happy with your school?" Abbey said, "Dad, I can't imagine myself anywhere else." I loved her answer! I loved that my daughter loved her school. And I loved how she had arrived there. The best part of it was, I got to walk beside the daughter God gave me to love. She let me, God showed up for us, and our journey together initiated us both into a deeper walk with him.

Maybe this tactic will help you stand with your daughter or son, as it did for me with Abbey. Instead of trying to predict or control the future, We Shall See frees you to walk alongside their dreams and discover just how big God wants to be in their life and yours.

Smart Phones, Social Media, and Cards

As early as nine or ten, in the explorer stage, your son's or daughter's vows and agreements, and ultimately what they come to believe, start to outweigh your authority in their lives. They've reached the "age of accountability," when their choices and beliefs begin to impact their world more than yours do. And you may not know what is really going on with them because you haven't asked, aren't engaged, or, worse, naively assume all is well.

Don't be ignorant; step into their world. In this day of smart phones, you'll be smart to learn how to use them. Find creative, conversational ways to ask your kids, "What apps do you like? What is your favorite social media? Whom do you follow? What podcasts do you listen to?" Do you know *why* your kids are choosing their sites and apps? How do they feel, and what are they learning, when they use them?

And . . . can you be a participant, a cunning voice, a good presence in the arena they are playing in? Technology and social media are dangerous games, yes, but you are a dangerous man, an oriented father. Strategically, you may be more successful going into their arena than trying to pull them out of it.

Most kids get their phones in the explorer stage. That is when the enemy doubles down on "You are on your own." Step in and block that lie with your presence. Your child's phone can be a weapon against you, but it's also one of your greatest tools. Do you text? Text your son. Do you email? Email your daughter. Do you take pictures? Take pictures of your kids, and send pictures to them. Get in their inbox.

And in the midst of all the high tech, don't forget handwritten I-love-yous. Pick up a card or write your son or daughter a note once in a while. Remember letters? There are more ways than texting and even talking to lovingly engage and get your thoughts, feelings, questions, and encouragement across their noses and into their hearts.

Make a Moment or Seize a Moment

I invite you to ask God one of these questions:

Where and how have I wounded my kids?

Where is my child on their masculine or feminine journey, and what do they need from me?

What is the glory of their life?

When God gives you an answer—a word, image, or memory—ask the Father for instruction on how to father. Then consider taking what God shows you to your child in the form of a question: "Sweetheart, can I ask you something?"

Let's say God has made you aware of a wound you inflicted. You can ask, "Do you remember when I said . . . ?" Be specific for both your sakes. If the event occurred last night, they are sure to remember; if it was last month or last year, you may need to fill in some details. Even if they don't remember, follow through with the story God brought to your mind. Tell what you remember about what happened, what you said and did, and how you handled your child's heart. Let him or her know you have been talking to God, and he brought the matter up.

And then? When you are both on the same page, ask for forgiveness. Even if the event happened decades ago, it is amazing what ground you can take back from the enemy. Partnering with God and your child, you can reclaim what your false self gave away and offer healing to a wound you were used to inflict.

Sometimes the right time to ask your leading question pops up spontaneously. Don't let the moment pass—seize it. Other times, some planning may be required to make it happen. Either way, curiosity alone makes most kids willing.

The more moments you seize in real time, the fewer you will have to circle back and try to make. However, bear in mind that your child may not remember the event you want to revisit. Or, especially if they're an adult child, they may not be ready to forgive. That's OK. Be brave and let them have the controls. You made the first move; now let them choose theirs. That's the way it should be.

Remember too, as you invite your children to open their lives to you, to open your own life to them. Sharing and vulnerability are a two-way street. Do your kids know any of your God stories? Do they know your trials and the tales of your over-coming and becoming? Sharing your heart's journey with your kids is a gentle but powerful way to help them know you, trust you, and be ready to turn to you and God in order to find their own way.

Making a moment is not just about recovering from past wounds. There's a fun and even joyous side to it as well. You can make a golden, lifegiving moment happen with every birthday, every anniversary, every holiday, and those special occasions when life or the calendar hands you an easy one—a graduation, an award, an accomplishment, and so on. Moments of healing and repair are always good; even better are moments you make or seize to deliver the powerful, validating package, *I see you, and I love what I see.*

Making Amends

My oldest daughter, Ashley, shared a story with me of a time when, as a little girl, she wore flip-flops to church. The clack, clack, clack of the sandals on the back of her heels was so fun as walked the sidewalk leaving church—until the moment I turned and growled, "What are you doing? Stop dragging your feet."

Maybe that sounds like no big deal, but it was to her, and therefore it is to me. My false self had shown up, and years later, thanks to my daughter's transparency, I needed to take responsibility for it. "That was when I learned you weren't safe," Ashley told me. Ouch! I get it, and I've paid for it. Sadly, so has each of my girls.

Making amends is different from trying to make it up to them. Making amends is owning what you've done so you can go forward better, whereas "making it up" has you striving to remedy the past. You can't, and you may just cause confusion if you try. Better to simply admit your fault and its impact and ask forgiveness. Better to say, "I was wrong, and I'm so sorry I hurt you. Please forgive me." But most dads—most men, for that matter—don't know how to apologize. You start by receiving God's love for your own heart. Healing for your heart leads to the tenderness, kindness, and patience you need to lovingly handle your kids' hearts. The soft words of God train us as dads to have soft words for our children.

Learning how to apologize takes practice. Living judiciously behind the scenes of their lives takes practice. Learning to live less concerned about who gets credit or who gets blamed takes practice.

As a dad, you're going to get a lot of practice.

Every day you can practice—and you should, for you never know when a big moment is coming. Getting the small stuff right is a whole lot more fun than having to make amends. But when you don't get it right, then making amends can set both you and your son or daughter free.

Discover Their Glory

Invitation is a powerful thing. The greatest thing you can invite your children to do is discover their glory. Helping them with that is part of your own glory and one of your missions in your role as their dad. Proverbs 25:2 says, "It is the glory of God to conceal a matter and the glory of kings to seek it out." That certainly applies to uncovering, validating, and initiating your kids in their individual glory.

In wanting to see and hear my daughter's hearts, I've invited myself to watch TV shows I might have normally missed, like *One Tree Hill*, *The Twilight Saga*, and *Downton Abbey*. (Well, maybe I would've watched *Downton* anyway.) I've listened to music I wouldn't normally have listened to (my girls play their phones in the car), and I've attended events I wouldn't normally have attended. I've seen Taylor Swift in concert.

Sitting down with your kids to watch and listen to what they watch and listen to; taking in their shows, songs, and events . . . all of it is a path to discovering their glory. These things lead to conversations, which lead to questions, which lead to discovering your children's hearts and where they are in their journeys. Ultimately, your goal is to come to see how each child uniquely reflects God's image. After all, they not only carry your DNA—they also carry his.

* * *

Being together is where the action is when it comes to kids. I've learned to care about what mine care about by discovering *why* they care. I've unashamedly invited myself into their world, and I've invited them into mine. Neither they nor I will ever outgrow the need for that invitation.

The apostle Paul writes,

> Fathers, do not provoke your children to anger [do not exasperate them to the point of resentment with demands that are trivial or unreasonable or humiliating or abusive; nor by showing favoritism or indifference to any of them], but bring them up [tenderly, with lovingkindness] in the discipline and instruction of the Lord. (Ephesians 6:4 AMP)

"In the discipline and instruction of the Lord" isn't just for them. It's for you as well. With your help and God's leading, each of your children can come to see, hear, and believe in their glory—who they are, how God uniquely made them, and what they have to offer the world.

As in your own journey, each stage of your son's or daughter's life needs a guide, an inviter, an interpreter, and an advocate. That's you. The Holy Spirit is involved; your job is to walk your child as far as you can until they can walk with the Spirit on their own. Even then, you are not replaced. The Spirit just takes a more direct role in your child's life, and you become a wonderful close second.

It's Never Too Late—Until It Is

"Fighting for the Hearts of Your Kids" is one of the last sessions at Zoweh's *The Heart of a Warrior* events, mostly because it is kinder to invite men to go to God with their own hearts *before* they go after their loved one's hearts. After one such presentation, a man was waiting for me offstage, and he didn't look happy. I took a deep breath and prayed, "OK, Jesus."

With a furrowed brow and leaking eyes the man said, "You're wrong,"

"I'm so sorry. What did I say?"

His voice shifted from anger to pain. "Eight months ago, I lost my eight-year-old daughter in a car accident. I was driving."

Fighting back tears, he continued. "Not a day goes by that I don't cry out to the Lord. Not a day goes by that I don't wish I could hold her, say something, anything, talk to her, tuck her in, watch her sleep, fix her breakfast."

There it was. A holy grief. Holy ground. I told the man how sorry I was for his loss and that I understood why he was so upset. "I hear you," I said. "You're right. It's never too late until it is."

Brother, your life is larger than any lecture. Your way is bigger than any instruction. If I could do it over again with my kids . . . oh, if I could do it over again . . .

I would talk less and listen more.

I would seize more moments, and I would make more moments happen by preparing for more, and I would ask more questions, ask more often what my kids are thinking and how they are feeling.

Above all, I would bless them with kind words, and with my reassuring presence, and with lots more gentle and affectionate touches. That's loving engagement!

Blessing with words of validation and initiation is our job as fathers. My advice: Bless each of your children once a day. Pray over them by name. Whether by text message, a phone call, email, a handwritten note, or what have you, use your resources and creativity to let them know you see them and love them.

Their glory is your mission. Over time, they will invite you to tell them stories of your discoveries in walking with God—how he is healing, training, validating, nd initiating you as a man. This is the privilege and opportunity you are looking for. Sow the seeds of such opportunities through the ways you invest yourself in each child each and every day. Tomorrow is not guaranteed for either you or them.

Go After Shame ASAP

It's never your business to *tell* your kids how they should or shouldn't feel. But . . . do *discover* how they feel, and why. Yes! That's where the gold is and where you'll find their hearts—and the battlefield in which to fight.

Taking notes got you through high school and maybe college, and it will help you in fatherhood as well. Listen for wounding moments, what the enemy is trying to do, and what God is up to in your kids' lives. Listen for them making vows and agreements. And write such stuff down. (When I catch something one of my daughters says, or the Spirit whispers, "There it is, a piece of her glory"—or a part of her heart, or a wound—I write it in my cell phone's note app.) Then when the time is right, you can ask questions that help them discover the truth for themselves.

In particular, be on the lookout for shame. The voice that once told your own young heart, "Something is wrong with you," wants to work in your children too. Not being invited to a party, being teased, experiencing the rejection of a breakup; or, when they're older, losing a job, struggling financially, or suffering a divorce . . . abuse and trauma come in all shapes and sizes. Left untreated, they spiral downward into shame.

Get in there, Dad, as quickly as possible. The sooner you offer your strong presence and loving words, the less time your child will spend in shame's prison. When you're able to ask questions and listen well so you really hear what is going on in your son's or daughters' life, and when you respond lovingly and affirmingly, you equip your child to fight the battles against shame that are certain to come.

When shame tells boys and girls that being hurt or needing help is weakness, and when they believe their father will withhold love and punish them instead, they learn to hide their lives from Dad. Make sure you're not that dad. I heard of one father who placed this note in his son's drawer:

> If you're scared to tell me something, just bring me this note as a reminder that I'm here to support you. I won't get mad; I will work with you on a solution.

That's a father preparing to meet his child's heart in the future. Even apart from his physical presence, that dad's voice speaks clearly and lovingly, proactively combatting the lies of shame. In the crucial moments when the accuser shows, he is confronted with the blessing of that father on his child. The son or daughter of a dad like that has way better than a fighting chance to grow up settled in their belovedness and free of shame.

Father's Day

Father's Day 2021 was one of the best in my life. We were circled up and the cards came in, each one written as if a Father of the Year award was being given. Oh, how I wished my daughters' loving words could be fully true, but I knew the backstory of those cards—my anger of years past, the mishandlings each of my children suffered. It has been hard to swallow and challenging to own. But the journey to Father of the Year has also involved some of God's most transforming work in training me to be a good king.

Father wounds are a big deal—the ones you received and the ones you inflicted. One day you will want your children to forgive you; therefore, I highly recommend you forgive your own father. More on this in the next chapter, for forgiveness is not always easy and never glib, and it is a far cry from denying injury or condoning abuse. For now, it's enough to understand that sowing and reaping, and judging not lest you be judged, are integral to how the spiritual realm works. Forgiving your father is part of how you fight for the hearts of your own kids. Part of doing your own work.

Your children desperately need you to do that work. It is how you establish a kingdom they will be safe to live in and honored to inherit. For as heirs to your throne, they will one day most certainly inherit what you have left behind, and I'm not just talking about estates and account balances. Their inheritance started long ago with the investments you made in their becoming who they truly are, in how they are known in heaven, and in the particular glory each child possesses and can bring to the world. That's a wealth every child is intended to inherit.

Every day is an opportunity for you to love your kids by walking with God and working on yourself. By doing the hard stuff—and the good stuff. By sharing your presence and your words. By speaking, providing, and being the blessing they long for and need. Do these things and you'll make every day Father's Day.

The Final Four

I'll conclude this chapter by sharing four rules of thumb God has shown me for going after my kids' hearts, no matter their age. By now these precepts may sound familiar—in fact, I hope they do. You've already come across the ideas they express any number of times in this book, especially in these last few pages, and I hope they have stuck in your mind. But they're so crucial that I want to draw them together and give you a quick recap.

1. *"You are worth my time."* Invite your kids along when you go somewhere. Make one-on-one dates. Attend their stuff whenever you can. In as many ways as you can, invest your presence in their lives.

2. *"I want to know your heart."* Learn to ask questions that invite them to share how they feel, what they think, and most importantly, what they believe.

3. *Bestow affection both in words and in touch.* Write notes, hold hands, put your arm around them, greet them with a gentle hug, give them a pat coming or going. Make a moment or seize a moment to validate, initiate, or heal.

4. *Listen.* Give your children your eyes and ears. It's one of the most loving and validating things you can give anyone.

* * *

The two institutions created by God for us, marriage and family, are the throne room of your kingdom. They are where you are first to bring your glory. They are the core of your mandate to reign and rule in love, the holy center from which you bring the kingdom of God to others.

Marriage and family are also where the enemy will powerfully attempt to steal identity, kill desire, and destroy love. Getting your heart back—receiving healing from God—is your training and the way you take back lost ground. It is how you win the battle for your life and then for your loved ones' lives. And it is how you establish your kingdom as a kingdom for good.

There are realities and subtleties to the fight. As Graham Cooke says, "You're not fighting to win; you've already won. You're fighting not to lose."

You are a king at war. In the final chapter, we'll look at aspects of the battle we haven't yet covered—what else you're up against, specific kingdom ways that lead to even more freedom, and the glory that lies beyond.

CHAPTER 17
Kings at War

You, dear children, are from God and have overcome them, because the one who is in
you is greater than the one who is in the world.
—1 John 4:4

Dark times lie ahead of us and there will be a time when we must choose between what
is easy and what is right.
—*Albus Dumbledore,* Harry Potter and the Goblet of Fire

Once, in long ages past, there was a holy war in heaven, a mutinous rebellion.
The war came to earth. And you and I are in it.

We were born into a world at war, for what goes on in the spiritual realm plays
out in the physical. Evil wants to make sure we never, ever come into the love of God,
much less the power God wants to entrust to us. For if we do, goodness will prevail,
and the kingdom of God will advance.

> **Do not let yourself be overcome by evil,**
> **but overcome (master) evil with good.**[1]
> —**Paul the Apostle**

We come to it at last.

When we were young in the masculine journey, we were taken captive by the
kingdom of darkness because we had no one to fight for us, teach us how to fight,

or model how to wield the authority of Christ against darkness. We had no one to protect us while also showing us the ropes, no one to train us up in how to guard our hearts.

This chapter is about learning how to defend yourself against evil. We turn our focus now to how you can stand your ground in the spiritual realm and join Jesus in the Great Revolution. Overthrowing evil and advancing the kingdom—*that* is supposed to be Christianity.

The kingdom of darkness threatens you every day, all day long. Like hit-and-run drivers, foul spirits crash into your life, then exit the scene, leaving you to deal with the damage. Utilizing a communication network of lies, the unholy trinity—Satan, this fallen world, and our false self—intimidate, diminish, and accuse. They labor tirelessly to bring fear, guilt, and shame to human hearts. To overcome the unholy trinity, we need God's help.

* * *

The worst form of punishment in our prison system is solitary confinement. On the inside they call it "time in the hole." The enemy have their own version of it. It has always been their objective: Isolate us from God; cut us off from others; punish us with "You're on your own"; then after the damage is done, blame it all on us. Separate, isolate, wound, then accuse—that's their strategy in a nutshell.

Unless you learn the art of war and take your place on the front lines of the kingdom conflict, you're vulnerable to their tactics. You must learn how to protect your heart (Proverbs 4:23) and then the hearts of those given you to love. Otherwise you, and certainly they, will come under the subtle control of the kingdom of darkness, whose favorite way to fight is covert.

In his book *Defeating Dark Angels*, Dr. Charles Kraft writes:

> Our churches are full of people in bondage, many of whom do not even know that believers are called by Jesus to set captives free. . . .
>
> One way or the other, many Christians remain ignorant of the enemy, his helpers and their schemes (2 Corinthians 2:11). . . . Demons cannot create something from nothing. They can only take advantage of what already exists. Emotional or spiritual problems provide the "garbage" that attracts the spiritual rats.[2]

In concept, overcoming is pretty simple: Get rid of the garbage—the lies that support the false-self system—and the "rats" starve.

What the Friends of Jesus Knew

Have you ever noticed the overtones of spiritual battle in the New Testament letters to the churches? Words like *enemy*, *battle*, *weapons*, *conflict*, and *evil*? Peter, James, John, and Paul warned their readers about the kingdom of darkness.

> Be alert and of sober mind. Your enemy the devil prowls around like a roaring lion looking for someone to devour. (1 Peter 5:8)

> So submit to [the authority of] God. Resist the devil [stand firm against him] and he will flee from you. (James 4:7 AMP)

> We know that anyone born of God does not continue to sin; the One who was born of God keeps them safe, and the evil one cannot harm them. We know that we are children of God, and that the whole world is under the control of the evil one. (1 John 5:18–19)

> God is strong, and he wants you strong. So take everything the Master has set out for you, well-made weapons of the best materials. And put them to use so you will be able to stand up to everything the Devil throws your way. . . . This is for keeps, a life-or-death fight to the finish against the Devil and all his angels. (Ephesians 6:10–12 MSG)

The New Testament Scriptures are full of such language, of exhortations and admonishments to "be careful," "pay attention," and "be courageous." The friends of Jesus knew. How did they come to know? Through experience. Through receiving firsthand teaching from Jesus, then watching Jesus encounter the enemy (i.e., demons), then experiencing their own encounters. This is how we too are to learn discernment and how to wield power and authority, enforce the kingdom's ways, defend against the opposition, and free those under the enemy's influence.

Really. The book of Acts reads like an old western where the good guys (the disciples) ride into town and the bad guys (the demons) duck for cover as the shoot-out begins. When the dust clears, townsfolk are amazed and grateful. "No worries ma'am, it's Jesus. It's all Jesus."

Every personal kingdom, yours and mine, needs an armory and tactics with which to fight. Why? To defend against attack. Because life outside the garden is a constant battle over what is false and what is true about you, God, and others.

Experiencing the love and life of Christ is the greatest confidence *in* battle and the greatest strategic weapon *for* battle that a man can possibly take *into* battle. It is what enables a man to fight *from* victory instead of *for* victory. Echoing 2 Corinthians 10:4, Neal Anderson, founder of Freedom in Christ Ministries, writes, "You can't outsmart or outmuscle the flesh or the devil on your own. Your weapons must be divinely powerful if you are going to win a spiritual conflict."[3] This is what the friends of Jesus know, practice, and enforce.

Training

With great intention, Jesus taught and brought the kingdom of God, and in doing so, he aggressively moved against both the spiritual and the physical establishments, for they are always intertwined. The Jewish religious leaders were taking people one direction; Jesus took them another. He allowed neither the Pharisees nor the Roman officials to dictate or deter his mission.

And he didn't take any crap from Satan or his fallen angels. They were the real enemy he came to overthrow. Jesus was no pacifist; he was a revolutionary. He fought simultaneously in both realms, the physical and the spiritual. Jesus told Peter in Matthew 16:19, "I will give you the keys of the kingdom of heaven; whatever you bind on earth will be bound in heaven, and whatever you loose on earth will be loosed in heaven." That's how it works for us too: position, power, and authority; binding and loosing.

Paul wrote, "We can break down what people think and every big idea that tries to stop people from knowing [experiencing] God. And we can make every thought a prisoner to obey Christ" (2 Corinthians 10:5 WE, my insertion). Do you know how to do this? Apparently, we are supposed to.

As with any skill, practice makes perfect. What voices are you contending with? When was the last time you demolished a stronghold or took a thought captive? What accusations, insults, and diminishments have you grown used to and are tolerating, allowing them to influence your choices and behavior? You have already been trained; the question is, by whom and for what? The enemy have their training program too. Remember, not every thought is your own.

What Do They Have on You?

Though we live in the world, we do not wage war as the world does. The
weapons we fight with are not the weapons of the world. On the contrary, they have divine power to demolish strongholds. We demolish
arguments and every pretension that sets itself up against the knowledge
of God, and we take captive every thought to make it obedient to Christ.
(2 Corinthians 10:3–5)

What you believe matters. Believe lies and those lies have authority over your
life. Believe the truth and you live free. Most of the lies got implanted along the way;
therefore the truth seldom just takes over. For there is a force behind sinning: spirits
who hate you and work with their "man on the inside," your false self, to bind and
control your will. They are hell-bent on stealing your worth, shackling your true self,
and infiltrating your kingdom, usurping authority over it by having authority over
you. Thereby they also strategically position themselves for the next generation, and
the next, and the next.

So . . . what are the father of lies and his fallen angels up to in your life? If you're
not sure, then in my experience you and your kingdom are already in trouble. "There
is no neutral ground in the universe," wrote C. S. Lewis. "Every square inch, every
split second, is claimed by God and counter-claimed Satan."[4] Because in this world,
there is a deliberateness behind "random" acts of violence, constant inconveniences,
and people sinning against one another (for the false self is all about influencing
people to sin).

Neal Anderson was one of the first to pull back the veil on spiritual warfare and
provide desperately needed training. He writes, "The major strategy of Satan is to
distort the character of God and the truth of who we are. He can't change God and
he can't do anything to change our identity and position in Christ. If, however, he
can get us to believe a lie, we will live as though our identity in Christ isn't true."[5]
Understand this and you're moving in the right direction.

Often when I'm sharing with a church audience about warfare, I'll ask, "How
many of you believe there is a Satan, foul spirits, and a kingdom of darkness?"
Hands fly up and heads nod. Then I ask, "So, what do you believe they have on you?
What are they doing to personally and specifically thwart you?" It gets pretty quiet.
Deer in the headlights—a whole herd.

General concepts and principles about spiritual warfare *are* helpful, just like the safety pamphlet in the seat back of an airplane is helpful. But what is more helpful is seeing the warfare for yourself. If you can't observe what the enemy are doing to you, you can't and won't fight. What do they have on you? What are they using? What are they doing to isolate you and separate you from receiving love?

Everyone has a history with the enemy (we spent six chapters looking at yours), but most have no idea how darkness has infected their life. This must change for freedom to be yours and for that freedom to be protected. You can own a house, car, computer, or bank account, but that doesn't mean someone isn't going to break in and try to steal. So it is with your heart.

Dark Spirits

"Dementors," created by J. K. Rowling for her Harry Potter series, latch on like leeches to their victims and suck all the happiness, hope, and life from their souls. Where did Rowling get the idea for such a character?

From our story.

When God created both heavenly and human beings, he created them eternal, but he didn't create them bad. Rather, he gave them the will and ability to choose. Satan and his fallen angels chose independence from God and thus became in character everything God is not. Yet darkness was still permitted to exist. Satan was allowed in the garden—and that's where many of us still keep him in our thinking. Despite overwhelming evidence both in the Bible and in the daily headlines, we've come to believe the prince of this dark world and his minions aren't active in our world today. That's their great achievement: getting us to buy the lie "We're not here."

You are being watched by unsympathetic eyes. Profiled, stalked, and hunted. You need to be just as observant. You have to see the snake before you can kill the snake. Dr. Ed Murphy writes, "Areas of [many Spirit-filled believers'] lives are in bondage to feelings, thoughts, and practices not compatible with their Christian faith. They know something is wrong, but few suspect the possibility of a direct demonic dimension to their problem. . . . It was also true of me. . . . I was ignorant of the operations of the evil spirit world."[6]

The earth—that is, this present world system—still belongs to Satan. But we belong to God. The apostle John says it plainly: "We know that we are children of

God, and that the whole world is under the control of the evil one" (1 John 5:19). Satan wants to deceive us into thinking we are his to control. But his method is all thick, dark smoke and sophisticated distorting mirrors intended to get us to make agreements with the lies of fear, guilt, and shame.

This is about far more than sinning or being sinned against. It is about claims on your life through the beliefs that drive or control it. How you interpret your experiences is what you will come to believe about yourself, God, and the world. It's how this war works and how it is to be fought. So it is imperative that a good king reclaim his will, learn to exercise it, and take on the constant and vigilant posture, "I will not be used. I will not be on the wrong side."

How Demons Work

The systematic theology taught in seminaries across the country does nothing to prepare pastors and biblical counselors—who daily teach and treat the hearts in pews and in their offices—to deal with demons. Yet the Bible consistently portrays their reality. They have no right to "possess" children of God who are filled with his Spirit, but their campaign to influence us is all too real. Their goal is control, and they'll take as much as we allow them.

So we need to be wise to their tactics and alert to their efforts (see 2 Corinthians 2:11). Charles Kraft writes, "While we need to be careful not to go to the extreme of blaming everything on demonization, we also need solid instruction concerning the important role demons play in sabotaging lives."[7]

That has been my own experience. Working with men the past two decades and seeing God bring healing and freedom has been an honor. Yet too many men were taking back lost ground only to lose it again months or years later. So I asked Jesus, "What am I missing? Is there something more I need to know?" His answer: demons. Jesus wanted to take me into a new training circle, introduce me to some new teachers and the realm of deliverance.

There are four ways demons can gain a foothold:[8]

1. *Conscious Invitation.* Some people literally and intentionally open themselves up to the presence and work of demons by inviting them in, "making deals with the devil."

2. *Invitation of Someone in Authority.* When messages from those who

mishandle our hearts lead us to agree with lies and respond with vows, demons actively support the results.

3. *Inheritance.* Ancestral sin can open the door for demons to work in a family tree, perpetuating generational curses of punishment, addiction, and moral failure in children and grandchildren.

4. *Cursing.* Judgmental or critical words spoken over you in your presence, or even in your absence, can powerfully influence your life. This also applies to the person doing the judging and criticizing. Cursing rather than blessing enables spirits to traffic between two people, creating a tie that binds and compromises both image bearers.[9]

VERY IMPORTANT: The process of deliverance doesn't start with going head-to-head with demons. It starts with healing. Healing has everything to do with exercising our authority in Christ in the spiritual realm.

Our Greatest Weapons

The great Chinese church leader Watchman Nee wrote, "Satan often uses the flesh to secure the consent of man, yet in each instance of enticement the enemy creates some kind of thought by which to induce the man. We cannot separate temptation and thought. All temptations are offered us in the form of thoughts. Since the latter are so exposed to the power of darkness, we need to learn how to guard against them."[10]

One of our greatest weapons is discernment; one of the enemy's greatest weapons is our lack of it. Another powerful weapon is our will. If you've never thought about this, it is likely you've also never really used your will against your enemy. Rather, they are probably using your will to see theirs done. You've got to consciously engage your will; other wise, you're running on the autopilot of your false self, guaranteed. And the enemy will use your false self to summon or collide into someone else's false self, and vice versa. That's how they operate.

Our greatest weapon of all is love, with all it implies: validation, worth, significance, belonging, and more. When we receive these things from God, then we can offer them to others on behalf of God. They're the countermeasure to the lies. Experiencing God's love is the first step toward healing, restoration, and, finally, transformation.

Taking out the garbage of lies gives us the opportunity to take out the rats as well and cancels their permission to be in our life. It's our first and best move. God has already made all the arrangements for rat removal. He is just waiting for us to discern where they are and engage our will with his offer to eradicate them.

Bringing the Cross and Resurrection

Learning requires failure. And life is full of learning. Few of us get something right the first time, and that's OK. Mistakes aren't necessarily sin. And when they are sin, payment has been made through the cross so we might learn the power of the cross. That is why the enemy hates the cross. Colossians 2:15 says,

> When He [Jesus] had disarmed the rulers and authorities [those supernatural forces of evil operating against us], He made a public example of them [exhibiting them as captives in His triumphal procession], having triumphed over them through the cross. (AMP, first brackets mine)

> He stripped all the spiritual tyrants in the universe of their sham authority at the Cross and marched them naked through the streets. (MSG)

Come on! The agents of shame, shamed? That's good stuff! Don't you love it when the villain gets his comeuppance—when the bullied finally gets the courage to swing back, and the bully takes one on the nose? When you see and exercise your power and authority against one of Satan's little, dark henchmen, you'll know when it works. You'll see and feel the shift. Bring the cross and demons have to submit.

Darkness also hates the resurrection. The life of God, the river of life, is in you, and it is to flow through you. Remember Jesus's promise: "I have come that [you] may have life, and have it to the full" (John 10:10). That's capital-*L* Life. Abundant Life is the offer of Christianity. It's what the enemy seeks to prevent you from having. But the cross defeats the enemy, and the resurrection makes sure they don't forget it. The question is, will we enforce it? You must claim the cross and resurrection.

How?

Declare it.

Speak it out loud against your enemy: "I take my place in your cross and resurrection, Lord Jesus. I claim its power and authority in my life, and through the work of the cross and resurrection, I declare my value and worth as my Father's beloved.

And I declare as well that my power and authority as God's agent in this world comes from and through the love of Christ for me and the life of God in me."

Give it a shot. Say it. Pray it out loud. How does it feel? Anything but good might be an indication your enemies are whispering what they can to make you feel silly or believe you are somehow unqualified. Not true. And now you know what to do.

Intimacy: The Key to Overcoming

Back in his college days, my friend Jim approached a cute girl at a party. After a moment of introduction and flirting, the gal's jealous boyfriend showed up. "Hey, what do you think you're doing? Trying to move in on my girl?"

Jim, now aware of the situation, backpedaled and apologized. But the boyfriend, still offended, asked Jim if he wanted to fight. Astonished, Jim replied no.

"Well, then, put your hands in your pockets."

Jim complied . . . and received a knockout punch in return.

The moral of the story: Never put your hands in your pockets during a confrontation.

Putting my hands in my pockets was exactly what I learned to do when intimidation, accusation, guilt, shame, and fear came calling. When you do what they say, it's only a matter of time before you're on the floor, wondering what the hell just happened. But they can only fight within the boundaries of how the battle works. They have dirty tricks, you bet, but they are not fighting unfairly. The opposite is actually true: We're the ones with the upper hand. Through Christ, the odds are stacked in our favor.

The authority is on your side as a son of God. It's not a fair fight—*if* you know how to fight. Fourteen times in the New Testament we are called overcomers. Being an overcomer in Christ implies there is something to overcome—and someone. Not just sin, not just false beliefs, but *them*: agents of darkness that work to create the false self and empower it with a constant diet of lies. But we don't have to live disoriented—ignorant, naïve, confused, and therefore oppressed.

"I'm not afraid of the devil," wrote Tozer. "The devil can handle me—he's got judo I never heard of. But he can't handle the One to whom I'm joined; he can't handle the One to whom I'm united; he can't handle the One whose nature dwells in my nature."[11]

Here, then, is the key: Overcoming, defending, and providing for your kingdom depend on your intimacy with God.

That's how God designed us to operate. "God's Way is not a matter of mere talk; it's an empowered life" (1 Corinthians 4:20 MSG).

Jesus, the Second Adam,[12] reclaimed what the first Adam gave away. This includes your ability to effectively and powerfully fulfill your roles and assignments in life, especially those of husband and father. In all circumstances, Jesus makes it possible for you to offer your glory as you walk intimately with him. And when you are attacked, when the enemy makes an attempt on your Life, you have both the heart and the equipment to fight back.

* * *

The ultimate answer to all our questions is, walk intimately with God. Listen for him. Pay attention. "If any of you lacks wisdom, you should ask God" (James 1:5). That's how wisdom is gained—by asking God. He speaks, we listen, then we move and we learn. This is to be the normal Christian life. There is always more going on than first meets the eye; therefore, a king must learn wisdom and discernment.

The more spiritually alert you are, the greater becomes your ability to discern. Then you can preemptively take the fight to the enemy. It's a great day when a man moves from defense to offense.

The Problem of Forgiveness

There's a reason I have waited till now to discuss in depth one of our most incalculably powerful weapons against the enemy. Forgiveness is often misunderstood and glibly prescribed in ways that can intensify a wound rather than heal it. And because of the depth of pain many of us have experienced, it can be an emotionally charged topic.

Asking a man to forgive before he is ready—before he has processed the wound, its message, the agreement, and the vow; and before he has understood what forgiveness looks like and does *not* look like—well, it's just not kind. It places a heavy burden on a heart that is already struggling. And it doesn't work.

Let's be clear about the level of forgiveness we're talking about. There's a huge difference between accepting a friend's apology for showing up late for coffee versus forgiving a parent's emotional, physical, or sexual abuse. The one is barely a scratch on the skin; the other is a knife through the heart. With the first example, "That's OK" is usually an appropriate response.* With the second, the way we were treated was by no means OK, and it was—and is—a very big deal. That kind of forgiveness is costly, particularly if the person denies any wrongdoing and shows no remorse for the damage he or she has done and might still be doing to us.

How do we forgive that kind of evil? How do we even start?

We'll search out answers in the next few sections. But let's begin with two reassurances:

- Your own heart is paramount and needs to be treated kindly. The person who hurt you is not more important than you.

- You are deeply loved by God. He understands—and he is with you and for you.

Please keep those two truths always in mind, because they're essential. And with that understanding, let's move forward, beginning by looking at what forgiveness is and clearing up a couple common misconceptions that keep people stuck in unforgiveness. It's crucial to get an accurate understanding, because forgiveness is part of your road to freedom. I'm not saying it's easy. Rightly understood, though, it's not one more weight to bear but, ultimately, a weight removed.

What Forgiveness Means

What is forgiveness, anyway? Webster's gives these senses of the word *forgive*: "to cease to feel resentment against (an offender) . . . to give up resentment of or claim to requital for."[13] The idea is, someone did something to us that puts them in our debt emotionally and relationally. But whatever the debt may be, we choose to relinquish our right to collect.

When someone wounds our heart, the hurting part inside us cries out for compensation. We need something either *from* the offender, like an apology, or *for* the offender, like punishment for what they did to us. Forgiveness takes that desire for payback and places it in God's hands. Far from minimizing or excusing the other person's words or actions, forgiveness requires an honest reckoning of their impact

---

* The exception is if an otherwise trivial incident fits into a what seems like a larger pattern of disrespect. In that case, a conversation may be in order so both of you can get clear.

on us. Then it says, "What you did to me was wrong, but I choose not to require payment. I give you to God and to the consequences of your words, actions, and choices."

Those who wound us *will* be held responsible. Just not by us.

By taking that stance, we entrust our need for justice to the only One who sees both us and that other person with complete clarity. I like how the Message renders the apostle Paul's words: "Don't insist on getting even; that's not for you to do. 'I'll do the judging,' says God. 'I'll take care of it'" (Romans 12:19).

Of course, we've got to believe God means what he says. Forgiveness is an act of faith. And rooted in faith, it also becomes a powerful act of our will, setting in motion healing, redemption, and freedom. By forgiving, we declare, "My heart belongs to God and to me. I will not let its well-being depend on the actions and attitudes of another person."

Two Things Forgiveness Does *Not* Mean

There's no cut-and-dried method for forgiveness, any more than there is for other aspects of healing. Sometimes forgiveness happens in a moment, in a flash of understanding and grace (the empowering presence of God to transform us). Other times, it's a difficult process. Either way, it'll help to dispel a couple misconceptions.

Forgiving Does Not Require Reconciliation

It's wonderful when forgiveness leads to the restoration of relationship. Sometimes it does, and the relationship may turn out better than ever because of the honesty, care, and courage involved.

However . . .

Some individuals are fundamentally harmful. People with certain personality disorders thrive on control, excel at deception, and enjoy hurting others. You're not going to change such a person, and it's not your mission to try. So note carefully:

Forgiveness does not require you to expose yourself to further abuse.

Please don't do it.

It's one thing to forgive a vicious dog for biting you, but for goodness' sake, don't climb back into the kennel with it. Or as Jesus put it, "Do not give what is holy to the dogs; nor cast your pearls before swine, lest they trample them under their feet, and turn and tear you in pieces" (Matthew 7:6 NKJV).

You don't need to trust the other person in order to forgive them. You do need to trust them to have a healthy relationship with them. So remember:

Forgiveness depends on you. It's entirely your choice to forgive . . . or not.

Reconciliation depends on them. It's up to the other person to earn your trust by showing themselves trustworthy.

The first goal of forgiveness is not to restore a difficult relationship. It's not even (no matter who insists it should be your priority) to save your marriage. It's to grieve, honor yourself, and go with Jesus to get part of your heart back. At some point, forgiveness will be part of that journey. It can make reconciliation possible, but it's no guarantee. Much depends on the other person, not just you. And that's not the point. The point is to unhook that person's hold on your heart. The point is freedom—for you and maybe someday for them.

Forgiving Does Not Mean Forgetting

You know that old maxim, "Forgive and forget"? How are you supposed to do that second half—the bit about forgetting?

Part of healing, and certainly of forgiving, requires you to remember what happened to you. You can't forgive what you don't remember. And forgiving doesn't erase the memory of what happened from your brain—it just loosens that event's grip on you as you loosen yours on it, and gives you a better way of viewing it. Now instead of a place of pain, it can become an overcoming, a victory in your life and a source of wisdom.

The virtue of a life experience doesn't come from forgetting it happened but from letting God use it to shape your character, your faith, and your insight into your life and the lives of others. Forgiveness weaves the darker threads of your story into the tapestry of your glory. Don't let those hard parts go to waste. Use them for the kingdom. It's like capturing the enemies' munitions and using them to shoot back.

The Power and Process of Forgiving

Unforgiveness holds on to blame and resentment, anger and pain, until they have a hold on you. It's like trying to punish the offender by locking yourself in prison. You're the one paying. You're the one still hurting over what was done to you.

You're the one who relives the pain whenever you're triggered by anyone or any-thing that symbolizes the wounder and the wound. Carrying all that ungrieved and unresolved hurt gets really, really heavy. That's why Lewis B. Smedes, one of the most prolific writers on forgiveness in the twenty-first century, wrote, "To forgive is to set a prisoner free and discover that the prisoner is me."[14]

Jesus, the author of life and the authority on love, is also the creative, compas-sionate designer of forgiveness. He knows that forgiveness is a part of loving relation-ships and is essential to our doing life together. Jesus died to get that point across. That's why Paul could write, "Bear with each other and forgive one another if any of you has a grievance against someone. Forgive as the Lord forgave you" (Colossians 3:13).

Forgiveness is a *huge* deal. It cost the Father his Son and Jesus his life, for the cross was its purchase price. What God did for us, we need to do for others—because all of us make mistakes, sin, and wound others. We all need to experience having our feet washed so we can learn how to wash others' feet. And we all will be invited to forgive our wounders as Jesus forgave his on the cross.

Few things are as strong and loving as forgiving. It is as far from passivity as the east is from the west. In an interview with Steve Harvey, Bishop T. D. Jakes said, "We think that forgiveness is weakness, but it's absolutely not; it takes a very strong person to forgive." Your kingdom needs forgiveness, and you need to know how it works, how to offer it, and certainly how to receive it. Sow forgiveness into your realm, and the gardens of life and love all around your kingdom will flourish.

* * *

Jesus talked about forgiveness a lot. It is one of the kingdom's secret weapons that isn't supposed to be a secret. It's meant to be part of our growing skill set as beloved sons. Yet when was the last time you forgave someone for what they did to you? When was the last time you asked someone to forgive you?

Oh, we dip our toe into the shallows now and then by saying "I'm sorry," but even there we struggle. Forgiveness—both granting it and seeking it—is a vulnerable place for men to go in their relationships. I keep a list in my own heart of those who have wronged me or hurt my family. The names don't come up often, but when one does, I am very aware of how I feel, how my body reacts, and where my thoughts go. Whether that person hurt me decades ago or just the other day, reliving the pain puts me at a crossroads. I can accept the enemy's invitation to unforgiveness, which produces anger, fear, and shame. Their goal: getting my false self to maintain and perpetuate the wounding. Or I can give the pain to God, as often as it comes up and as often as it takes, to see forgiveness accomplished. Those crossroad moments are always an invitation to either more hurt or more healing.

Forgiveness, you see, is often a process. True, it can sometimes happen in a moment and completely. But often we experience its release over time as choice builds upon choice to forgive. The journey begins with a single step, and that first step may be the hardest. It could be as basic as asking yourself this question: If I had the power to punish the offender or, at the extreme, send that person to hell . . . would I? If you can answer no to at least one of those options, you're on your way.

* * *

"How many times must I forgive?" Peter asked Jesus. "Seventy times seven," Jesus answered. In other words, "As often as it takes until you've got the job done."*

Wounding and sin are very serious in the kingdom, and therefore so is forgiveness. In order to pull it off, we need an advocate, someone who modeled it to whom we can entrust our pain. That's Jesus. Declaring to him, "I no longer require payment," surrenders the matter and the other person to the Lord. Forgiveness is his relief program—and yours.

One of the Most Loving Things We Can Do

It hurts to be hurt, and anger is a natural response. Can we be angry? Sure, absolutely, and we need to be real about it, not stuff it. The danger is when anger crosses the line into resentment, judgment, rage, and even revenge. That is why Paul wrote,

> Be angry [at sin—at immorality, at injustice, at ungodly behavior], yet do
> not sin; do not let your anger [cause you shame, nor allow it to] last until
> the sun goes down. And do not give the devil an opportunity [to lead you
> into sin by holding a grudge, or nurturing anger, or harboring resentment,
> or cultivating bitterness]. (Ephesians 4:26–27 AMP)

Jesus said in Luke 6:45, "A good man brings good things out of the good stored up in his heart, and an evil man brings evil things out of the evil stored up in his heart. For the mouth speaks what the heart is full of." So . . . what is stored up in

---

* Since the number seven in the Bible often signifies completion, Jesus's hyperbolic response says a lot in a mouthful.

your heart? Unforgiveness binds one life to another in a bad way. Forgiveness unties unhealthy bonds and allows God to work in two people.

* * *

My friend Tom was working on forgiving his dad, and he asked Jesus to weigh in. He did . . . in a way Tom didn't expect. Instead of telling him what he needed to forgive his dad for, Jesus kindly but plainly said, "You have judged him ruthlessly and mercilessly."

Tom knew his father wounds had led to agreements and vows, and those had bred the resentment that festered in him. Tom didn't just resent how his dad had made him feel. He resented who his dad was.

With tears, Tom laid down his right to be angry. It was a holy time and a holy prayer: "I release my dad. I forgive my dad for what he did and didn't do." Tom named those things specifically—and in letting go of them, he freed both his father and himself from the unforgiveness he had harbored so long. Tom said, "I knew something had lifted, shifted. I could feel it in my heart."

What happened next was wild. Something in the universe *had* shifted. A wound was treated and a blockage opened. The very next day, Tom's dad called him. Tom said, "My dad never calls me. We had the best conversation we've ever had, and I know why."

Choosing to freely forgive a wounder for what he or she did and how it has affected us is a powerful and courageous move of love. It brings part of our story to the surface, allowing God to bring the final elements of healing to our masculine heart and creating life-giving possibilities that otherwise would never exist.

It's been said that we want mercy for ourselves and justice for others. God wants those things too, but his idea of justice is based on a far, far greater knowledge than ours. Our wounders have a wounded past too, and God takes it into consideration. It doesn't excuse their mistreatment of us, but it can explain their behavior, or at least some of it. Understanding their story may release unexpected empathy, even mercy, in our heart and make it a little easier to forgive them.

Compassion says, "Not only would I not punish that person if I could, but I want them to experience God's love so they too can heal and become everything he created them to be."

Unforgiveness is a weapon of the enemy. Forgiveness is the weapon of a good king. Jesus not only taught forgiveness, but he practiced it in the most agonizing and unjust circumstances imaginable. It was on the cross that he spoke the words that have resounded throughout history: "Father, forgive them, for they know not what they do."

In Closing: A Benediction

You have crossed the checkerboard. You are a king with a kingdom. But you don't wear the crown for your benefit alone. There are many other players still on the board, some for you to fight for and some to fight against. You are a king at war. The war has been won, but you must go and claim your victory every day, everywhere, and in every way.

You cannot do this on your own. You need God, and you must learn to walk intimately with him. You also need friends—allies, other oriented kings, warriors, and elder-sages. The sooner you can find them, the better for you, your heart, and your kingdom, and for theirs.

Remember who you are.

Remember Whose you are.

Remember why you are—to be loved by God, to love others and fight for their hearts, and to reveal your God-given glory to the world around you.

Walk in the freedom, the wisdom, the life, the love, and the power and authority that flow from Jesus, the King of kings, to you. This is your new normal. For you are one of his kings—a royal presence on life's grand checkerboard, where your story connects with many others in the Larger Story of the kingdom.

My prayer for you is this ancient one:

May the Lord bless you and keep you.
May the Lord make his face to shine upon you and be gracious to you.
May the Lord lift up his countenance upon you and give you peace.

And may you reign and rule in fierce love,
like the One whose image you bear.

You are a good man becoming a good king.
Long live the king!

King Me

EPILOGUE

Teach us to number our days, that we may gain a heart of wisdom.
—*Psalm 90:12*

All shall be done, but it might be harder than you think.
—*Aslan*

The Scriptures tell us that in Christ, through Christ, and by Christ we are free. *Free.* "In him and through faith in him we may approach God with freedom and confidence" (Ephesians 3:12). The legislation has been passed in heaven. Yet freedom is far from practiced or enforced.

In this fallen and hostile world, freedom is more than threatened; it is accosted. Freedom is something we have, but freedom is also something we must fight for. You have to own something before you can protect it.

Freedom is the objective of the Christ follower, the kingdom man. Freedom is what good kings enjoy, offer, and defend. And freedom is the reason Jesus came. Quoting the prophet Isaiah, Jesus described his mission:

> "The Spirit of the Lord is on me,
> because he has anointed me
> to proclaim good news to the poor.
> He has sent me to proclaim freedom for the prisoners
> and recovery of sight for the blind,
> to set the oppressed free."
>
> (Luke 4:18)

Jesus paid a great price to fulfill that prophecy and obtain our freedom. Life with God is to be lived *free*.

It is for freedom that Christ has set us free. Stand firm, then, and do not let yourselves be burdened again by a yoke of slavery. (Galatians 5:1)

I like how my friend Tom often shares it: "Freedom is the ability to exercise our will for good." It's why Paul wrote to the Romans, "Don't let evil get the best of you; get the best of evil by doing good" (Romans 12:21 MSG).

Overcoming evil with good—that is the job of a good king. It is our Father's invitation to us. And a heart free to accept and fulfill that invitation becomes a man dangerous for good.

You Will Be Tested

In 1892, sixty thousand people—more than the capacity of Yankee Stadium—attended the three-day memorial for a man widely regarded as the finest preacher of the nineteenth century: Charles Spurgeon. It was Spurgeon who wrote, "The trumpet still sounds the note of war. You may not yet sit down and bind the wreath of victory about your brow—no garlands of laurel and songs of victory for you, yet—you have still to wear the helmet and bear the sword. You must still watch and pray, and fight."[1]

Spurgeon's words express a profound truth. Apart from it, life will not make sense. You will misinterpret and mishandle your life and the lives entrusted to you again and again unless you view them in the context of war. Lacking orientation in the ways of the kingdom, you will pray for the wrong things; you will say and do the wrong things; and worst of all, you will be unable to receive God's counsel against the ploys of the enemy. You will remain disoriented. It is that simple.

The lack of orientation is everywhere. So consider these five truths in the journey of becoming a good king:

1. God is at work.

2. You are his son.

3. We are at war.

4. Orientation, healing, and training take time.

5. It's all about freedom.

Each stage of the masculine journey has its warfare, and therefore each stage has its woundings. No one gets through this journey unscathed. Too many things have happened to you that are not good. Sin never is.

If we could fix it on our own, there would be way more settled, strong, and kind men moving about the planet. Right now, that is not, the case. Most men are still asleep. But you are not most men. I pray that by now, if you've arrived at this page, you are well on your way to being an oriented man. A man living like Jesus, with nothing to hide, nothing to prove, and nothing to fear.

God isn't done with you, and therefore, neither is your enemy. For all we've tried to tame the Christian life with theology and academics, it remains wild and dangerous, wonderful and hard, an adventure to be taken and a battle to be fought. It is far from tame.

Until He Returns . . .

From time to time I must be reminded that this present world is not my home. It is not yours either. Our home is being built, and when it is ready, Jesus will return. "As lightning that comes from the east is visible even in the west, so will be the coming of the Son of Man" (Matthew 24:27). Oh, what a day that will be! The Savior of the world, the King of all kings, will appear and end suffering, wounding, and pain, end this war, end the fallenness. Scripture says we will be changed in a moment, and a new heaven and new earth will appear.[2]

Paul looked forward to that day when he wrote to Timothy,

> In the future there is reserved for me the [victor's] crown of righteous-
> ness [for being right with God and doing right], which the Lord, the
> righteous Judge, will award to me on that [great] day—and not to me only,
> but also to all those who have loved and longed for and welcomed His
> appearing. (2 Timothy 4:8 AMP)

This is what we long for because it is what we were made for. Until then, we live with hope, struggle forward, fight the good fight, heed the warnings, and learn how to love and lead, provide and protect, reign and rule—for these are the things a good king does.

Becoming such a king takes practice. Learning how to reign and rule means recovering from our past and being prepared for what lies ahead. It is complicated, even overwhelming for a time, but the extraordinary life we were made for is worth learning. The storms, trials, and struggles are for the remaking of you and me. One day it will be done. The work of restoration will be accomplished. And we will finally see Jesus face to face.

Until then—until the parting of the eastern sky ends the Great War, and the celebration that never ends begins; until all things are remade like new, and the enemy's desolation is swallowed up by God's restoration and a world made perfect— we practice, we train, we fight. We look for God in every moment of every situation, trusting that he is wanting to entrust us with more.

The great question now is, Knowing what you know, how will you live among those who don't?

The answer: Lovingly. Kindly. Patiently.

Jesus said, "I am coming soon. Hold on to what you have, so that no one will take away your crown" (Revelation 3:11 NLT). Wait, crowns can be taken? Yes, they can. But you can do this, friend. Together with God, you can *over*come and *be*come, so that you can be entrusted with more. It's the kingdom way. God's love is unconditional, but his trust has conditions.

So, as a good king, remember this:

God *wants* you.
Hearts *need* you.
And lives are *depending* on you.

You were made to be loved and to reign with Christ forever and ever.
And forever starts now.

THERE WILL NO LONGER BE NIGHT; THEY HAVE NO NEED
FOR LAMPLIGHT OR SUNLIGHT, BECAUSE THE LORD GOD
WILL ILLUMINE THEM; AND THEY WILL REIGN [AS KINGS]
FOREVER AND EVER.

—REVELATION 22:5 (AMP)

Acknowledgments

Life is a team sport. We were never meant to go it alone. Yet since it is in relationships that we often get hurt, every man is in need of a great comeback. To see the restoration of his heart, a man needs trusted teammates to walk alongside him, caring, listening, provoking, and loving him back to life. There is no greater team with whom to partner than the Trinity. The triune God made us for himself, and in him we find our way home. Thank you, Father, Son, and Spirit, for loving and leading me on this journey of intimacy with you—a journey on which I am becoming more and more my true self.

Thank you, Robin, for three-decades-plus of walking with me and with God. Thanks for teaching me how to listen to the music of the kingdom, sing the words of hope, and learn the steps of love. Your queenly ways invite me again and again to be a good king.

Thank you, Ashley, Hannah, and Abbey, for your patience, kindness, and love. Thank you for all the second chances that have empowered me to do better and be better. You are each beautiful inside and out, and it is an honor to call you my daughters and watch you grow in strength and kindness. You are the best part of my kingdom.

Thank you to my friend and editor, Bob. You are an amazing king and well on your way to becoming one of the great elder-sages. You make things better—words, books, and me. And thanks to my brother in arms, Cole, who makes words, formatting, and graphics look easy. That's a big part of your glory, my friend.

Thank you, Brothers. You know who you are—the like-hearted, moving in the same direction. Each of you is a gift to me. You are the men the Trinity most often partners with to deliver goodness to my heart.

And finally, to the Zoweh Team in the trenches: to you who are aspiring to live in redemptive community in a kingdom God has entrusted to us as both students and teachers, and as friends, kings, and queens—thank you. You are the hearts God so often partners with to train me in becoming a good king, dangerous for good.

Notes

Chapter 1: The Hope of Every Boy's Heart

[1] Oswald Chambers, *My Utmost for His Highest, Updated Edition,* ed. James Reimann (Grand Rapids: Discovery House, 2005), January 16.

[2] Michael Thompson, *The Heart of a Warrior: Before You Can Become the Warrior, You Must Become the Beloved Son* (Grand Rapids: Heart & Life, 2015); John Eldredge, *Wild at Heart: Discovering the Secret of a Man's Soul* (Nashville: Thomas Nelson, 2001).

[3] From a November 2003 talk by Eldredge at Young Life's Frontier Ranch in Frazier, CO.

[4] C. S. Lewis, *God in the Dock: Essays on Theology and Ethics, ed. Walter Hooper* (Grand Rapids: Eerdmans, 2014), 108. First pub. as *Undeceptions: Essays on Theology and Ethics* (London: Bles, 1971).

[5] C. S. Lewis, *The Problem of Pain* (New York: Macmillan, 1944; HarperCollins, 2001), 47. The 2001 edition is the one cited.

[6] Dictionary.com, s.v., "initiation," accessed May 26, 2022, https://www.dictionary.com/browse/initiation.

Chapter 2: Good Kings

[1] See Gen. 1:26, 28.

[2] *Merriam-Webster's Collegiate Dictionary*, 11th ed. (2003), s.v. "lord."

[3] Dallas Willard, *The Divine Conspiracy: Rediscovering Our Hidden Life in God* (New York: Harper Collins, 1998), 25.

[4] This and the preceding quote are taken from *Rocky Balboa*, directed and written by Sylvester Stallone, starring Stallone, Burt Young, and Antonia Tarver (Metro-Goldwyn-Mayer, Columbia Pictures, and Revolution Studios, 2006).

[5] Dallas Willard, *Hearing God: Developing a Conversational Relationship with God*, rev. ed. (Downer's Grove, IL: InterVarsity Press, 2012), 35.

[6] Willard, *Hearing God*, 39.

Chapter 3: The King of Kings

[1] Dallas Willard, *The Great Omission: Reclaiming Jesus's Essential Teachings on Discipleship* (New York: HarperOne, 2006), 7.

[2] Willard, *Great Omission*, 94.

[3] C. S. Lewis, *The Joyful Christian: 127 Readings* (New York: Touchstone, 1996), 50.

[4] N. T. Wright, "Look at Jesus," The Work of the People, video, 3:44, accessed November 3, 2022, https://www.theworkofthepeople.com/look-at-jesus.

[5] Oswald Chambers, *Bringing Sons Into Glory: Studies in the Life of Our Lord*, 2nd ed. (Grand Rapids: Our Daily Bread, 2020), 17.

[6] John Eldredge, *Beautiful Outlaw: Experiencing the Playful, Disruptive, Extravagant Personality of Jesus* (New York: FaithWords, 2011), 139–40.

[7] Cf. Luke 3:22 and 4:3.

[8] See Matthew 4:8–10.

[9] See Luke 4:23–27.

[10] C. S. Lewis, *Mere Christianity* (New York: HarperCollins, 2001), 46.

[11] Dallas Willard, *Hearing God: Developing a Conversational Relationship with God* (Westmont, IL: InterVarsity Press, 1999), 108.

[12] Lewis, *Mere Christianity*, 225–26.

[13] George MacDonald, *Knowing the Heart of God: Devotional Selections from Sermons, Novels, and Poems of George MacDonald*, ed. Michael Philips (New York: Rosetta Books, 1996) 176, 381.

[14] Eldredge, *Beautiful Outlaw*, 11.

[15] Dallas Willard, quoted in John Ortberg, *Soul Keeping: Caring for the Most Important Part of You* (Grand Rapids: Zondervan, 2014), 23.

Chapter 4: The Larger Story

[1] Madeleine L'Engle, *Herself: Reflections on a Writing Life* (New York: Crown, 2001), 360.

[2] Sue Monk Kidd, *The Secret Life of Bees* (New York: Penguin, 2002), 158.

[3] C. S. Lewis, *God in the Dock: Essays on Theology and Ethics,* ed. Walter Hooper (Grand Rapids: Eerdmans, 2014), 13. First pub. as *Undeceptions: Essays on Theology and Ethics* (London: Bles, 1971).

[4] J. R. R. Tolkien, *The Two Towers*, The Lord of the Rings, bk. 2 (George Allen & Unwin, 1954; New York: Houghton Mifflin Harcourt, 1993), 320–21. Quote is from the Houghton Mifflin Harcourt edition.

[5] The first two brackets are my insertions. The last bracket is part of the AMP text.

[6] John Eldredge, *Wild at Heart: Discovering the Secret of a Man's Soul* (Nashville: Thomas Nelson, 2001), 67.

[7] Jonathan Edwards, *Jonathan Edwards on Evangelism*, ed. Carl Wolf (Eugene, OR: Wipf and Stock, 2013), 86.

[8] George MacDonald, *The Hope of the Gospel* (London: Ward, Lock, Bowden and Co., 1892), 4.

Chapter 5: The Heart of a King

[1] L. Frank Baum, *The Wonderful Wizard of Oz* (Orlinda, CA: SeaWolf, 2019), 42. First pub. 1900 by George M. Hill (Chicago).

[2] C. S. Lewis, *The Four Loves* (New York: Harcourt Brace, 1960), 155–56.

[3] Dan Allender, *To Be Told: God Invites You to Coauthor Your Future* (Colorado Springs: Waterbrook, 2005), 40.

[4] C. S. Lewis, *Mere Christianity* (New York: HarperCollins, 2001), 205.

[5] Gordon Dalby, Robert Hicks, and John Eldredge have written extensively about similar stages. See Gordon Dalby, *Healing the Masculine Soul: God's Restoration of Men to Manhood,* rev. ed. (Nashville: Thomas Nelson, 2003); Robert Hicks, *The Masculine Journey: Understanding the Six Stages of Manhood* (Colorado Springs: NavPress, 1993); and John Eldredge, *Fathered by God: Learning What Your Dad Could Never*

Teach You (Nashville: Thomas Nelson, 2009).

[6] Søren Kierkegaard, in Clare Calisle, *Philosopher of the Heart: The Restless Life of Søren Kierkegaard* (New York: Picador, 2019), 15.

Chapter 6: Boyhood

[1] Antoine de Saint-Exupéry, *The Little Prince* (Hawthorne, CA: BN Publishing, 2010), from the dedication.

[2] Henri Nouwen, *The Life of the Beloved: Spiritual Living in a Secular World* (New York: Crossroad, 2002), 12.

[3] From a November 2003 talk by Eldredge at Young Life's Frontier Ranch in Frazier, CO.

Chapter 7: Explorer and Warrior

[1] C. S. Lewis, *On Stories: And Other Essays on Literature.* (Boston: Houghton Mifflin Harcourt, 2002), 39.

[2] Sreechinth C, *Wisdom of Native American Legends: Sayings of Wooden Leg, Red Cloud, Sitting Bull, Black Elk, Quanah Parker, Red Cloud, and Others* (Wiefelstede: UB Tech, 2018), 33.

[3] G. K. Chesterton, The Society of G.K. Chesterton website, accessed June 14, 2022, https://www.chesterton.org/quotations/war-and-politics/, quoted from *Illustrated London News*, January 14, 1911.

[4] Robert Bly, *Iron John: A Book about Men*, 3rd ed. (Boston: Da Capo, 2004), 158.

Chapter 8: Lover

[1] Herbert Kretzmer, "Bring Him Home," original French lyrics by Alain Boublil, from the stage play *Les Miserables* (English adaptation, London: Cameron Mackintosh, 1985). Based on the 1862 novel by Victor Hugo.

[2] Brent Curtis and John Eldredge, *The Sacred Romance: Drawing Closer to the Heart of God* (Nashville: Thomas Nelson, 1997), 147.

[3] Robert Bly, James Hillman, and Michael Meade, eds., *The Rag and Bone Shop of the Heart: A Poetry Anthology* (New York: HarperCollins, 1992), 3.

[4] Proverbs 16:22. The KJV calls it a "wellspring."

[5] Statistics per The Recovery Village, https://www.therecoveryvillage.com/process-addiction/porn-addiction/pornography-statistics/; "20 Stats About the Porn Industry and Its Underage Customers," June 14, 2022, Fight the New Drug, https://fightthenewdrug.org/10-porn-stats-that-will-blow-your-mind/; Jeremy Wiles, "15 Mind-Blowing Statistics About Porn and the Church," July 11, 2022, Conquer Series, https://conquerseries.com/15-mind-blowing-statistics-about-pornography-and-the-church. All sites accessed July 28, 2022.

Chapter 9: King

[1] Francis Bacon, *The Philosophical Works of Francis Bacon,* ed. John M. Robertson (New York: E. P. Dutton, 1905), 747.

[2] Bob Goff, *Live in Grace, Walk in Love: A 365 Day Journey* (Nashville: Thomas Nelson, 2019), 87.

Chapter 10: Elder-Sage

[1] J. R. R. Tolkien, *The Return of the King* (New York: Random House, 1955), 160.

[2] C. S. Lewis, *Yours, Jack: Spiritual Direction from C. S. Lewis* (New York: HarperCollins,, 2008), 28.

[3] *Merriam-Webster*, s.v. "elder (*n.*)," accessed April 4, 2021, https://www.merriam-webster.com/dictionary/elder.

[4] *Merriam-Webster*, s.v. "sage (*n.*)," accessed April 4, 2021, https://www.merriam-webster.com/dictionary/sage.

[5] T. S. Eliot, *Four Quartets*, "Part II: East Coker," Philoctetes website, accessed April 13, 2021, http://philoctetes.org/documents/Eliot%20Poems.pdf.

[6] Robert Hicks, *The Masculine Journey: Understanding the Six Stages of Manhood* (Carol Stream, IL: NavPress, 1993), 22.

Chapter 11: The Healing Path: Trailhead

[1] Jane Travis, "12 Things I've Learned in 12 Years As a Counsellor," *Jane Travis* blog, accessed August 6, 2022, https://janetravis.com/10-lessons-ive-learned-in-10-years-as-a-counsellor/.

[2] Brené Brown, "Shame vs. Guilt," Brene's website, January 15, 2013, https://brenebrown.com/articles/2013/01/15/shame-v-guilt/.

[3] Dallas Willard, *Hearing God: Developing a Conversational Relationship with God*, rev. ed. (Downer's Grove, IL: InterVarsity Press, 2012), 20.

Chapter 12: Becoming You

[1] See Mark 2:1–12.

Chapter 14: The Glory of a King

[1] Rick Warren, *The Purpose-Driven Life: What on Earth Am I Here For?* (Grand Rapids: Zondervan, 2002), 21.

[2] C. S. Lewis, *The Weight of Glory: And Other Addresses* (New York: HarperOne, 2001; first pub. New York: Mcmillan, 1949), 46.

[3] Gary Barkalow, *It's Your Call: What Are You Doing Here?* (Colorado Springs: David C. Cook, 2010).

[4] *Les Misérables*, Scripts, 1998 screenplay based on the novel by Victor Hugo, directed by Billie August, written by Rafael Yglesias, accessed Nov. 6, 2021, https://www.scripts.com/script/les_miserables_12459.

[5] Gary Barkalow, *It's Your Call: What Are You Doing Here?* (Colorado Springs: David C. Cook, 2010), 60.

[6] Barkalow, *It's Your Call*, 63.

[7] Quote in the afterword of Viktor Frankl, *Man's Search for Meaning* (Boston: Beacon Press, 2006), 165. First English-language edition published in 1959 under the title *From Death-Camp to Existentialism*.

Chapter 15: The Queen

[1] Verena Dobnik, "Will New York Invite the 'Fearless Girl' Statue to Stay on Wall Street?," *USA Today*, March 27, 2017, https://www.usatoday.com/story/news/nation/2017/03/26/new-york-invite-fearless-girl-statue-stay-on-wall-street/99677644/.

[2] Stasi Eldredge, *Becoming Myself: Embracing God's Dream of You* (Colorado Springs: David C. Cook, 2013), 55.

[3] Jan Meyers Proett, *Beauty and the Bitch: Grace for the Worst in Me* (Colorado Springs: Bondfire Books, 2013), 5–6.

[4] "GNP/GNI by Country 2022," World Population Review, accessed October 24, 2022, https://worldpopulationreview.com/country-rankings/gnp-by-country.

[5] Figures derived from "The Real Price of Beauty in the US," *Booksy*, February 4, 2020, https://booksy.com/blog/us/the-real-price-of-beauty-in-the-us/#:~:text=%243 5.46%20on%20average.-,Cosmetics,month%2C%20or%20%241%2C380%2 per%20year.

[6] Ezekiel 28:12.

[7] *Cambridge Dictionary*, accessed December 5, 2021, s.v., "romance," https://dictionary.cambridge.org/us/dictionary/english/romance.

[8] See Ephesians 5:25–32 and Revelation 21:2. New Jerusalem is the church of Jesus Christ—you, me, and all our brothers and sisters in Christ.

[9] For eye-opening insights on how the Bible portrays woman as man's vital and coequal *ezer*, check out "God Created Woman As an Ezer Kind of Helper (Genesis 2:18)," *Theology of Work Project*, https://www.theologyofwork.org/key-topics/women-and-work-in-the-old-testament/god-created-woman-as-an-ezer-kind-of-helper-genesis-218.

Chapter 16: Heirs to the Throne

[1] This quote proliferates on the internet and is commonly attributed to Billy Graham, but I've been unable to track it down to one of his actual writings or speeches. Perhaps one of my readers can. It certainly has the ring of something Dr. Graham would have said.

Chapter 17: Kings at War

[1] Romans 12:21 AMPC.

[2] Charles Kraft, *Defeating Dark Angels: Breaking Demonic Oppression in the Believer's Life*, rev. ed. (Ada, MI: Chosen Books, 2016), 23, 50.

[3] Neal Anderson, *Victory Over the Darkness: Realize the Power of Your Identity in Christ*, rev. ed. (Ada, MI: Bethany House, 2020), 160.

[4] C. S. Lewis, *Christian Reflections* (Grand Rapids: Eerdmans, 1967), 33.

[5] Anderson, *Victory Over the Darkness*, 46.

[6] Edward Murphy, *The Handbook of Spiritual Warfare*, rev. ed. (Nashville: Thomas Nelson, 2003), *xv*.

[7] Kraft, *Dark Angels*, 153.

[8] While the following descriptions are mine, I owe thanks to Dr. Kraft for the four italicized terms and the concepts they reflect. See *Dark Angels*, 78–82.

[9] See, for instance, Luke 6:37 for Jesus's description of how judgment boomerangs on the judge. The Message puts it eloquently: "Don't pick on people, jump on their failures, criticize their faults—unless, of course, you want the same treatment. Don't condemn those who are down; that hardness can boomerang. Be easy on people; you'll find life a lot easier."

[10] Watchman Nee, *The Spiritual Man*, vol. 1 (Anaheim: Living Stream Ministry, 1998), 499.

[11] A. W. Tozer, *God's Greatest Gift to Man: Tozer's Very Last Sermon* (New York: Christian and Missionary Alliance, 1995), 28.

[12] See 1 Corinthians 15:22, 45.

[13] *Merriam-Webster*, s.v. "forgive," accessed February 27, 2022, https://www.merriam-webster.com/dictionary/forgive.

[14] Lewis Smedes, *Forgive and Forget: Healing the Hurts We Don't Deserve* (New York: HarperOne, 1996), 133.

Epilogue

[1] Charles Spurgeon, "Mature Faith—Illustrated by Abraham's Offering Up Isaac," in *Spurgeon's Sermons Volume 15: 1869*, ed. Anthony Uyl (Woodstock, ON: Devoted Publishing, 2017), 155.

[2] See, respectively, 1 Corinthians 15:51–52 and Revelation 21:1.

Also from Michael Thompson
and Zoweh

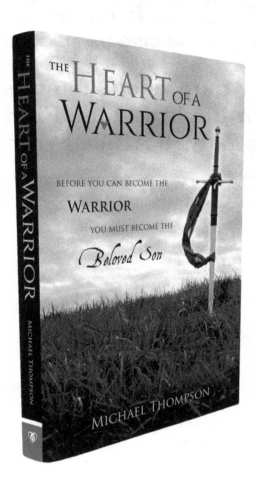

The Heart of a Warrior delivers a much-needed message to men!

- John Eldredge, bestselling author of *Wild at Heart*

RESCUING HEARTS

ZOWEH
ALLIES

ADVANCING THE KINGDOM

Every man needs friends and allies in his kingdom. Find yours on the Zoweh Allies Frontlines.

The mission of Zoweh Allies is to connect kindred hearts and invite men into deeper intimacy, oneness, and connectedness with God and each other through redemptive friendships, missions, and battles.

The Zoweh Allies Team also wants to partner with you to create a battle plan for the hearts of men wherever you meet with them—at church, at home, or out and about. Contact the Zoweh Allies Team for help creating a Battle Plan for your men's group.

zoweh.org/allies

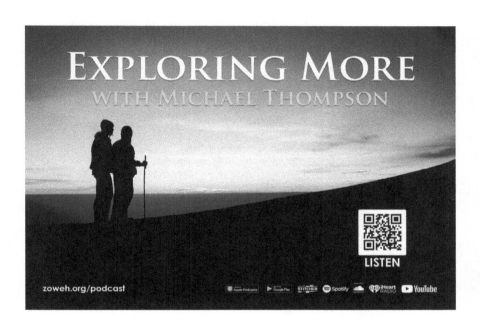

EXPLORING MORE
WITH MICHAEL THOMPSON

LISTEN

zoweh.org/podcast

FREE RESOURCES

The Heart of a Warrior

The Heart of a Warrior Expedition Leader's Guide

Fathering: Fighting for the Hearts of Your Children

A Biblical Theology of the Heart

The Masculine Journey Collection

SCAN ME

Discover more than 30 FREE resources and tools for you to listen to, read, lead, and pray on your heart's journey.

ZOWEH